THE PHILOSOPHY OF
MARTIN HEIDEGGER

THE
PHILOSOPHY OF
MARTIN HEIDEGGER

J. L. Mehta

HARPER TORCHBOOKS
Harper & Row, Publishers
New York, Evanston, San Francisco, London

This edition includes Chapters I, VIII, IX, and X of the original, hardcover, edition published in India by the Banaras Hindu University Press, Varanasi. Reprinted here by arrangement.

First TORCHBOOK edition published 1971.

STANDARD BOOK NUMBER: 06-131605-9

Designed by C. Linda Dingler

Die Wanderschaft in der Wegrichtung zum Fragwürdigen ist nicht Abenteuer sondern Heimkehr.

—MARTIN HEIDEGGER

CONTENTS

PREFACE

The finitude of human thought lies in the fact that it is prompted by a profound need to raise and answer questions about ultimate truth and is at the same time incapable of arriving at any definitive, eternally valid formulation. It is always *unterwegs*, under way, both in the thinking of individual philosophers and in the collective, historical thinking of an epoch and a people, though hardly ever aware of itself as being so and treading sometimes with the arrogant mien of being in possession of a total and final vision. It is ever on its way, groping and fumbling, towards a dimly perceived goal, not only in regard to the conditions of historical or biographical development but also in respect of the moves, techniques and methods followed and of the vocabulary, idiom and language forged in the smithy of thinking from time to time. In the sphere of thought concerned with ultimates, the individual and the historical, the method and the language are all integral parts of the "way" of thought. The following pages attempt to show how this conception of philosophy as a "way" and as being "on the way" is explicitly recognized and concretely exemplified in the thinking of the great German philosopher Martin Heidegger. By the characteristic movement and dynamism of his thought, by the way his own thinking takes up and fuses with the wider historical movement of Western philosophy, by his sensitiveness to questions about method and their implications for the matter under investigation and by his self-conscious and sophisticated employment of language, Heidegger's philosophy demonstrates how all these factors combine, in their inextricable unity, to make up the way of all human, mortal thinking.

Hegel realized that in philosophical thinking it is not the naked result, in itself a mere corpse, but "the result along with the process of arriving at it" that really matters and, indeed, constitutes the matter. But Hegel's attempt, as later Husserl's, to bring philosophy nearer to the form of 'science', that goal where it can lay aside the name of love of knowledge and be actual *knowledge,* is seen by Heidegger to be a mirage, an abandonment of the basic stance of thought, that of questioning and listening, and its surrender to one of its own derived forms. That is why for him "the true shape in which truth exists" can be neither system nor 'science', as Hegel thought, but must be an ever incomplete project of thought and an interminable "being under way". Heidegger's own thinking is incomplete in more than one sense; it baffles and fascinates, and yet by its very incompleteness, it stimulates, provokes and invites. It is incomplete in the sense of not being conceived as a 'system'; it is complete in execution, both in respect of his main work *Being and Time* and to his later writings, which claim neither to be comprehensive nor final. His thinking is open to past thought and carried out in its medium but remains an inconclusive dialogue with this thought, by no means exhausting all that remains unthought in it. It strains towards the future but does no more than touch the fringe of "what is yet to be thought."

Another mark of the finitude of human thought is that it is time-bound and conditioned by the cultural and historical situation in which and from which it springs forth, even while seeking to transcend it towards a higher generality. That is why, as Hegel again saw, "to understand what exists is the task of philosophy" and why philosophy must, in part at least, be "its time comprehended in thought." This is what makes Heidegger into a critic of the present time as the era of technology, of the modern period as the age of subjectivism, and of the entire metaphysical tradition of the West since the time of Plato as determining our present homelessness and oblivion of our true foundations. It is the explicit awareness of this finitude that makes him keenly sensitive to the origins of this tradition, to its uniqueness and to its difference from other traditions grounded in other modes of illumination. And it is for this reason that Heidegger is able to achieve a finitude of transcendence that goes beyond the limits of the present and of the tradition that has brought it to pass, into a realm which is not that of a merely empty and timeless universality but which is concretely and directly relevant to our thinking here and now. Maurice Merleau-Ponty said, "The true place of philosophy is not time, in the sense of discontinuous time, nor is it the eternal. It is rather the 'living present'." The philosophical thought of a Nietzsche, a Whitehead, a Sartre and a Merleau-Ponty is dedicated to this living present, in all the concrete eternity in which it can be experienced. In Heidegger's thought, philosophy assumes this place with explicit awareness of its own presuppositions.

Philosophy, Whitehead remarks, is the one avocation denied to omniscience. But it is the very finitude of philosophical thinking that enables it to transcend the immediate horizon which circumscribes it in each particular case. The horizons of language and culture, of period and history, of tradition and race both enable thinking and limit and divide it. And yet there is such a thing as a fusion of horizons in which the past and the present meet, in which what is alien is appropriated and otherness is overcome, though only as a process and a task that never comes to an end. Such fusion, however, requires the labour of the concept to be raised to the philosophical level and indeed constitutes the very core of the philosophical consciousness, as Hans-Georg Gadamer's analysis of what he calls the hermeneutic experience has so brilliantly shown. If the philosophical quest is not to be the vain pursuit of a phantom, of a shadowy and idealized abstraction, its labours must be directed at the achievement of a concrete universality experienced and experienceable in thought. The only completeness that such experience can possess is its openness to new experience for, as Gadamer insists, the dialectic of experience attains its fulfilment not in knowledge but in that openness for experience which is set into free play by experience itself. This openness is precisely the wayfaring of philosophy, its interminable being on the way as also its own way of being. To have taken this step beyond Hegel is not the least of Heidegger's achievements.

The main themes of Heidegger's thinking are the traditional themes of *philosophia perennis:* Man, World, Being and Truth, and Language which encompasses them in the medium of thought. But he seeks to think of these for a new time, in a new way and in a new language. That is why his writings have aroused, ever since the publication of *Being and Time,* the most animated controversy in his own country, simultaneously inviting angry rejection, unscrupulous appropriation, widely diverging interpretations, unquestioning discipleship. The reasons for this have become evident only with the gradual emergence of a tolerably coherent Heidegger-interpretation during the last few years. A philosophical theory or view, even when different from one's own and speaking a different language, can be understood and appreciated. A well-rounded system of thought, even when generating the most unexpected consequences, can be acknowledged and admired in respect of its logical structure or of the imaginative vision that sustains it. A novel, sophisticated method of philosophical inquiry, self-justifying in its execution, can still be accommodated within the limits of what is intellectually admissible. But a thinking such as Heidegger's, which is all the time "on the way", never amounting to a 'theory' or doctrine, yielding no 'world-view', lacking the logical coherence and fixed contours of a 'system' and pursuing no recognizable 'method', is hardly kind on the reader. And when this thinking goes on to put into question the very concept of philosophy, with its theories, views, systems and methods, leaving hardly anything in terms of which it can be assimilated, it is bound to invite, in minds that are long made up, a gesture of prompt and total rejection. The only alternative, in this case, is to recognize that in Heidegger's thinking a long tradition of philosophy, viz. the Western metaphysical

tradition, comes to a final critical awareness of its own foundations and limits. To recognize this, however, is to open and surrender oneself to his deep questioning. Such submission is ex-
posure to the agony of being torn and divided, of awaiting a new
healing, interminably long in coming. Perhaps philosophy as a
form of love knows no other alternative. Perhaps in this realm it
is otherwise than in the sphere of sound common sense, for
which, as Hegel remarked, a stained stocking is always prefer-
able to a torn one.

Speaking of the fundamental reversal of the modern European
subjectivistic form of thought initiated by Heidegger, Johannes
Lohmann compares him with Copernicus and Darwin, very
much as Freud has often been, for striking a blow against our
habitual anthropocentric outlook and for dislocating the centre of
man's being away from his ego. The resistance to such a reversal
of long ingrained habits of thought which Copernicus, Darwin
and Freud encountered has been no less powerful in the case of
Heidegger, and it can begin to be overcome, in mortification and
courage of renunciation, only when the reverberations of the immediate impact of his work have subsided. For the student who
approaches Heidegger's writings with a background of Anglo-
American philosophy alone, there is the additional difficulty of a
failure of communication. If Heidegger is a "metaphysician on a
grand Teutonic scale", as John Passmore asserts, he is so in an
altogether different sense than that of "classical" or "neoclassical"
ontology; and he speaks in an idiom quite foreign to contemporary Anglo-American philosophizing. Heidegger's approach is
"phenomenological" in a broad sense of the term, not ratiocina-
tive or argumentative. It may, however, be pointed out that,
despite differences in starting-point and contextual milieu, contemporary analytical philosophy is in pursuit of aims which are
not themselves basically different from those of phenomenology.
Both analytical philosophy and phenomenology subserve at bottom a common *logos,* discourse aimed at disclosure of what is
hidden and implicit in experience, in the way we understand

things, in language. What Moore and Price seek, what Wittgenstein and Wisdom, Ryle and Austin achieve, is illumination
and disclosure of hidden structures, helping us, in F. Waismann's
words, "to open our eyes, to bring us to see things in a new way."
In his own way, and perhaps in a profounder sense, this is just
what Heidegger does all the time, bringing some "state of affairs"
into view, letting what *is* come to light.

It is significant that in the English speaking countries Heidegger's thought has evoked much greater interest in theological
circles than amongst professional philosophers. The reasons for
this lie partly in what Gilbert Ryle calls "the laicizing of our
culture" in the post-Victorian English-speaking world. As he has
described it, "the fires of philosophical theology and anti-theol-
ogy" were out already in the middle 1920's in English academic
circles and "the theoretical imbroglios that stimulate philosophy
came out of the work not of Renan, Newman, or Colenso, but of
such people as Cantor, Clark Maxwell, Mendel, Karl Marx,
Frazer, and Freud." But the imbroglio that has stimulated Heidegger's thinking has been that of philosophy itself and of the
bios theoretikos which launched Western metaphysics on its long
course by asking, with Aristotle, "the ever-puzzling question":
what is Being? The attempt to answer this question has been
inseparably linked up, throughout the career of Western philosophy, with the theological question about God and metaphysical
thought has marched along with a background of unresolved
tension between the manifestation of the Divine in the experience
of faith on the one hand and the effort to conceptualize it in the
experience of thought on the other. This is also the tension, deliberately accepted, behind all of Heidegger's thinking, for with
that background alone could he possibly re-think, or philosophically 'repeat', the fundamental quesion of Western metaphysics
and so move forward towards a new beginning and a fresh
answer. The religious question, however, is not merely a clerical
concern and reflection on it is not bound up with cultural vicis-
situdes exemplified in the process of laicizing or secularization

nor with the rise and fall of metaphysics and anti-metaphysics. From the earliest dawn of history, the dimension of the Holy has entered, in all cultures and traditions of mankind, into man's understanding of himself and his world, of Being and Truth and into his language and thinking. The incorporation of this in an "experience of thought" is a demand no less insistent or legitimate than the pursuit of wisdom itself. The embarrassments of science do not necessarily provide the sole quarry for philosophy, nor is the latter confined to questions conceived as narrowly theoretical. And revolutions in philosophy are sometimes more profoundly inspired than becomes apparent on the surface. Despite Stuart Hampshire's recent attempt at a valiant stand against Jean-Paul Sartre's philosophy, trends of a different kind are already beginning to emerge in the philosophical climate of England and the United States. Progress in the solution of purely theoretical problems is laudable and, indeed, essential to philosophy as an academic discipline. But it can neither replace nor repress disciplined reflection on the larger issues bound up with human existence as such and with man's innate craving to understand what is handed over to him as tradition and task.

The present book is substantially a reprint, with minor corrections, of the author's *The Philosophy of Martin Heidegger* (Varanasi, India: Banaras Hindu University Press, 1967), leaving out the six chapters dealing with Heidegger's *Being and Time* in that work. These chapters were written in 1962, just before the English translation of this book appeared in the same year. They have been omitted here as excellent expositions of *Being and Time* are now available to the English reader. This classic but incomplete treatise, it is generally agreed, is Heidegger's *magnum opus*, the starting-point and centre of his philosophical itinerary. Its author was praised, in 1929, by Gilbert Ryle for showing himself "to be a thinker of real importance by the immense subtlety and searchingness of his examination of consciousness, by the boldness and originality of his methods and conclusions, and by the unflagging energy with which he tries to think beyond the stock categories of orthodox philosophy and psychology." It has been described as epoch-making (H-G. Gadamer), as one of the few really original and authentic philosophical works of our time (John Wild), as perhaps the most celebrated philosophical work which Germany has produced in this century (Macquarrie and Robinson), as this astonishing torso (H. Spiegelberg). It also constitutes the indispensable point of departure for Heidegger's later thought, which may in fact be regarded as carrying out, in a language more appropriate to its deepened insight, of the original plan of *Being and Time* and providing the answer to its main question. Heidegger's later thinking can be understood in its real import and significance only in the perspective opened out by this "work of break-through," just as that work can be understood properly only when it is read as marking a stage on Heidegger's way of thought and integral to it. The present exposition is based on the conviction that, as Heidegger has himself recently remarked, only by way of his earlier thought can one gain access to what was to be thought later but that the thought of the earlier Heidegger is rendered possible only as contained in his later thought. Chapters II and III seek to follow up the original plan of *Being and Time* by dealing, on the basis of Heidegger's subsequent writings, with the topics that were to be considered in the unpublished Division III of Part I and in Part II of that work, i.e., with the 'reversal' and the 'destruction' respectively. In chapter II an account is also given of the three important essays written soon after *Being and Time*, essays which not only throw light on the objectives of this work but also give clear indication of the different directions from which Heidegger's thought was converging, even at this time, on his central problem, the question about the sense of Being. In chapter IV an attempt is made to give a systematic exposition of this question and of the manner in which Heidegger answers it in his later writings. It lays no claim to completeness or finality, for Heidegger's thought still continues to be *unterwegs* and all that he has written has not yet seen the light of day. Such an attempt would not perhaps have been possible a few years ago and it may have to be supplemented in important respects in the future. Writing about Nietzsche, Heidegger says, "The nearer in time a thinker is to us, so as to be almost contemporary, the longer is the way to what he has thought, the more unavoidable the need for taking this long way." This applies especially in Heidegger's case and an attempt such as the one made here can, therefore, be only provisional and hesitant, a necessary first step which may have to be retraced, particularly in respect of accentuation and explicitness on particular points, if and when a better perspective emerges with the passage of time. Such uncertainty and, consequent upon that, the need to resist the temptation to tie up loose ends prematurely, is not peculiar to the task of expounding this philosopher's thinking alone but is necessarily bound up with all that is creative and contemporary. As in the preceding chapters, I have primarily aimed at exposition and even this confines itself largely to letting Heidegger himself speak. It is, of course, true— as Heidegger insists—that there is no such thing as an exposition that is not also, necessarily and intrinsically, interpretation. And this, in fact, comes into view in this chapter which closes with some questions addressed to Heidegger by way of criticism. If I have avoided *explicit* interpretation, in terms of and by comparison with concepts and doctrines in the Indian philosophical tradition, it is only because such interpretation demands a critical examination not only of the subject of the interpretation but also of the tradition, standpoint and presuppositions on which the interpretation is based. The time for such an attempt is not yet ripe.

What I have aimed at here is neither polemic nor apologetics but only straightforward exposition, with only occasional critical comment in the form of footnotes, on what I regard as errors and misinterpretations in some recent writings on Heidegger. I have resisted being dragged, therefore, into the controversies that have raged around his writings or identifying myself with any particular school of Heidegger-interpretation. The controversial literature, polemical and partisan, that his writings have generated is extensive and not without interest. But it is intelligible only in the context of the wide ramification of schools, points of view and, to use Collingwood's phrase, the variety of parish-pump loyalties and alignments prevailing, like everywhere else, in the present-day German philosophical scene. The significance of Heidegger's thought, the present writer is convinced, extends much farther and goes much deeper than these squabbles, often reminiscent of the *querelle des anciens et des modernes*. As Heidegger has remarked in his *Vorträge und Aufsätze*, the unique thing which a thinker at any time succeeds in saying (and so showing) is never such as to permit of being logically or empirically proved or refuted. It is also not a matter of belief or faith. It can only be brought into view through a thinking that questions. What is seen in this manner is manifested always as question-worthy. And this applies to the central thought of every thinker: something seen, and yet a riddle, questionable. To let Heidegger's thought emerge in all its question-ability and question-worthiness, as "something seen, and yet a riddle"—nothing more than this has been attempted here. If reference is frequently made to recent secondary literature in my footnotes, this is only to remind the reader that, in the case of a contemporary writer at least, an awareness of the immediate context in which his thought emerges and becomes effective cannot be altogether dispensed with. An exposition of this thought, so self-consciously tradition centred, by one who can only approach it from the outside and view it from the standpoint of his own tradition is not perhaps without its own advantages.

This work could not have been written without the benefit of the ten months I spent at the Universities of Cologne and Freiburg during 1957–1958. I am greatful to the *Alexander von Humboldt-Stiftung* for the award of a grant which made this stay possible. I acknowledge thankfully the stimulus I received, in lectures and private conversation, from Professor Dr. Ludwig

Landgrebe at Cologne and Professor Dr. Eugen Fink at Freiburg. My special thanks are due to Professor Dr. Walter Biemel, not only for the many instructive conversations I had with him at the Husserl-Archiv at Cologne and at his house but also for giving me liberally of his time in explaining, line by line, some very difficult Heidegger texts. Above all, I am profoundly grateful to Professor Martin Heidegger for allowing me the privilege of meeting and talking with him, more than once, in his house, for his cordiality and for his kindness in arranging contacts helpful in my study of his thought.

The Bibliography of Heidegger's writings given at the end is arranged in the order of publication. However, in view of the often considerable disparity between the years of publication and of composition or conception, the dates of the latter are also mentioned. Anyone interested in the living movement of creative thought should find this instructive in regard to the 'way' of Heidegger's thought. Titles of some writings, as yet unpublished but known only to a few scholars and mentioned by them, are given in the text. Discussing, in *Nietzsche*, the writings kept back from publication by this philosopher, Heidegger has pointed out the difference between communication of work done in the special sciences, where promptness is all-important, and that of philosophical thoughts. As he remarks there, "In contrast to 'science', the situation in philosophy is entirely different. . . . (What the great thinkers create) has, even in the manner of communication, its own time and laws. The urgency of publishing and the dread of being too late do not obtain here, for it is of the very essence of every genuine philosophy that it be misunderstood, necessarily, by its contemporaries. Even in relation to himself, the philosopher must cease being his own contemporary." This perhaps also explains his own practice in the matter of publication, found so baffling, and at times confusing, by students of his thought.

Except where otherwise indicated, all renderings from the German originals are by the author.

References to Heidegger's writings in the footnotes are to the German originals. Page references to English translations (E.T.) are given where possible. The editions used are mentioned in the Bibliography (IIA) at the end.

J. L. MEHTA

THE PHILOSOPHY OF
MARTIN HEIDEGGER

chapter one

HEIDEGGER'S WAY OF THOUGHT

"The poems composed by every great poet are attempts to put into words one single poem. His greatness depends on the extent to which he has entrusted himself to this unique poem, for it is this which enables him to maintain the purity of his poetic utterances by keeping them within the ambit of their single origin. This unique poem in a poet remains unuttered. None of the individual poems, nor all of them together, say everything. And yet each poem speaks out of this unique uncomposed poem and each time says what is the same."[1] What Heidegger says about the poet is also true of the thinker, as he has himself remarked elsewhere[2], and it is supremely true of Heidegger himself. All his writings, from first to last, revolve around one idea, whatever the ostensible theme may be which at the moment happens to occupy him. This central thought is the unuttered thought of Being, the hidden source within him of all that he has said, but which no particular formulation fully and adequately expresses and which is not exhausted by all his writings taken together. Heidegger's 'philosophy', therefore, though systematic in the extreme, is not a system and, by reason of the very task it has set before itself, cannot be one. It is rather a trail blazed, a path traversed, a way taken by thought[3], as he calls it, toward the one

1. *Unterwegs zur Sprache*, pp. 37–38.
2. *Was heisst Denken?*, p. 20 (E.T., p. 50).
3. For an elucidation of Heidegger's philosophy as a "way", see Ottow Pöggeler's book, *Der Denkweg Martin Heideggers*, 1963, pp. 7–15.

goal of enshrining in language, or rather preparing to do so, the unuttered thought of Being. It reaches out into the unexpressed future but it does so through a close and devoted attention to the way this unuttered thought of Being *has* been at work in the history of the European philosophical tradition. The unexpressed and unthought spring of Heidegger's own thinking is the hidden wellspring of the European philosophical tradition itself and of the course of its unfoldment in history. One may therefore rightly say, with Otto Pöggeler[4], that in Heidegger's thinking "European thought reaches out beyond its own self and surpasses itself. With unparalleled energy he leads European thought forward, neither going back to any of its past forms nor rejecting it out of hand." Rooted in this tradition and speaking out of it, Heidegger yet subjects it to deep questioning and in so doing prepares the way for a new perspective on that tradition and a fresh appropriation of it[5].

4. "Sein als Ereignis," *Zeitschrift für Philosophische Forschung*, XIII (1959), p. 600.

5. See Walter Schulz's well known article, *Über den philosophiegeschichtlichen Ort Martin Heideggers* (*Philosophische Rundschau* I, 1953/54), where a serious attempt is made for the first time to view Heidegger's philosophy in a historical perspective. Schulz sees it as "the inner ending of the process of Western metaphysics", as representing the end of a tradition and therefore incapable of being either assimilated into it or criticized in terms of any phase of that. Western metaphysics, he believes with Heidegger, exhibits a meaningful historical pattern moving towards an end and, secondly, that this culmination is reached in our own times and becomes visible in the philosophy of Heidegger. Attempting as it does to interpret man in his wholeness entirely out of himself and not in terms of any other entity, *Being and Time* is, in this sense only, "a work of the philosophy of subjectivity and indeed its culminating work." This can be explicitly seen in the essay *What is Metaphysics?* in which the metaphysical tradition is shown as culminating in 'Nothing'. Schulz says therefore that this essay is "the metaphysical endwork of traditional metaphysics" and that the 'Nothing' of that essay is the "end-point of tradition", not only its culmination but its terminal point, after which it passes over into another beginning. Heidegger's philosophy thus represents the historic moment of the self-abrogation, the 'reversal', of the metaphysical tradition and is itself conditioned by this tradition.

Cf. also the recent full-length study (*Heidegger und die Tradition*) by Werner Marx showing, with particular reference to Aristotle and to Hegel, how Heidegger seeks to go beyond the entire metaphysical tradition and to initiate a new way of thinking about Being and Man.

Heidegger's thinking, even more than Hegel's, is profoundly historical in character but, unlike the latter's, its way is one of questioning rather than of construction. The way followed by his thought is the way of an inquirer, of one who is tireless in his questionings, not that of "a dubious prophet seeking dim and distant goals."[6] In asking or questioning lies the piety of thought, Heidegger says; in the eyes of faith such asking is folly but it is in this 'folly' that the essence of philosophy is to be found. However, as Heidegger was to realize, this questioning is itself rooted in a prior 'listening', which is therefore the primary and proper gesture of thought.[7] On this voyage of inquiry there are not only

6. It would therefore be a mistake to approach the philosophy of Heidegger as the work of a solitary Teutonic genius, an 'outsider' thinking profound and original thoughts even though, unlike Wittgenstein, he has fathered no school and is himself part of no 'movement'. Ludwig Landgrebe, Eugen Fink and Hans-Georg Gadamer, each from a different perspective, have shown how Heidegger's thought is part and parcel of the larger movement of European thought, "an achievement and a part of the progress of philosophy" (to use John Wisdom's words about Ryle's work!). In this respect he is more like Wittgenstein than like Whitehead, though it is only the latter Wittgenstein who seems to be at all aware that he is attacking old-established habits of mind, rooted deep in history. The extreme unhistorical attitude of his *Tractatus* phase finds explicit utterance in *Notebooks 1914–1916* (p. 82c): "What has history to do with me? Mine is the first and only world! I want to report how *I* found the world."

7. Cf. *Einführung in die Metaphysik*, pp. 5f. (E. T., pp. 5f.) where Heidegger discusses the character of "asking as a primordial power", what is implied in real questioning and how the questioning spirit differs from the attitude of religious belief, the security of faith which has its own particular way of standing in truth. The passion for genuine questioning is for Heidegger the distinctive mark of philosophical thinking, as represented, for example, by Socrates, "the purest thinker of the West". About the Greeks, Heidegger says, "The Greeks saw in the ability to ask the whole aristocracy of their existence; their ability to question was for them the standard for differentiating themselves from those who were not capable of it and did not want it. These they called barbarians" (*Die Frage nach dem Ding*, p. 32; E.T., p. 42). In Heidegger, however, the passion of questioning is eventually subordinated and made subservient to the sensitivity of 'hearing'. Pure questioning is inspired by the quest for the *radix*, the root, of everything. But this quest itself, i.e., philosophy, is rooted in the metaphysical conception of Being as Ground. Once this is abandoned, the nature of thinking as questioning is itself modified. As Heidegger says, explaining the statement in *Die Frage nach der Technik* that the devoutness of thinking lies in questioning, "Every question is always raised within (the horizon of) the promise held

no ready-made answers; the questions themselves have to be creatively formulated afresh. In the light shed by the question itself, the thinker forges a path towards its answer, travels a little distance, looks back from there to the original question and reformulates it from the new vantage point. He proceeds thus from one station of thought to another, giving voice to the un-uttered thought, saying what has not been said before and yet leaving behind him an inexhaustible 'unsaid' as a task for pos-terity. The unity of Heidegger's thought is the unity of a *way* taken by thought, not a unity of positions or of doctrine; it is the unity of a quest and not that of a method followed or of discover-ies made on the way. "To follow one star, only this. To think is to concentrate on one thought, motionless like a star fixed in the heavens above the world", as he puts it in a little collection of epigrams[8]. A "wanderer in the neighbourhood of Being", Hei-degger moves, in his thought, sometimes along what appears to be a well laid out path, sometimes into forest paths that lead nowhere, but always seeking the adequate word in which Being may find utterance, even when it involves the most radical de-parture from our accustomed ways of thinking and speaking.

Heidegger's main work *Being and Time* is a milestone on this 'way' of inquiry, embodying, in his words, the result of a few steps taken towards the goal of a fresh formulation of the *ques-tion* of Being. The book, published in 1927 as *Being and Time*, Part I, still remains a torso and in the preface to its eighth edition (1957) even the promise of a second part is finally withdrawn as being unfeasible unless the whole of the first part is completely recast. This does not, however, mean in any way a rejection and a disowning of this early work; on the contrary, as Heidegger re-marks there, "the way taken by this book is even today a neces-sary one, if the question of Being is to move us in our depths."

---

out by that which is put into question. . . . The primary and proper gesture of thought is not questioning; it is rather the hearing of the promise of that which is to come into question." (*Unterwegs zur Sprache*, p. 175).

8. *Aus der Erfahrung des Denkens*, p. 7.

The work has proved epoch-making in contemporary Continental thought and its title *Being and Time* has become, as Eugen Fink remarks[9], the watchword of this century. Because of the sheer originality of its approach, the novelty of its terminological apparatus and its incompleteness, it became a centre of heated controversy and its aims were widely and variously misunderstood until, after a quarter of a century, it established itself as a classic in modern German thought[10]. Soon after its appearance, a generation which had lost all its spiritual moorings and to which the central tradition of European thought and religion had lost its meaningfulness, saw in this work a document which showed the way for extracting the meaning of human existence by an analysis of this existence itself. Its main objective, the problem of Being, was overlooked as inessential and *Being and Time* was appropriated by the Existentialists as one of their major texts. Others, with more academic pretentions, canvassed with equal vigour the view that Heidegger was primarily a thinker of Being, an ontologist. But the ontologists who claimed him as one of their own never cared to inquire whether the 'Being' of which Heidegger was in pursuit was what they understood by this term. Judging his aims in the light of their schooling in the European metaphysical tradition, they completely missed seeing that it was precisely this age-old meaning of Being that he was putting into question. Still others, realizing that Heidegger's thought, going beyond metaphysics, could not itself be interpreted in the sense

9. *Zur ontologischen Frühgeschichte von Raum-Zeit-Bewegung*, p. 42.

10. Some idea of the impact of this work on contemporary European thinkers and of the large polemical literature to which this book and Heidegger's subsequent writings have given rise can be had from the bibliography compiled by Hermann Lübbe (*Bibliographie der Heidegger-Literatur, 1917–1955*, containing 880 titles). A supplementary bibliography (1960; later enlarged into a book) has been brought out by Guido Schneeberger.

Brief accounts of early misunderstandings about *Being and Time* and of the stages through which· the interpretation of Heidegger has passed are given by Peter Fürstenau (*Heidegger*, 1958), and by Schulz and Pöggeler in articles referred to above. See also Max Müller, *Existenzphilosophie im geistigen Leben der Gegenwart* (2nd Ed. 1958).

of traditional ontology, held that his main theme was not a petrified and empty concept of Being but 'world', a new concept of the world to replace the old and outmoded Christian, metaphysical conception as it culminated in the European Nihilism depicted by Nietzsche. Heidegger, for them, was the mythologist and herald of this new world of the future. Finally, the Phenomenologists who were unwilling to go all the way with the Master, hailed this work as striking out a new and more fruitful direction in Phenomenology and gave to it the label of 'Hermeneutic Phenomenology'. But, as Pöggeler has well pointed out, what Heidegger actually *thinks* cannot be grasped through any of these catchwords. To label him as an existentialist, the propounder of a heroic nihilism, as a myth-maker, as a metaphysician in the traditional sense or a phenomenologist, or as a pseudo-theologian or a mystic, is to overlook him as a thinker and to miss completely the originality and the profoundly revolutionary character of his thinking.[11]

I THE DEVELOPMENT OF HEIDEGGER'S THOUGHT

With the publication of *Being and Time* Heidegger achieved a 'break through' into the dimension proper to his own independent thinking and into an explicit awareness of his own intellec-

11. The basic precondition for an appreciation of Heidegger, it may be added, is the realization that he cannot be interpreted, and therefore should not be judged, in terms of the thought of any preceding stage in the history of Western philosphy. When approached from a fixed standpoint, whether rationalistic or empiricistic, idealistic or realistic, mystical or positivistic, he can only be 'used' or criticized and dismissed but never truly understood. Further, Heidegger's relationship to the Western metaphysical tradition is in a profound sense, ambiguous. He is critical of this tradition and often 'unfair' to its leading philosophers; leaving it behind, he carries thought forward into a new dimension. But this criticism and overcoming of metaphysics does not, like contemporary positivism, 'prove' it to be an error and so eliminate it (only to restore it in the subtle form of logical analysis!). Far from rejecting or denigrating metaphysics, Heidegger only seeks to exhibit its limits—though in a different sense and manner than Kant—and bring to light the truth (as he calls it) or basis on which metaphysics itself stands. In this sense he prepares rather for a reappropriation of the whole metaphysical tradition on a deeper level of thinking; his overcoming of metaphysics is really a rejection of its claim to ultimacy.

tual mission as a thinker. But for a right understanding of this work it is not only necessary to keep in view the path taken later by his thought but also to have some idea of the path that led up to it. As he says in a dialogue with a Japanese professor published recently,[12] our past (*Herkunft*) always remains our future (*Zukunft*) and that *from* where we have come is always what comes *towards* us. Hence, a brief account of Heidegger's development before the publication of his main work may be appropriately given here. Born in 1889, Heidegger underwent a Catholic theological education in a Jesuit seminary at Konstanz. His preoccupation with the problem of the relation between the word of the Holy Scripture and theologicalspeculative thought led him to pay close attention to Hermeneutics, a philological discipline developed in the service of Biblical exegesis, which was to play, in a widened sense, an important role in the methodology of *Being and Time*. In his closing years at the gymnasium, "in 1907 to be more precise, I came across the problem of Being in the shape of a dissertation by Franz Brentano, the teacher of Husserl, entitled *Of the multiple meanings of Being according to Aristotle*, written in 1862."[13] This book was not only the "first guide in my study of Greek philosophy during the gymnasium period" but, in combination with his deep theological studies, it initiated that movement of thought which was to become soon a lifelong passion and bear rich fruits, illustrating Hölderlin's words in the *Hymn to the Rhine*: ". . . For, how you begin is what you will always remain." It is this theological background of his studies—Brentano was a Catholic Aristotelian—that gave the

12. *Unterwegs zur Sprache*, p. 96.
13. *Unterwegs zur Sprache*, p. 92. *Von der mannigfachen Bedeutung des Seienden nach Aristoteles*, long out of print, is now available again in a reprint (Olms, Hildesheim, 1960). The title page of this work carries as a motto the sentence from Aristotle: *to on legetai pollachos* ("what *is*, becomes manifest, in respect of its Being, in many ways", in Heidegger's rendering). "Latent in this phrase is the *question* that determined the way of my thought: what is the pervasive, simple, unified determination of Being that permeates all of its multiple meanings? . . . What, then, does Being mean?" (Heidegger's "Preface" to William J. Richardson's *Heidegger*, 1963, p. x).

dimension of depth to his philosophical questionings. As he himself says, referring to his theological antecedents, "Had it not been for these theological origins, I would never have come upon the way of thinking."[14] Later, Heidegger was to come into intimate contact with the new Protestant theology also at Marburg, during the period when *Being and Time* was under preparation.[15] The influence of Søren Kierkegaard, the Danish philosopher whose works had become recently accessible in Germany through the Diederich's translation, as providing the existenziell basis for Heidegger's existenzial analytic, is quite patent and acknowledged by him in *Being and Time*.[16] Such key terms of the analytic as existenz, anxiety, situation, resoluteness and choice, death, authenticity, repetition, possibility, the anonymous 'one' and the 'moment' have obviously been suggested by Kierke-

14. *Ibid.*, p. 96.
15. According to Hans-Georg Gadamer (Cf. his "Introduction" in the Reclam edition of *Der Ursprung des Kunstwerkes*), Heidegger's *opus magnum, Being and Time,* grew out of his "fruitful contact, full of tensions, with contemporary Protestant theology after his call to Marburg in the year 1923." How profoundly Heidegger's own work has, in turn, influenced contemporary theology is writ large in the pages of Rudolf Bultmann and Paul Tillich, distinguished theologians who have, however, confined themselves to the existential concepts and idiom of *Being and Time.* For the way the later Heidegger has been appropriated by the theologians, see *Denken und Sein— Der Weg Martin Heideggers und der Weg der Theologie* by Heinrich Ott, successor to Karl Barth at Basel. This book not only deals exhaustively with Heidegger's relevance to contemporary theology but also gives a lucid account of the whole range of Heidegger's thought as it was available in print until 1959. *The Later Heidegger and Theology,* Edited by James M. Robinson and John B. Cobb, Jr. (1963) contains a number of essays discussing the relevance of the later Heidegger to theology. The focal essay is by Ott. Cf. also *An Existentialist Theology* by John Macquarrie is a comparison of Heidegger and Bultmann. Heidegger's impact on Catholic theology is attested by Max Müller, *Existenzphilosophie im geistigen Leben der Gegenwart,* 1949 and Joseph Möller, *Existenzialphilosophie und katholische Theologie,* 1952, and Gustav Siewerth, *Das Schicksal der Metaphysik von Thomas zu Heidegger,* 1959.
16. The distinction between existenziell and existenzial is basic in Heidegger. The former term refers to the ontic, the factual and the experienced, whereas the latter refers to its ontological and transcendental condition and significance. 'Existence' and its derivates are spelled with a 'z' in order to indicate their special technical use.

gaard. But, as Heidegger insists, the Dane's contribution to thought does not go beyond the sphere of the existenziell and it has no further relevance to Heidegger's basic problem. In taking over these concepts, therefore, Heidegger modifies them radically for his own purposes.[17] Another experience of the young Heidegger, all-important for his development and destined to play an important creative role in his later work, was the impact of art and poetry upon him, in particular, the poetry of Hölderlin and Trakl. The publication, in 1910, of Hellingrath's edition of Hölderlin's translations from Pindar and, in 1914, of Hölderlin's later hymns, Heidegger says, "had on us students at that time the effect of an earthquake."[18] It appears as if at this time Heidegger was assimilating, with equal avidity and energy, the European cultural heritage in the fields of religion and theology, of art and poetry and of philosophical thought from the Greeks to the present day. In the European religious and literary tradition profound insights into the truth of life and reality find expression which the central metaphysical stream of thought has been unable, strangely enough, to incorporate into itself. Perhaps, as Heidegger was to discover later, the very origin and nature of metaphysics has prevented this, forcing it to move only along a track laid out for it in its beginnings and rejecting as unworthy of thought everything that did not fit in with its conceptualizing, representational ways. Only when thinking goes back into the foundations of metaphysics, to a level deeper than that of metaphysics and theology alike, can it imbibe into itself the truly creative work of religion and poetry, transmuting it and assimilating it in such fashion as to remain loyal, at the same time, to its own path of inquiring and questioning.

It is significant that even while preparing his Ph.D. thesis, Heidegger was absorbed in extensive logical studies and pub-

17. About the concept of existenz in *Being and Time,* for example, Heidegger says (*Nietzsche II,* p. 476) that here neither the concept in Kierkegaard's sense nor that in the sense of *Existenzphilosophie* is involved.
18. *Unterwegs zur Sprache,* p. 182.

lished a detailed critical survey of recent work in this field
(*Neuere Forschungen über Logik*),[19] showing his familiarity
with the whole range of logical studies, including even the
mathematical logic of Russell and Whitehead.[20] His later rejection of formal-logical argumentation in philosophy and attempts
to probe into the metaphysical foundations of the very concept of
logic are obviously not based on total ignorance of what logic is
about. By this time Heidegger had come to attach "far-reaching
significance to Husserl's circumspect and most felicitously formulated investigations" (i.e. *Logische Untersuchungen*) which are
credited with breaking the spirit of psychologism in logic. In 1912
he also published an article on "The problem of reality in modern
philosphy", giving an indication of his concern with the problem
of Being for the first time, though the approach here is still that
of traditional epistemology. The most important personal influence on him during this period, however, was that of the great
Neo-Kantian value-philosopher Heinrich Rickert, who preceded
Edmund Husserl at the university of Freiberg.[21] Heidegger's
Ph.D. thesis, written in 1914 under the supervision of the Catholic philosopher A. Schneider, dealt with "The Theory of Judgment according to Psychologism (*Die Lehre vom Urteil im
Psychologismus*)" and sought to establish the need for purifying
logical theory of all psychological considerations as being com-

19. In *Literarische Rundschau für das katholische Deutschland*, xxxviii
(1912).
20. See Spiegelberg, *The Phenomenological Movement*, Vol. I., p. 292.
The account of Heidegger given here, though very readable and informative,
has been sharply criticized by H-G. Gadamer (*Die phänomenologische
Bewegung*, in *Philosophische Rundschau*, XI, 1963).
21. As H-G. Gadamer has pointed out in his 'Introduction' to the German
translation of R. G. Collingwood's *Autobiography* (entitled *Denken*), the
philosophical climate in Germany during the early years of this century
differed in essential respects from that in England. For the background
of contemporary German philosophy, characterized largely by a reaction
against the dominant Neo-Kantianism, see also Gadamer's 'Introduction' to
the Reclam ed. of Heidegger's *Der Ursprung des Kunstwerkes*. Werner
Brock's *Introduction to Contemporary German Philosophy* and the standard
histories, Windelband-Heimsoeth, Stegmüller, Knittermeyer, all contain
accounts of Heidegger as also of the contemporary philosophical landscape.

pletely irrelevant to it.[22] In *Being and Time* and throughout his later work Heidegger resolutely shuts the door upon the psychological and the subjective as only clouding the inquiry, irrespective of whether the inquiry is understood as phenomenology, ontology or 'essential thinking'.

Heidegger's Habilitation thesis, dedicated to Rickert, was published in 1916 and was entitled, *Die Kategorien- und Bedeutungslehre des Duns Scotus* (*Duns Scotus' Doctrine of Categories and Meanings*). The main problem which concerns him here is the interrelation between logic, language and metaphysics and how the first two lead ultimately into the problem of Being and to the many ways in which Being is expressed. There are foreshadowed thus in this work the twin problems of language and of Being which were to preoccupy him constantly later on, for as Heidegger explains in retrospect,[23] "the *theory of categories* is the usual name for the discussion of the Being of essents[24] and the *theory of meanings* means the *grammatica speculativa*, the metaphysical reflexion on language in its relation to Being." What seems to have attracted him to this thinker of the Middle Ages is again the dimension of depth in medieval logic, metaphysics and mysticism, though he also sees clearly the limitations of medieval philosophy, its lack of methodological awareness and the absence of an independent questioning spirit. "The Middle Ages lack what constitutes the characteristic feature of the modern spirit: the liberation of the subject from his ties with his environment, the firm establishment in his own life."[25] This sense of the limits of the medieval consciousness, with all its richness

22. For details regarding Heidegger's academic career, see Paul Hühnerfeld, *In Sachen Heidegger,* pp. 40–42.

23. *Unterwegs zur Sprache,* p. 91.

24. This neologism, borrowed from Ralph Manheim, has been used throughout this work to render the German *"das Seiende"* for reasons explained by Manheim in the "Translator's Note" in his English translation of *Einführung in die Metaphysik;* 'entity', 'what is', 'all that is', 'beings' have also been used in many places alternatively.

25. Quoted in Spiegelberg I, p. 295.

and depth, perhaps accounts for Heidegger's growing interest in Husserl's phenomenology—already evident throughout in this early work—as a possible way out of the limitations, not only of the medieval intellectual approach but also of the dominating epistemological, Neo-Kantian trend in German philosophy during this period. The Duns Scotus book foreshadows, as Herbert Spiegelberg has remarked,[26] Heidegger's preoccupation with the problems that were soon to be central in his own thought, the problems of Being and of Historicity. The need of a 'translogical metaphysics' as the real optics of philosophy, going beyond the logical problems of categories and meanings and the hope of an early, more detailed study about Being, Value and Negation is here announced by Heidegger. So also is the need of a historical philosophy of the living spirit, as it underlies the whole logico-epistemological sphere, including within it the problems of categories and meanings, a need which becomes acute in view of the pointlessness of mysticism (as mere irrationalistic *Erleben* or experience) and the powerlessness of philosophy as a mere rationalistic structure.

Heidegger's concern with the problem of time is directly testified by the title of the Habilitation lecture he delivered at Freiburg University in 1915 (published, 1916) on the concept of Time in Historiography ("Der Zeitbegriff in der Geschichtswissenschaft"). The concept of time in history is here "contrasted sharply with that of natural science in a way which shows Heidegger's familiarity with the science of Einstein and Planck."[27] Even at this stage the urgent need for a conception of time deeper than that of chronology is explicitly voiced by Heidegger. Thus the basic themes of Being, Time and History, as they were to occupy him in *Being and Time* have already appeared on Heidegger's field of vision as of central importance. Nevertheless, he has not yet found his own language; though seeking a "philosophy of the living spirit", he is still shackled in the idiom of traditional

26. *Ibid.*, p. 296.
27. *Ibid.*, p. 297.

metaphysics and expresses himself in terms of eternal values and timeless meanings—ways of speaking later to be attacked so vehemently by himself.

The realization must have soon followed that in order to carry through his project of a "break-through into the true reality and the real truth"—so he puts it in the book on Duns Scotus—it was necessary that the metaphysical tradition should not just be taken for granted and accepted uncritically. It has to be examined thoroughly as to its ultimate presuppositions and assimilated afresh by going back to its very origins in Aristotle, Plato and indeed right back to the earliest Greek thinkers before Socrates. The dimension of historicity essential for such an inquiry was opened up to Heidegger through his intense preoccupation, at this time, with the work of Wilhelm Dilthey and his friend Count Paul Yorck of Wartenburg, thinkers who were themselves on the trail that led beyond metaphysics to that level of depth, ever present in the realms of poetry and religion, which has always accompanied metaphysics as its "anti-metaphysical shadow" throughout the European spiritual tradition. But, as Pöggeler has pointed out[28], even before his contact with the work of Dilthey, Heidegger had been prepared for its philosophical appropriation by his encounter with the dimension of the historical through an intensive study of primitive Christianity and the religious thought of St. Augustine. His lectures on the Phenomenology of Religion while he was a *Privatdozent* at Freiburg dealt with early Christianity as evidence of the factual experience in life of the dimension of history and it is from his way of understanding the religious consciousness of early Christianity that, as Pöggeler puts it, Heidegger attains the guiding point of view for his own conception of 'facticity' and factual existenz. Taking religion as a matter of factually realized life-experience (*Erlebnis*), Heidegger believes, at this stage, that it should be kept free of all metaphysical conceptualization, very much as Augustine, Luther,

28. See Pöggeler, "Sein als Ereignis," op. cit., p. 604, and *Der Denkweg Martin Heideggers*, pp. 36–45.

Pascal and Kierkegaard have attempted in different ways to argue. In his lectures (unpublished) on *Augustine and Neo-Platonism,* Heidegger followed Luther in taking up an extreme anti-metaphysical position and attempted to show how in the philosophy of Augustine an original and basic religious experience is perverted by being conceptualized in terms of uncritically accepted metaphysical ideas. According to Heidegger, it is the merit of Augustine that he thinks on the basis of factual life-experience but he goes wrong when, instead of letting this experience come to a natural conceptual blossoming, he tries to impose upon it concepts which have their origin in alien soil. By interpreting the original Christian experience, in other words, in terms of Neo-Platonic metaphysics, Augustine falsifies that experience. To penetrate into its pristine truth once again requires, therefore, first a 'destruction' of the Augustinian conceptualization by means of an analytical interpretation of it. The profound impact upon Heidegger of this realization—how unexamined metaphysical concepts distort and falsify basic life-experience—cannot be overestimated. Seeking to reflect on the reality or Being of Time and of God on the basis of lived experience, Augustine lapses into the representational thinking of metaphysics as it has unfolded itself since Plato, and hence conceives time in Aristotelian terms and Being as 'constancy of presence' in the Greek manner. This conception of Being is the basic presupposition on which the entire tradition of metaphysical thinking in the West rests, a presupposition of which metaphysics itself is aware indeed but not *as* a presupposition. Never subjected to the scrutiny of thought, it has remained up till now the dogmatically accepted foundation of this whole tradition—the Unthought (*das Ungedachte*) of Western philosophy. To understand the character of this foundation, the problem of Being, what it means to be, must be explicitly faced as a *problem* and its consideration be taken up at the point where Plato, Aristotle and the early Greek thinkers have left it unexamined and unexplained in all its fateful implications. This is the problem which Heidegger sets himself to explore now, having attained by 1923, if not earlier, a clear awareness of the path he was henceforth to follow.[29]

Before we come to this, however, it will be appropriate to make a brief mention at this point of the role which two schools of thought contemporaneous with Heidegger's development, the Philosophy of Life and Phenomenology, have played in his thinking. Both Dilthey's *Lebensphilosophie* and Husserl's *Phänomenologie* were attempts to extract a meaning out of life and consciousness and build this up conceptually by investigating them from within, immanently, without any presuppositions and without taking any help from the discoveries and constructions of science and metaphysics respectively. Heidegger combines both of these approaches in his analytic of *Dasein* (man), putting them within the framework of the transcendental method of Kant. Reacting, like many other thinkers of his age, against both the Absolute Spirit of Hegelian rationalism and the claim of natural science to provide a comprehensive conceptual framework for all knowledge, Dilthey sought to base himself on Life as the ultimate bed-rock from which all philosophy must proceed. Instead of interpreting life in terms of the ready-made abstractions of epistemology or by applying to its concepts derived from the natural sciences, we must start from life as "the first and ever

29. See *Sein und Zeit*, p. 72 (E.T., f. 490), for reference to his lectures dating back to 1919 on the 'hermeneutics of facticity'; also *Unterwegs zur Sprache*, p. 95.

Heidegger has explained in his recent "Preface" in Richardson's *Heidegger* (pp. x–xiv) how the way from his first encounter with the question of Being ("whence does Being as such, not merely beings as beings, receive its determination?")" in Brentano's dissertation to this clear awareness was a long and devious one, "a tangled process, inscrutable even to me." As he says there, "Meanwhile a decade went by and a great deal of swerving and straying through the history of Western philosophy was needed for the above questions to reach even an initial clarity." Three insights which were decisive in preparing the way to such clarity were: a gradual clarification of the real meaning and scope of the principle of phenomenology, the understanding of *aletheia* (truth) as non-concealment, based on a renewed study of the Aristotelian treatises (especially Book ix of the *Metaphysics* and Book vi of the *Nicomachean Ethics*) and the recognition of the fundamental character of *ousia* (The Being of what is) as *presence*.

present reality." As Dilthey puts it, "Life is the basic fact and it must be the starting-point of philosophy. That is what we know from within, something behind which one cannot go. Life cannot be brought before the bar of a Reason sitting in judgment."[30] Life manifests itself in complexes of 'lived experience' (*Erlebnis*), teleological unities of meaning which are objectivized in the cultural productions of man. In an individual, these 'lived experiences' are connected together into the structural unity of his life-history but since the individual's life, as constituted by these unities of meaning, is itself embedded in the wider historical process in which it is only an element, it can only be in terms of the latter that this personal life-experience can be finally understood. "For, man does not understand his own self by means of any kind of rumination upon himself . . . only through an understanding of the historical reality generated by him does he obtain a consciousness of his capacities, for good or for ill."[31]

To know what life means is therefore to understand the essentially historical objectivizations of life as they are studied by the 'human sciences' (*Geisteswissenschaften*). Towards the establishment of the epistemological autonomy of these sciences, of history in particular (as against the prevailing epistemology which was solely oriented to the natural sciences), Dilthey in large measure directed his efforts. According to him, the unities of meaning embodied in life-experiences are the ultimate constituents of knowledge in the historical, human sciences and to get at them what we require is understanding (*Verstehen*) from within rather than causal explanation as practised in the natural sciences. "Only his history tells man what he is", Dilthey says[32]; human nature is human history and the book of life, to be read, needs, not causal explanation but *Verstehen*, understanding of the way life itself has explicated itself in history. To designate the method by which the book of life may be read and compre-

30. *Gesammelte Schriften,* VII, p. 359.
31. *Ibid.,* III, p. 210.
32. *Ibid.,* VIII, p. 224.

hended, Dilthey adopted the term 'hermeneutics', borrowing it from the great religious philosopher, Friedrich Schleiermacher. The concept of 'hermeneutics', a discipline concerned with the understanding and interpretation of literary texts, in particular the Holy Scripture, entirely from within and in terms of what is contained within them, was widened by Schleiermacher to include all expression of the human individuality. Every written document or spoken word could be understood, by interpreting its parts in terms of the whole and the whole in terms of the parts, as the expression of the psychology of the writer or speaker, and the aim of the hermeneutic art in the wider sense was to reproduce, through a study of the expression, this inner psychology.[33] Dilthey extended this concept of hermeneutics to the whole of historical reality and in all its manifestations. The historical process, thus interpreted from within and not in terms of thought-constructions imported and imposed from without, reveals itself as made up of meaningful structural unities, ultimately definable in terms of the 'lived experience' (*Erlebnis*) of individuals but itself a supra-individual meaningful expression of Life. Art, religion and philosophy are direct manifestations of Life, part of the Objective Spirit, not as Hegel thought, embodiments of the Absolute Spirit; it is in their historical unfoldment, not in the speculative knowledge of the Hegelian Concept, that Spirit progressively attains to self-awareness. Life, in other words, becomes progressively aware of itself, by means of concepts immanently developed, as it unfolds itself in the objectivizations of history. Hermeneutics as it is understood by Dilthey is thus not concerned with the ultimate truth of these historical manifestations of man's self-understanding. It brings to light the finitude of man's knowledge—and this is its great value—but in giving equal validity to the different ways in which man has understood life in different ages, it remains stuck up in a rela-

33. Schleiermacher's *Hermeneutik* has been recently re-edited by Heinz Kimmerle (Heidelberg, 1959).

tivism of world-views (*Weltanschauungen*), without any criterion of truth by which they may be judged.[34]

Heidegger rejected the psychological concept of *Erlebnis*,
along with all that was subjectivistic in Dilthey's way of thinking
and he had no use for the Neo-Kantian epistemological orientation of Dilthey—he intended his main work to be a Critique of
the Historical Reason—and the traces of the concept of method
in natural science still present in him. But his vision of the historicity of things, his conception of understanding and of hermeneutics as immanent self-interpretation of Life were absorbed
by Heidegger in his own thinking, not without undergoing profound modification in the process. Historicity and understanding
are central operative concepts in *Being and Time* and are also
thematically discussed there in considerable detail. In his later
writings they continue to play an important role, though in a
radically modified form. The concept of hermeneutics is itself
further widened by Heidegger, so that it ceases to be merely a
theory of the method of interpretation and becomes identical
with the basic activity through which man understands and
interprets his experience. After *Being and Time*, where the application of this concept is limited to the interpretation of Dasein,
the term 'hermeneutics' is dropped by Heidegger, in conformity
with the change in his attitude towards the whole conception of
method as such. Nevertheless, the hermeneutic approach, in a
transmuted, deepened and still further widened form, is evident
throughout in all his later writings also. As the remarkable discussion of the 'hermeneutic circle' or the circle of understanding
in *Being and Time* shows, this work truly carries forward the
work of Dilthey, not merely in regard to the problem of his-

34. A thorough discussion of the views of Dilthey will be found in
Gadamer, *Wahrheit und Methode*, pp. 205–228. Unlike G. Misch (*Lebens-
philosophie und Phänomenologie*) and O. F. Bollnow (*Dilthey*) and like L.
Landgrebe (*Philosophie der Gegenwart*), Gadamer brings out the philo-
sophical limitations of Dilthey. See also Pöggeler, *Der Denkweg Martin
Heideggers*, chapter 2 entitled, "Metaphysik and Geschichte".

toricity but also in elucidating and developing the notions of understanding and interpretation.[35]

With its intensely questioning spirit and the radicalism of its approach, Edmund Husserl's phenomenology has played a vital role in the development of Heidegger's thought. His keen interest in this discipline even before his personal contact with Husserl in 1916; his intimate association with the latter for more than a decade, during which period Heidegger not only lectured on phenomenological topics but also edited Husserl's *Lectures on the Phenomenology of the Inner Consciousness of Time;* the publication of *Being and Time* in Husserls' *Year book of Philosophy and Phenomenological Research* and its dedication, in book form, to the Master—all these are facts which give clear evidence that, for some years at least, phenomenology loomed large in the thoughts of Heidegger.[36] What is more important, in *Being and Time* itself, towards the commencement and again at the end,

35. In the dialogue on language in *Unterwegs zur Sprache,* Heidegger explains the deeper sense in which, connecting *hermeneuein* with Hermes, the messenger of the gods, he understands Hermeneutics. "Hermeneutics means, in *Being and Time,* neither a theory of the art of interpretation nor interpretation itself, but rather an attempt to determine the nature of interpretation primarily in terms of the essence of the hermeneutical . . . (this) means primarily not interpreting but rather the bringing of message and tidings." (See *Unterwegs zur Sprache,* pp. 95–98, 120–126.)

The concept of a philosophical hermeneutics (philosophy regarded as understanding and interpretation) has recently been worked out on a monumental scale by Hans-Georg Gadamer, an early pupil of Heidegger and a scholar of extraordinary range. His work (*Wahrheit und Methode*), inspired by the insights and approach of Husserl, Dilthey and Heidegger, culminates in a discussion of language as the basis of a hermeneutic ontology. Written in a sober, academic, non-Heideggerizing style, this work is indispensable for a grasp of the aims, methods and achievements of the type of philosophy which is concerned not so much with argumentation as with understanding. It is no less valuable as providing a perspective for the understanding of Heidegger's thought and for its illuminating comments on many aspects of that. Gadamer's book also gives a critical account of the development of the concept of hermeneutics from Schleiermacher, through Dilthey, to Heidegger.

In a recent article (*Hermeneutik und Historismus, Philosophische Rundschau,* IX, 1961), Gadamer has discussed critically recent work in the field of theological, juristic and philosophical hermeneutics.

36. For details regarding these facts, see Spiegelberg, op. cit. pp. 275–283.

philosophy is defined as "universal phenomenological ontology" and an illuminating analysis of the meaning of 'phenomenon' is given, along with a discussion of the 'provisional', preliminary concept of phenomenology—the final elucidation of the idea of phenomenology being postponed for later consideration. In *Being and Time*,[37] Heidegger explicitly acknowledges his indebtedness to Husserl: "The following investigations have become possible only because of the ground laid by E. Husserl, with whose *Logical Investigations* phenomenology came into its own." Heidegger adds in a footnote, "If the following investigation takes a few steps forward in the disclosure of the 'things themselves', it is to E. Husserl that the author's thanks are due; he gave to the author during his period of apprenticeship at Freiburg his forceful personal guidance and freest possible access to unpublished studies, thus familiarizing him with the most diverse areas of phenomenological research." What is the extent and scope of Heidegger's indebtedness to phenomenology and to what extent has he appropriated its basic insights into his own work?

Husserl's aim in building up this new discipline was to provide philosophy with a truly secure foundation and establish it as a 'strict science' (*strenge Wissenschaft*) by means of a more radically conceived Cartesian procedure. Suspending all epistemological assumptions and metaphysical presuppositions, he sought to have a glimpse of the 'things themselves' (*Sachen selbst*) as they are revealed in pure, primordial experience, uncontaminated by 'theories' and ready-made concepts. To this end, all linguistic expressions and complexes of meaning are traced back to what is ultimately given in consciousness and 'constituted' by its own acts, to the exclusion of everything that cannot be described in terms of these acts and is imported from 'without' (e.g., the findings of science, metaphysical ready-made concepts). In this phenomenological reduction, as it was termed, consciousness is

37. *Sein und Zeit*, p. 38 (E.T., p. 489).

studied in respect of its intentionality, i.e., of the different ways in which it is directed towards its immanent objects in acts by which these objects are constituted. There is a strict correlation between the modes of consciousness and modes of being (i.e., types of immanent objects) as they are connected together in intentional acts. To be, for Husserl, is thus to be a correlate of an act of consciousness, the pure *ego cogito;* it is to be an object. Unlike psychology, which describes concrete experience in its particularity and is an empirical science, the 'phenomena' of phenomenology, the 'things themselves', are universal essences and it is the purpose of the 'eidetic reduction' to bring these to light by an act of direct intuition (*Anschauung*, looking at). To arrive, through a consideration of the particular and the concrete, at the direct intellectual 'seeing' of the essential structures given in consciousness, the phenomenon in its non-empirical purity, is the primary, not the ultimate, aim in phenomenological inquiry. In the earlier *Logical Investigations* phase of phenomenology it was this primary task that was in the forefront; later, the problems of a 'transcendental' reduction of all objects of consciousness—with all belief in their external reality suspended or 'bracketed'—to its constitutive acts dominate the inquiry.

Husserl's dream was to establish philosophy as a strict science, not indeed in respect of the naturalism and objectivism characteristic of the modern natural scientific approach, which he strongly deprecated, but in the sense of bringing to bear upon philosophy a rigour, a clarity as to basic principles and a methodological self-consciousness which would provide it with a new, unshakeable foundation, free from all unexamined presuppositions. Such a foundation Husserl thought he had found in the subjectivity of the pure ego and pure consciousness, the 'wonder of all wonders', on which a rationally grounded system of philosophical knowledge, completely autonomous, could be built. For Heidegger, this quest of a certified, rationally grounded system is a philosophical chimera, the outcome of that subjectivistic, anthropocentric attitude which has come to dominate philosophy since the modern age was ushered in by Descartes and which is itself the mark of an epoch in the history of Being, an epoch characterized by the oblivion and the all but complete 'withdrawal' of Being. In taking the pure ego or consciousness as the ultimate *fundamentum absolutum inconcussum* and as an allegedly presuppositionless beginning, Husserl fails to be critical and radical enough, for he does not inquire into the mode of Being of consciousness (*Bewusstsein—being* conscious), as Heidegger pointed out in his comments on Husserl's drafts for the *Encyclopaedia Britannica* article on Phenomenology.[38] Husserl does not inquire into the subjectivity of the subject; though he has often described the task of phenomenology as the achievement of critical self-awareness and as an overcoming of the naïvete of the natural attitude, his own work does not carry this process through to its end. Heidegger's thought brings to the surface the unexamined presuppositions in Husserlian phenomenology, as Ludwig Landgrebe and Eugen Fink, with their intimate knowledge of both Husserl and Heidegger, have shown.[39] In that sense it may be regarded as carrying the phenomenological start made by Husserl to its logical conclusion. Further, when Husserl takes the 'acts' of consciousness as the acts of a timeless, universal and absolute ego, he falls into the idealistic error of thinking that it can 'constitute' the world solely out of itself, without any anchorage in something factually given, something that it presupposes and cannot spin out of itself. For Heidegger, on the contrary, the factual, existing man is the basic fact and the source of all projects of the understanding. The 'facticity' of man con-

---

38. See Walter Biemel, "Husserls Encyclopaedia Britannica Artikel und Heideggers Anmerkungen dazu" in *Tijdschrift voor Philosophie*, XII (1950). The various drafts of this article, along with Heidegger's comments and a letter to Husserl are published in *Phänomenologische Psychologie* (*Husserliana*, IX, 1962). Heidegger collaborated with Husserl in the preparation of the earlier drafts and the difference between their conception of phenomenology that emerged in consequence can be seen clearly from the material contained in this volume. Cf. in particular, pp. 256, 247, 517 ff. and 600–602.

39. Landgrebe, *Phänomenologie und Metaphysik, Philosophie der Gegenwart* and subsequent articles; Fink, *Sein, Wahrheit, Welt*.

sists in this that the possible ways in which he can understand himself and the world presuppose, and are limited by, the actual historical situation in which man at any time happens to be and the particular tradition he happens to inherit. This is the meaning of the 'hermeneutics of facticity' which Heidegger substitutes, in *Being and Time*, for Husserl's transcendental reduction[40] and the reason why he prefers to employ the method of 'interpretation' rather than that of reflexion in his inquiries. The place of the absolute ego of Husserl is taken by the factual, thrown Dasein regarded as the clearing (*Lichtung*) of the disclosure of Being— not the absolute subject but Being is the ultimate ground (looked at from the point of view of man, at least) of all 'constitution'.[41]

Heidegger would agree with much of Husserl's requirements "not to hunt deductively after constructions unrelated to the matter in question, but to derive all knowledge from its ultimate sources, from principles seen authentically and understood as insights; not to be diverted by any prejudices, by any verbal contradictions or indeed by anything in the world, even under the name of 'exact science,' but to grant its right to whatever is clearly seen, which thus constitutes the 'original', or what precedes all theories, or what sets the ultimate norm."[42] But the demand for a reduction to pure subjectivity he cannot concede, because

40. Cf. Landgrebe's article, "Husserls Abschied vom Cartesianismus," now included in his book, *Der Weg der Phänomenologie*.
41. Heidegger's dissatisfaction with the notion of the transcendental ego as the source of constitution is clearly expressed in his letter to Husserl (in Husserl's *Phänomenologische Psychologie*, pp. 601–602): "What is the mode of being of that entity in whom 'world' gets constituted? This is the central problem of *Being and Time*. . . . It needs being shown that the mode of being of a human being is totally different from that of all other essents and that precisely because it is such a mode of being that it contains hidden within itself the possibility of transcendental constitution. Transcendental constitution is a central possibility of the factually existing self. . . . The constituting subject is not nothing, hence it is something and has being—although not in the sense of something given. The inquiry into the mode of being of the constituting source is not to be evaded."
42. Quoted in Spiegelberg, op. cit. p. 128.

such a demand is itself conditioned and determined by the metaphysics of modern subjectivism as it has developed in ignorance of its own roots; its own 'facticity', the givenness of the historical situation out of which it has arisen, remains opaque to it. The historical roots of the concept of subjectivity and the foundations of the metaphysical tradition within which it has arisen remain invisible to Husserl (except, to some extent, in his last phase, when he attempted another new beginning with his *Crisis of the European Sciences,* a work of self-criticism, not perhaps wholly uninfluenced by Heidegger, though still opposed to him). Heidegger does not believe, as Husserl does, in the possibility of a radical start in philosophy, a beginning with a clean slate, by going straight to the 'facts themselves'. Philosophical inquiry for him is essentially historical; wherever one starts, a traditional concept is always presupposed though one may not be aware of it and hence the 'things themselves' never offer a pure, eternal essence. What is purely intuited in the Husserlian *Wesensschau* is always historically determined and therefore penetrating to the essential and original phenomenon always needs going back to the historical beginnings. For this reason philosophy cannot be a science in the sense of an attested, certain and universally and eternally valid body of objective truths. The compelling validity and objectivity of intuited essences is an illusion, for, as Heidegger shows in *Being and Time,* knowing is a mode of man's own being-in-the-world and a form of the project of understanding, a project (*Entwurf*) which is itself a thrown (*geworfen*) project in the sense that it is determined by tradition and the past. Not pure 'intuition' (deriving from the primacy of 'seeing' in the Greek conception of Being as objective presence) nor the Husserlian intentionality, but care (*Sorge*) as the being of man is what brings about the disclosure of essents.[43] The whole doctrine of intentionality shows itself as untenable, being based on a preconceived notion of a pure

43. Cf. *Die Phänomenologische Idee der Intentionalität* by A. de Waelhens in *Husserl und das Denken der Neuzeit.*

cognitive awareness standing over against a world of objective entities. To penetrate into this historical dimension of the pre-suppositions of thought, to inquire how and why European philosophy is compelled, in the terminal phase of its meta-physical tradition, to formulate its problems within the Cartesian framework and to show how the tenability of this framework itself rests on an unawareness of its own origins, is just the task which Heidegger sets before himself in his thinking.

Heidegger takes from Husserl a method for bringing to light the structures hidden in experience, the 'phenomena' as he him-self conceives them, a way of seeing what *is,* without losing sight of all that is presupposed in such 'seeing' and without claiming that such seeing can ever disclose eternal and ultimate 'Truths'. As he makes amply clear in *Being and Time,* phenomenology is for him only a method and even as such it finds application only in the analysis of human existence. For Husserl's conception of philosophy as a strict science, for the transcendental reduction and for the host of 'constitution' problems in phenomenology Heidegger has no use. After *Being and Time,* even this methodo-logical apparatus is discarded in consequence of a clearer aware-ness of his own task and of the impossibility of realizing it without giving up the language and concepts of traditional metaphysics and theory of knowledge.

Though in *Being and Time* Heidegger defines philosophy as "universal phenomenological ontology, taking the hermeneutics of Dasein (i.e., human existence) as its point of departure", he never identified himself with phenomenology as a school nor ac-cepted any of the 'programmatic' conceptions of this discipline as put forward by Husserl from time to time. The kind of phenom-enological description and analysis conducted in this work has been characterized, at one time by Heidegger himself[44], as 'hermeneutic phenomenology' but this, as he makes clear, does not mean that he was aiming at initiating a new trend within

44. *Unterwegs zur Sprache,* p. 95.

phenomenology. "I attempted, on the contrary, to arrive rather at a deeper conception of the essence of phenomenology in order to give it in this way, on purpose, its place in the framework of European philosophy", Heidegger says, adding[45] that with the help of hermeneutics, understood in a deeper sense than the traditional, "I was enabled to characterize the phenomenological thought that opened for me the way to *Being and Time*." If, following Heidegger's elucidation in this work, we understand phenomenology as a way of bringing into view the being of whatever is, a way of thinking that can lead us to see, and hear, into the nature of things, a way of bringing this to light, then Heidegger is and has always been a phenomenologist. He does not infer, deduce or generalize, offers no 'logical' arguments, 'proves' nothing. Yet, through his analyses and explorations in depth, through the reconnoitering movement of his thought, going in circles around the matter in question, he brings into view coherent structures lying buried under the surface of our everyday experience as well as the presuppositions, the light of Being, involved in the way we interpret and understand this experience.[46] In *Being and Time*, this is done with some methodolog-

45. *Ibid.*, p. 122.
46. See *Vorträge und Aufsätze*, p. 134: "From the Sciences to Thinking there is no bridge but only a leap. It brings us not only to another side but to a wholly different locality. What it opens up can never be proved, if proving means deriving, on the basis of suitable assumptions, propositions about some state of affairs by means of chains of deductive inference. He who wants to prove or have proved to him that which is known only in so far as it manifests itself while at the same time concealing itself, he who still desires this does not by any means judge in accordance with a higher or more stringent measure of knowledge. He merely *reckons* with a standard and that, too, an inappropriate one. For, to that which lets itself be known only in such a way that in its self-concealment it manifests itself, we can also come up (be equal) only so that we point to it and, with that, enjoin ourselves to let that which shows itself appear in its own unhiddenness. This simple pointing is a distinctive mark of thinking, the way to that which it is given to man to think, once and for time to come. Everything permits of being proved, i.e. of being derived from suitable assumptions. But very little is amenable to pointing, to being emancipated into arrival by being pointed to, and this also very seldom."
Cf. also *Der Satz vom Grund*, pp. 40–41, for Heidegger's remarks on "axiomatic thinking."

ical fanfare (though surprisingly little of the technical apparatus devised by Husserl is in evidence). Later even this is given up as inessential and the manner becomes less academic, simpler and more evocative. But always, from first to last, the one thing that engages Heidegger is the task of bringing into view, through meditative thinking and the employment of language adequate to embody it, what and how things *are* and in what their Being consists. For, as he says, "The one thing that counts, now as before, is to bring to light the Being of the things that are (essents), not, it is true, in the manner of metaphysics but so that Being itself comes out, shining forth, into view."[47]

Although Heidegger has been profoundly influenced, in certain ways, by the work of Dilthey and Husserl, his own thinking cannot be understood merely as a continuation and radicalization of motives present in these philosophers. He takes these philosophers as contemporary points of departure for his own thinking, as opening for him a 'way'. But having once in this manner launched himself into the mainstream of European thought, he goes further back and lines up, as it were, with Nietzsche—the

---

47. *Ibid.*, p. 122. The question whether Heidegger is to be called a phenomenologist has been widely debated. Landgrebe and Fink, both loyal and veteran phenomenologists, both aware of the strains within Husserlian phenomenology and alive to the need of an inner transformation of it, look upon Heidegger as to a large extent accomplishing this. For a lucid discussion of the whole problem, see Spiegelberg's *The Phenomenological Movement, Vol. I*, as also the excellent review of this work by Richard Schmitt (*Review of Metaphysics*, March, 1962). In various articles published recently, Schmitt has been doing valuable liaison work trying to bring together Continental Phenomenology and English Analytical Philosophy. It still remains, however, to be realized fully how very much off the mark Gilbert Ryle was in his attacks against Phenomenology (beginning with his review of *Sein und Zeit* in *Mind*, 1929). As regards the continuity of the philosophical development from Dilthey through Husserl to Heidegger see, besides the works of Landgrebe mentioned earlier, Hans-Georg Gadamer: *Wahrheit und Methode;* also Gadamer's recent review article on the Phenomenological Movement (*Philosophische Rundschau*, XI, 1963). But, as Gadamer himself remarks in his book (p. 243), "The true precursor of Heidegger's way of posing the problem of Being and of the opposition to the direction of inquiry in Western metaphysics which it signified, could, therefore, be neither Dilthey nor Husserl but much rather Nietzsche."

last great thinker of the metaphysical tradition—and taking up the thread from this herald of "a provisional transition" from this tradition, himself executes the actual transition to another mode of thinking. We can say, in fact, of Heidegger (as he does about Nietzsche) that "in his thinking all motives of Western thought, but all transformed, are skilfully gathered together" *and* transcended so that the entire thought of the West is appropriated in its real truth through the transition. His roots go back into the Greek origins of Western philosophy and there is hardly any major facet of European thought which has not acted as a stimulus to his own development. But to attempt to trace out in detail the variety and extent of the influences that have gone into the making either of his main work or of his later writings would be premature at this stage. Some indication of Heidegger's indebtedness to medieval thought has been given above. The influence of the early Greek thinkers, Heraclitus and Parmenides, is patent in his later writings. The extent to which Plato has stimulated his thinking is evidenced not only by his essay on "Plato's Theory of Truth," by the discussion of the Good (*Agathon*) in *Vom Wesen des Grundes* and in *Nietzsche* but also by the ever-recurring discussion of the Platonic Idea in his later writings. The very formulation of Heidegger's central problem, the meaning of Being, derives from Plato and from Aristotle. A close reading of Heidegger's writings reveals, in fact, the figure of Aristotle as a pervasive presence; the Stagirite, as a thinker who has laid down the basic pattern of the entire tradition of Western metaphysical thought, is, as it were, the invisible partner in the dialogue of Heidegger's philosphy. Kant's influence is writ large on *Being and Time* and evidenced further not only by his books on Kant but also by the way he keeps coming back to Kant in his writings. Hegel's importance as a challenge to the thinking of Heidegger is not confined to the problem dealt with in the last chapters of *Being and Time;* how much of Heidegger's philosophizing is a continuing debate with Hegel is made evident by a reference to his essays, "Hegel's Concept of Experience," "Identity and Difference" and "Hegel and the Greeks".[48] Among philosophers who are nearer to our own times, it is above all Nietzsche, with his criticism of the Platonic-Christian tradition and the nihilistic culmination of this tradition in his own thought, that has provided the springboard for Heidegger's quest and which in some measure explains the intensity and the passion with which he seeks to bring into view the thread that runs through the history of Western metaphysics, connecting its beginning (Plato) with its end or consummation in Nietzsche. The powerful impact of the letter on Heidegger's thought and the way in which Nietzsche's philosophy is the key that has enabled Heidegger to lay hold of the inner meaning and significance of the Western metaphysical tradition has become apparent in its full scope only with the recent publication of his two-volume *Nietzsche*.[49]

48. Egon Vietta mentions (*Die Seinsfrage bei Martin Heidegger,* 1950) "the famous lecture-course, "Schelling, On the Nature of Human Freedom," held in 1936." Some indication of his preoccupation with Schelling is given in Chapter IX of his recent *Nietzsche*. Paul Tillich and Walter Schulz have drawn attention to the parallels between Heidegger and Schelling. See in particular, the latter's *Die Vollendung des Deutschen Idealismus in der Spätphilosophie Schellings.*

Vietta gives the titles of some other unpublished lecture-courses of Heidegger and reproduces in the above mentioned book valuable extracts from letters written to him by Heidegger. This book is a popular exposition, much of it in dialogue form, written in a "non-academic" style, but nonetheless useful for an understanding of what the philosopher is driving at.

See also Richardson (*Heidegger*) and Pöggeler (*Der Denkweg Martin Heideggers*) for more titles of Heidegger's unpublished Lectures and Seminar courses. The latter discusses in addition some unpublished works, quoting from them freely, in the main body of his book.

49. Heidegger worked and lectured extensively on some of the dialogues of Plato during the period when he was engaged in writing *Being and Time,* as for example, the *Sophist,* with a quotation from which this work begins, and the *Philebus* which, according to Dr. H. Boeder (personal communication) has had some influence on the analyses of *Befindlichkeit* and *Stimmung* in *Being and Time.* According to Eugen Fink (oral communication), Aristotle's *Nicomachean Ethics,* BK VI, has profoundly influenced the analyses in this work, in particular the Aristotelian concept of *phronesis.* In seminars, Heidegger has discussed in detail Augustine's *Confessions,* especially the portions dealing with Memory and with Time and also Aristotle's *Physics* (oral communication from Prof. Heidegger), recently published in part under the title *Vom Wesen und Begriff der Physis.* The writings of Heidegger's pupils and followers, such as H-G. Gadamer (*Wahrheit und*

The central problem of *Being and Time* is to raise afresh the question of Being, in a sense in which it has never been raised, having been bypassed throughout the whole history of European metaphysical thought. Metaphysics deals with the essent *qua* essent (*on e on*) and offers a *logos* (statement) about the *on* (the essent, what is). Concerned with the is-ness (*Seiendheit, ousia*) of the essent, it seeks all the time to represent essents as such in their totality. And it does this in a two-fold manner, representing, in the first place, the totality of essents as such in respect of their most general features and at the same time, secondly, this totality in the sense of the highest and therefore the most divine essent. Because it seeks to represent the essent *qua* essent, metaphysics has intrinsically had this two-fold onto-theological character ever since Aristotle developed the conception of a "First Philosophy" (*prote philosophia*) in his *Metaphysics*. As Heidegger says[50], "Regarded as dealing with the truth of essents as such, metaphysics has a two-fold form. But the ground of this two-foldness, let alone its origin, remains unknown to metaphysics, not as a matter of chance or due to negligence but necessarily. . . . As metaphysics, it is by its very nature shut out from a knowledge of Being, for it represents the essent (*on*)

Methode), Volkmann-Schluck (*Plotin als Interpret der Ontologie Platos*), Walter Bröcker (*Aristoteles*), K. Oltmanns (*Meister Eckhart*) and others, give some idea of the concentration with which Heidegger has studied the great Western thinkers. Heidegger has lectured extensively on most of these, from the Pre-Socratics to Nietzsche; extracts from some of these lecture-courses have been published and a few of them in entirety. It is known that he has occupied himself intensively with the interpretation of Aristotle (Cf. W. Szilasi, "Metaphysik und Geschichte der Philosophie," in *Martin Heideggers Einfluss auf die Wissenschaften.*) So far, however, only the exegesis of the introductory chapter of the Second Book of Aristotle's *Physics*, mentioned above, has been published. For a systematic presentation of the philosophy of Aristotle influenced by Heidegger's lectures, see the book by Bröcker mentioned above. A commenentary on Aristotle's *peri hermeneias* still remains unpublished.
50. For the whole of this paragraph see the "Introduction" to *Was ist Metaphysik?*. Cf. also "Hegels Begriff der Erfahrung" in *Holzwege*, pp. 161–163 (E.T., pp. 105–108) for the ambiguity in *on* and its significance for metaphysics.

as it has become manifest in the light of Being, without being in a position to attend to what has concealed itself in this very *on* as it became unconcealed. . . . On what has thus concealed itself in the *on* metaphysics remains grounded, in order to be able to devote itself to the representation of the essent *qua* essent (*on e on*)." The truth of Being, in other words, is the light in and through which beings become manifest, enabling metaphysics to represent them; but in illuminating the essent, Being itself, directing our gaze on the essent, keeps itself hidden.[51] Focussing on the truth of beings but itself grounded on the truth of Being, metaphysics is unable to perceive this latter fact. Further, metaphysics, in inquiring into the nature of what is, is always oriented to essents within the world, to what can be encountered within it and seeks to represent the essent as such and as a whole in terms of that. Its representational thinking takes the Being of essents as 'presentation', i.e., it understands it in terms of the present, as sheer presence (*Anwesenheit, ousia*). Metaphysics has always understood Being, therefore, in the light of Time, in terms of a particular mode of it, namely, the present. But it has simply assumed this way of taking Being and taken it for granted, without inquiring into it; nor has it sought to examine its basic presupposition about time itself as an eternal succession of 'nows'. In traditional metaphysics both Being and Time have remained unquestioned presuppositions. Hence, Being as presence is the Unthought (*das Ungedachte*) of metaphysics, the foundation on which metaphysics itself stands and therefore beyond its reach. We must ask, therefore, with Heidegger, "How then does it stand with Being and Time? Must not the one as well as the other,

51. This is what Heidegger often calls the "oblivion of Being" (*Seinsvergessenheit*). But this should not be understood, he points out (*Zur Seinsfrage*, p. 34; E.T., p. 91), as if Being were an umbrella left somewhere due to the forgetfulness of a professor of philosophy. Forgetting is not exclusively an omission or something merely negative; nor must it be understood solely in terms of an act of the human subject. Forgetting is rooted in self-concealment (*Verbergung*) in which what is forgotten is at the same time preserved.

Being as well as Time, must not both, in the way they are related together, become problematical, first of all problematical and eventually questionable? Does this not then show that in the innermost core of what is regarded as the central conception of European metaphysics, something essential in the nature of Being has never been thought about? The question of *Being and Time* is a signpost to this Unthought of all metaphysics. On this Unthought rests metaphysics and therefore what remained Unthought in metaphysics is due to no shortcoming of metaphysics itself."[52]

In *Being and Time,* Heidegger seeks to render problematic what has thus been taken for granted, to think this 'Unthought' of the Western philosophical tradition, to get back into the ground of metaphysics and find out if it is possible to have a more radical and deeper comprehension of Being. The meaning of Being has so long been glimpsed through the veil of a particular modality of time, the present, itself understood in terms of a particular interpretation of Being. Is it possible to break out of this circle or, as Heidegger would prefer to put it, break *into* this circle and comprehend more originally, and formulate in words, what Being itself means?

To answer this question it is necessary not only to examine what time is but to reopen the problem of Being in such fashion as to show its intrinsic connection with time. But since Being is always the Being of beings and, further, since the meaning of Being is manifested only within the comprehension of one essent, man, it is necessary that the inquiry should be anchored to man in his aspect of being open to Being, as the locus where Being and its meaning are disclosed, i.e., to *Dasein* (which is Heidegger's technical term for man in his aspect of being open to Being). The traditional way of understanding Being in terms of objective presence, in terms of entities given in the world, must be shown to be one-sided and superficial by demonstrating that

52. *Was heisst Denken?*, p. 42 (E.T., p. 103).

man's mode of being is radically different and that it provides us with a deeper conception of Being from which the former can itself be derived. The being of Dasein, of man in his overtness, must be brought into view as also the temporal horizon within which man's being discloses itself. And the way man comprehends Being, the conditions of the possibility of such comprehension, must be laid bare and it must be demonstrated how the comprehension of Being always moves within the dimension of time. The being of Dasein himself, it may turn out, lies in temporality and an 'analytic' of Dasein may yield a way of understanding time that is deeper, more primordial than the common view based on an ontology of objectively given essents. On the basis of time as thus understood in its real, primordial sense, the true meaning of Being itself may then be determined. The analysis of Dasein is thus the path to be gone over in order to arrive at the meaning of Being.

This is the path taken by *Being and Time*. The work, originally published as the first part of a larger study, begins with a general exposition of the question about the sense of Being. This includes a discussion of the necessity, the structure and the pre-eminence of this question and a statement of the double task—the analysis of Dasein and the 'destruction' (or analytical scrutiny) of the history of Ontology—involved in working out the question of Being. An account of the phenomenological method pursued in the inquiry is also given here. The first part of the inquiry proper opens with a preparatory analysis of Dasein. This includes a statement of the general character of the task and an accout of the basic constitution of Dasein as being-in-the-world; a detailed analysis of the concept of 'world', including an examination of the Cartesian conception of the world, and of man's togetherness, selfhood and anonymity; an analysis of the different ways in which man is 'in' the world and open to it, i.e., an analysis of man's existenzial constitution, including accounts of attunement or mood, understanding, interpretation, judgment and language; the everyday modes of man's openness to world and his aban-

donment to it. The preparatory analysis culminates in an exposition of the being of Dasein in terms of care or concern (*Sorge*),
to which is added a discussion of the problem of 'reality' and of
truth. Then follows an account of Dasein in his temporal aspect,
constituting the second Division of *Being and Time*. The problem
of the wholeness of Dasein and its relation to death is first dealt
with. Heidegger follows this up with an examination of how man
can be authentically himself, along with an analysis of conscience; an elucidation of Dasein's ability to be authentically
whole in terms of 'resoluteness'; an account of how temporality
constitutes the ontological meaning of care. This is followed by
an interpretation of the different elements in Dasein's constitution in terms of temporality. Next, an examination of the
historicity of man's mode of existence serves to bring out the
rootedness of history itself in the primordial temporality of Dasein.
Finally, in the last chapter of *Being and Time*, an attempt is
made to bring out the nature of original, primordial time by an
account of the vulgar conception of time and a demonstration of
its derivative character.[53]

As Heidegger remarks in the Introduction to *Was ist Metaphysik?*, "The thinking attempted in *Being and Time* sets out on
the way to prepare an overcoming of metaphysics", not in the
sense of abolishing metaphysics but in the sense of going back to
the ground of metaphysics, inaccessible to metaphysics as such, by
recalling the truth of Being itself. Because, Heidegger goes on to
say, this treatise, in dealing with the question of existenz ultimately aims at penetrating to the truth of Being—the hidden
ground of all metaphysics—it is entitled, not 'Existenz and Time'
or 'Consciousness and Time' but 'Being and Time'. The 'and' in
this title is not to be understood as meaning a juxtaposition of
two separate, distinct things. "In *Being and Time*, Being is not
something other than time, for 'time' here is the first name (*Vor-*

---

53. Magda King provides a very helpful introduction to the central ideas
of *Being and Time* in her *Heidegger's Philosophy* (1964). Her lucid and
careful 'guide' stops short, however, with Division One of *Sein und Zeit*.

name) given to the truth of Being." Time and Being are brought together, Heidegger explains further, because the Greeks, in whose thinking Being first disclosed itself, thought of Being as the presence of what is present, as *einai,* which means "to be present (*Anwesen*)". "The essence of this 'being present' is hidden deep in the earliest names of Being (*einai, ousia*). . . . In 'being present' there prevails, unconceived and hidden, the present duration, i.e., time. Being as such is accordingly unconcealed (revealed) through time. Thus time points toward the unconcealedness, i.e., the truth of Being." Time in this sense is, of course, not what metaphysics thinks about it; it is to be taken as "the first name, yet to be pondered upon, of the truth of Being, yet to be realized."[54] This hidden presence of time is betrayed not only in the earliest metaphysical name for Being but also in the last, the Eternal Recurrence of the Same. The history of Being, in the epoch of metaphysics, shows a pervasive sway of time which has never been subjected to thinking.

Similarly, in *Kant und das Problem der Metaphysik,* Heidegger explains that the interpretation of Dasein in terms of temporality is motivated solely by the problem of Being as such.[55] The fundamental ontological approach to the foundation of metaphysics in *Being and Time* must be understood in the sense of a repetition, of the renewal of a problem long buried in obscurity and yet ever alive. The opening quotation from Plato's *Sophist* is not meant, Heidegger says, for decoration but as a reminder that in classical metaphysics the battle of the giants over the Being of what is has already broken out. In this battle, Being is in some sense understood though not explicitly inquired after. The metaphysics of antiquity takes the *ontos on* as *aei on,* i.e., as unvarying and permanent, and as *ousia* in the sense of 'presence', a sort

54. As Heidegger later pointed out (Richardson's *Heidegger,* "Preface," p. XIII), even the delineation of temporality as ecstatic-horizontal which is given in *Being and Time* fails to reach the innermost character of time which can prove adequate from the point of view of the problem of Being.
55. P. 216 (E.T., p. 247 f.).

of immediate 'having' of the essent. Here the understanding of Being is based on a project in terms of time, as constancy of presence. From the very beginning thus the battle over Being is waged within the horizon of time. Why is Being understood, in this spontaneous and self-evident manner, in terms of time? The conception of time as developed by Aristotle, itself based on a comprehension of Being as presence, and generally taken for granted after him, gives no answer to this question. Hence the necessity, Heidegger says, for raising the old problem again and for an examination of the finitude of Dasein's constitution in such a manner that temporality as its basic transcendental structure comes clearly into view.

As will be evident from a look at the full plan of the projected work given in chapter II, section 8, of *Being and Time,* its published part breaks off at a crucial point. Even the analytic of Dasein is not complete, for, as Heidegger repeatedly points out in the course of the text, although the being of Dasein has been found to lie in care and the latter itself shown to be rooted in temporality, the entire analysis leading to this result must be considered as being provisional until a final reinterpretation in terms of a clarified concept of Being is forthcoming. The temporal horizon, within which the new concept of Being was to be determined, has indeed been laid bare. But the next step, the movement back from Time to Being, is not taken and the third Division of *Being and Time,* Part I, entitled "Time and Being" was held back for reasons which Heidegger left shrouded in obscurity for a long time. This has given rise to much misunderstanding as to the intentions and aims of Heidegger and also to the curious result that *Being and Time,* as published, became, even against the wishes of the author, a major contribution to the literature of Existentialism and the main *problem* of the work, in the service of which the analysis of human existence was conducted, was largely overlooked. The second part of the work was, of course, never published. *Being and Time* is thus a fragment; for reasons to be explained later its continuation was rendered

impracticable and yet, since its publication, Heidegger has ceaselessly travelled on the 'way' of his thought, "on his way, a wanderer in the neighbourhood of Being."[56] On this 'way' he has left
behind him the approach and language of *Being and Time* and,
nevertheless, as will be shown in what follows, his thinking does
eventually arrive at its destination, i.e., at a re-awakening of the
question of Being and a tentative formulation of a new conception of Being. The project of a 'phenomenological destruction of
the history of Ontology', the regressive scrutiny of the history of
the concept of Being, as planned for the second part of *Being
and Time* has actually been carried out by Heidegger on an
extensive scale in writings published since then.

The major part of *Being and Time,* as actually published,
comprises the analytic of Dasein, i.e., an analysis and interpretation of human nature. The powerful impact that the work had on
the related fields of psychology and psychiatry, of philosophical
anthropology, especially in its prevalent existentialistic garb, and
of theology, as newly influenced by the discovery of Kierkegaard,
is, therefore, quite understandable. But the way an original
philosophical work—which, as Nietzsche said, is in its essence
always 'untimely'—is received by contemporaries and its immediate impact (or absence of impact, as in the case of Hume's 'still-
born' *Treatise*) has hardly any relation to its real aims and to the
basic inspiration behind it. It is a mark of Heidegger's greatness
as a thinker that he did not allow himself to be swayed from his
central aim by the wide-ranging and epochal contemporary reception of his work. As he has himself remarked,[57] "If there is
such a thing as a catastrophe in the creative activity of great
thinkers, it lies not in the fact that they suffer shipwreck and
make no advance but rather in that they 'move on', i.e., let themselves be influenced by the immediate appeal, which is always
the result of a misunderstanding, of their thoughts. What is fatal
is always the mere advancing 'further', instead of staying behind

56. *Brief über den 'Humanismus,'* p. 93.
57. *Nietzsche I,* pp. 337–338.

at the source where one started." Unconcerned with the contemporary impact of his work and with the general failure in
appreciating its real import, Heidegger has remained loyal to his
own initial insight and left, in a real sense, his 'followers' always
far behind him. From the point of view of his Being-centred
thought, a particular interpretation of man and hence the mode
of his existence in history, is only the essential consequence of the
nature of truth and of Being itself prevailing at a particular time.
For this reason, the nature of man can never be adequately determined in its roots through the metaphysical interpretation of
man as a rational animal. "This was the insight", Heidegger explains,[58] "responsible for the treatise *Being and Time*. The
essence of man is determined in terms of the essence (*wesen*,
used as a verb, 'be-ing') of the truth of Being by Being itself. In
the treatise *Being and Time* an attempt is made to determine the
nature of man solely in terms of his relationship to Being, on the
basis of the question about the truth of Being and not any more
about the truth of essents. This essence of man is described there
in a precisely defined sense as *Da-sein*. In spite of the fact that at
the same time, as required by the context, a more fundamental
concept of truth was developed, the work has not succeeded in
the least in awakening even an elementary comprehension of the
issue raised here. This failure to understand is due, on the one
hand, to the ineradicable and deep-seated habituation to the
modern way of thinking. Man is conceived as a subject and all
reflection on man is taken as anthropology. On the other hand,
the reason for this failure lies in the nature of the attempt itself.
Because it has grown out historically and is not something 'arti-
ficial', it derives from what has been hitherto existing. But at the
same time it seeks to struggle out of it and therefore, necessarily
and continuously, still harks back into the grooves of the past,
even calling on it for help, but for the purpose of saying something quite different. Above all, the path thus struck out breaks

58. *Nietzsche II*, p. 194.

off at a crucial point. The reason for this breakdown lies in the fact that this path, and the attempt, without intending it, is faced with the threat of itself becoming, once again, a perpetuation of subjectivity and of becoming itself a hindrance to the decisive steps still to be taken by way of completing the account satisfactorily. Any turn towards 'objectivism' and 'realism' is still subjectivism: the question about Being as such stands beyond the reach of the subject-object relation."

Still thinking within the 'fundamental-ontological' framework of *Being and Time*, Heidegger published in 1929 a study of Kant entitled *Kant und das Problem der Metaphysik* (*Kant and the Problem of Metaphysics*), in part fulfilment of the task originally assigned to the projected second part of *Being and Time*. Heidegger seeks, in this book, to interpret the *Critique of Pure Reason* from his own fundamental-ontological point of view and to bring to light, by way of a valuable analysis of Kant's theory of the transcendental power of imagination, the role that Time plays in the Kantian ontology as its implicit and unthought foundation. In the same year was published the widely known Inaugural Lecture, *Was ist Metaphysik?* (*What is Metaphysics?*), to which later (1943) a Postscript and then (1949) an Introduction were added. This lecture is in the main a discussion of the concept of Nothingness and aims at showing how the Nothing, as the other to all that is, constitutes Dasein's transcendence as experienced in the first instance when we seek to ascend from beings (essents) to Being. Another article published the same year, in a volume presented to Husserl, is entitled *Vom Wesen des Grundes* (*On the Essence of the Ground*), where again the direction of the inquiry is from Dasein to its self-transcendence in the project of a ground of everything that is. The main topics discussed are the concepts of ground, freedom, transcendence and world. In all these writings Heidegger's main purpose is to press forward with the task of forging a path that might lead from the internal ontological constitution of Dasein to Being regarded as sheer transcendence, very much in the manner of *Being and Time*.

After these writings of the first phase (1927–1929), there is a long period of silence until the appearance of the *Brief überden 'Humanismus'* (*Letter on Humanism*) in 1947, announcing a shift in perspective, a "change in thinking", and revealing the full scope and the far-reaching character of this change. The few essays actually published during this period give only the barest indications of the change that was coming over Heidegger's thought and of the crisis which made him abandon the path, though not the ultimate objective, of *Being and Time*. The Rectoral Address he delivered in 1933 at the Freiburg University[59] reflects Heidegger's involvement, for a brief period, in politics and containing as it does (in Spiegelberg's words) his "supreme appeal to the will as the lever for shaping man's destiny in his universe", it can hardly be said to mark a change in the basic approach of *Being and Time*. In a sense, as Spiegelberg has remarked,[60] this speech "represents the high watermark and possibly the turning point of Heidegger's trust in the capacity of human being to force Being to surrender its secret", a trust of which Nietzsche's will-to-power is the symbolic expression.[61] It was with the metaphysical implications of this doctrine that Heidegger's thought was to wrestle in the years to come, with far-reaching consequences to his own thinking about Being and to his whole perspective on the history of Western Philosophy. This

59. *Die Selbstbehauptung der deutschen Universität.*
60. *The Phenomenological Movement*, Vol. I, p. 309.
61. This way of putting, it must be admitted, is not quite fair to Heidegger who has, from the beginning, sought to interpret Will in terms of Dasein's openness to Being. I am myself inclined to accept without qualification Heidegger's own interpretation of what he was aiming at in *Being and Time*. The thinking attempted there "remained captive to contemporary modes of representation and language and this also led to inadequate explanations of its own intentions" (Richardson, *Heidegger*, "Preface"). But, as he adds, "Any one who is prepared to observe the simple fact that in *Being and Time* the problem is set up outside the sphere of subjectivism— that the entire anthropological problem is kept at a distance, that the entire issue is governed solely and emphatically by the experience (i.e. the awareness) of man as *Da-sein* (i.e., as the place where the disclosure of Being occurs), with a constant eye to the question of Being—he will also see that the 'Being' into which *Being and Time* inquired cannot remain something that is posited by the human subject." Cf. Richardson, *Preface*.

influence of Nietzsche on his thought was, however, to be apparent only much later, with the writings published since 1950 and, in all its scope, with the publication of his *Nietzsche* in 1961. The new trend in his thought was signalled by the appearance, in 1936, of an essay on the poet Hölderlin, followed by another in 1943, and their publication together in a book entitled *Erläuterungen zu Hölderlins Dichtung* (*Explanations of Hölderlin's Poems*) in 1944 and with two more essays added, in 1951. Heidegger recurs to Hölderlin again and again in his later writings, and has published another independent essay on him in 1958–60.[62] In addition to his preoccupation with Hölderlin he has also written essays on other German poets such as Rilke, Mörike, Trakl, Hebel and George, as well as an important study, "Der Ursprung des Kunstwerkes" ("The Origin of the Work of Art," in *Holzwege*, 1950).[63] The relevance of Heidegger's interest in

62. *Hölderlins Erde und Himmel*, (*Hölderlin-Jahrbuch, Bd.* XI).
63. Within the scope of the present work it has not been possible to deal at length either with Heidegger's interpretations of Hölderlin, Rilke and other poets or with his views on art. Else Buddeberg's monograph, *Denken und Dichten des Seins—Heidegger/Rilke*, is an excellent introduction to both the thinker and the poet. In his widely read *The Disinherited Mind*, Erich Heller quotes Angelloz (*Rainer Maria Rilke*, 1936) as reporting a remark by Heidegger to the effect that "his philosophy is merely the unfolding in thought of what Rilke has expressed poetically"—which should be taken with considerable qualification. Heidegger's much greater closeness to Hölderlin is brought out illuminatingly in Beda Allenmann's monograph, *Hölderlin und Heidegger* and borne out by Heidegger's own statement (Cf. "Wozu Dichter?" in *Holzwege*) that Rilke's poetry belongs to and expresses the realm of the truth of essents as it has unfolded itself since the consummation of Western metaphysics in Nietzsche, whereas Hölderlin, dwelling in the region of the manifestness of Being, is a harbinger and forerunner, a poet who overflows into the future and moulds it.
    Heidegger's views on art constitute a radical criticism of traditional Aesthetics and are aimed at liberating the philosophy of art from the categories of metaphysics. The essay, Der Ursprung des Kunstwerkes," in which these views are developed, is equally important as marking a significant stage in the growth of Heidegger's own thoughts about World and Thing, Being and Truth. Cf. Gadamer's Introduction in the Reclam ed. of this essay. In his thorough study of Kantian aesthetics (*Die Bedeutung von Kants Begründung der Aesthetik für die Philosophie der Kunst*), Walter Biemel has shown how 'aesthetics', when thought through to the end, is transformed into a reflection in which art emerges as a 'happening of truth', as Heidegger contends.

poetry and the poetic essence to his thought and how this interest is integrally bound up with the changed conception of thinking as such, will emerge more clearly in the discussion below of his view on the relationship between thinking and composing (*Denken und Dichten*).

Also published during this period (1942), the essay, "Platons Lehre von der Wahrheit" ("Plato's Doctrine of Truth"), like the book on Kant, pursues the 'phenomenological destruction' proposed originally to be dealt with in the second part of *Being and Time*. Its main purpose is to show how, in consequence of his conception of the Being of things as *idea*, the nature of Truth also undergoes a radical transformation at the hands of Plato, a change of which Plato himself has no awareness. Another essay, published in the following year, is "Vom Wesen der Wahrheit" ("On the Nature of Truth") which in certain important respects goes beyond the brief discussion of truth in *Being and Time*. Both of these essays, however, were originally written in 1930–31, though the second one, repeatedly revised before publication, gives some inkling of the necessity behind the change in thought that was taking place in Heidegger at this time. Many courses of lectures which he actually delivered during this period, such as *Einführung in die Metaphysik* (*Introduction to Metaphysics*, 1935) lectures on Nietzsche delivered between 1936 and 1940, and on Aristotle's Physics in 1940, were not published until much later; so also with some articles and essays, such as "The Origin of the Work of Art," "The Age of the World-picture," essays on metaphysics and the history of Being, "Hegel's Concept of Experience," "Nietzsche's saying—God is dead," "Aletheia," "Nihilism and the History of Being," "Serenity," "The Overcoming of Metaphysics," the essay on Anaximander and "From the Experience of Thinking". During the years following the publication of *Being and Time*, Heidegger seems to have realized with increasing clarity how much of the start made in that work was dependent on the language and approach of traditional metaphysics and how the reversal from Time to Being and back to the re-interpretation of man and the world in terms of a 'clarified' and more basic sense of Being could not be effected without abandoning that language and that approach. By 1936, he seems to have fully realized that metaphysics, as concerned with the truth about essents, is itself grounded in the truth of Being ('truth' being understood in the basic sense of 'unhidden-ness') and is therefore powerless to explore and formulate the nature of this ground. In consequence, Heidegger was forced to move away from the original approach of *Being and Time*; instead of seeking to approach Being through the openness and transcendence inherent in man, he now tries to define man in terms of Being. The language of traditional metaphysics having proved inadequate, and indeed a hindrance, to his basic objective of rethinking the Truth of Being, Heidegger is now groping for a new language, a new way of speaking and thinking about Being, about man and about man's relationship to Being. Not until he has found this language and is in secure possession of the new perspective, does Heidegger announce the shift in his approach in the *Letter on Humanism*. Because Heidegger published little during the period 1930–1946, the consequent ignorance of the path his thinking had travelled since *Being and Time* led to widespread misunderstanding about the nature of the transition from the earlier to the later position as depicted in the *Letter*. But, as will be evident from the discussion of the 'reversal' in chap. II, this later position is not so much a 'break' in thinking as a continuous development resulting from immanent self-criticism. From the very beginning, the inquiry in *Being and Time* was conceived as circular in character—from the preconceptual comprehension of Being to the analysis of Dasein and its being (i.e., care, rooted in time) and from zeit (time) back to a clarification and determination of the sense of Being. The 'change in thinking' in the second phase of Heidegger's thought, therefore, does not constitute an abandonment of the basic aims of the inquiry; what is abandoned is rather the language of traditional metaphysics, its unavoidably representational and conceptual thinking and its belief in the necessity of a rigid methodology (i.e., the final abandonment of the conception of philosophy as a scientific discipline).[64]

The second part of *Being and Time* was to deal with a phenomenological 'destruction' of the history of philosophy, i.e., with the task of taking to pieces the whole fabric of Western metaphysics as it has historically developed. The main purpose of this was to show how at each important stage of its evolution it covered up more and more thoroughly the original impulse behind it, the thought of Being as it had flashed into the vision of the early Greek thinkers. To extricate this 'Unthought' out of the intellectual accumulation of the centuries, to recall this original vision and become aware of its inadequacy was the only way to a re-opening of the inquiry into this neglected problem and to take it up again for further building where it was left before Plato. This historical inquiry cannot, in fact, be separated from the systematic conceptual analysis of the problem of Being, as will be evident even from the historical discussions in the published part of *Being and Time*. Going back into the ground of metaphysics, Heidegger was to realize more clearly afterwards, is a going back in both the conceptual as well as the historical sense. This kind of regressive investigation of the history of philosophy is conducted by Heidegger both in the *Being and Time* phase (e.g., in the studies on Kant and Plato already mentioned) as well as later. Sometimes the historical discussions are included within more comprehensive systematic inquiries, as in the case of *Introduction to Metaphysics* (1953), with its interpretations of Heraclitus, Parmenides and Aristotle, of *Was heisst Denken?* (*What is Called*

---

64. Cf. Heidegger's "Preface" in Richardson's *Heidegger*, where the nature, the inherent necessity and the implications of the 'reversal' are explained at length. Heidegger again insists here, seeking to put an end to "the baseless and ceaseless prattle" about the 'reversal', that "The thinking of the reversal *is* a change in my thought. But this change is not a consequence of altering the standpoint, much less of abandoning the fundamental issue, of *Being and Time*." The basic question of *Being and Time,* far from being abandoned by reason of the reversal, is "fulfilled in a decisive manner in the thinking of the reversal."

Thinking?, 1954), in which the exposition is accompanied by constant reference to past thinkers, and of *Der Satz vom Grund* (*The Principle of Ground*, 1957), containing an elaborate discussion of Leibniz. *Vorträge und Aufsätze* (*Lectures and Essays*, 1954) contains interpretations of the concepts of *Logos* and *Aletheia* in Heraclitus, of *Moira* in Parmenides, of Nietzsche's Zarathustra as well as discussions of Kant. *Identität und Differenz* (*Identity and Difference*, 1957) seeks to differentiate Hegel's approach from Heidegger's own and another essay on "Hegel and the Greeks" (1960) is devoted to an examination of Hegel's interpretation of Greek philosophers. "The nature and concept of *Physis* in Aristotle" (1960) discusses the Aristotelian concept of Nature and its metaphysical implications. Finally, *Nietzsche* (2 vols., 1961) gives not only a full-scale interpretation of Nietzsche's philosophy but also contains detailed studies of Plato, Descartes and Kant. Heidegger's latest publications (1963) are important studies on Kant, one an essay (entitled, *Kants These über das Sein*) and the other a full-sized book (entitled, *Die Frage nach dem Ding*) dealing with Kant's doctrine of Transcendental Principles. For Heidegger, essential philosophical thinking is remembrance (*Andenken*) and hence the analysis of any concept necessarily involves an attempt to recall its genesis—analysis and interpretation are for him inextricably linked together. Moreover, the historical genesis, evolution and transformation of concepts is, according to Heidegger, itself rooted in what he calls the "History of Being", the self-revelation of Being in history. This history, as reflected in the creative thinkers of the West, begins with Anaximander, with whom an 'epoch' of Being is initiated in the West, blossoming forth in its full richness in the thought of Parmenides and Heraclitus. With Plato's interpretation of Being in terms of 'idea' there begins the epoch of the oblivion of Being and the rise of the metaphysical tradition, which is henceforth to dominate European thought. With Aristotle, in whom the original vision in some ways flashed out again, even while 'metaphysics', turned away from Being and busy with the truth of beings, is taking shape, Greek thought comes to its great end. Descartes marks the beginning of the epoch of subjectivism and the total 'withdrawal' of Being, the era of modern nihilism which unfolds itself steadily through the thought of Leibniz, Kant and Hegel, culminating finally in the total nihilism of Nietzsche.

As already stated, the aim of Heidegger's historical and critical interpretations is to bring into view what has remained 'Unthought' in the thinking of the great philosophers of the past and to formulate it in words. This work of interpretation—it might well be termed regressive interpretation—is not primarily an affair of historical scholarship but is rather creative in a profound sense.[65] As an explicit 'repetition' (*Wiederholung*) of obscure beginnings, it is at the same time a challenge to think anew and

---

65. Inevitably, for this reason, Heidegger's interpretations of past thinkers and of the 'basic words' of philosophy such as *aletheia, logos* and *physis* have drawn the wrath of classical scholars, orthodox 'academic' philosophers and theologians alike. Only bare mention of a few names in this context can be made here: P. Friedländer and G. Krüger on the interpretation of *aletheia,* of Plato and of Greek philosophy in general; E. Cassirer and H. Levy on that of Kant; B. Liebrucks and van der Meulen on Heidegger's interpretation of Hegel and W. Marx on that of Aristotle and Hegel; K. Löwith on that of Nietzsche. Heidegger has always acknowledged the 'correctness' of these criticisms but is yet, in a profound sense, left untouched by them. The 'hermeneutic' problem involved is too large to be dealt with here. But cf. Gadamer's comments (*Wahrheit und Methode,* pp. 472–473) on Löwith's criticism and on Heidegger's 'impatience' with philosophical texts. W. Marx's study of the relation between Heidegger and Aristotle (in *Heidegger und die Tradition*) is sympathetic and discerning. Equally valuable for an understanding of Heidegger's way of interpreting the pre-Socratic philosophers is the recent monograph by George Joseph Seidel entitled *Martin Heidegger and the Pre-Socratics.*

How far the sober, academic fields of classical scholarship, philology and linguistic science and the interpretation of individual philosophers are themselves being slowly but profoundly influenced by Heidegger's ideas, it is too early to judge. But reference may be made, beside the writings of van der Meulen and Marx mentioned above, to the work of Johannes Lohmann in the field of linguistic science (articles in *Lexis*), that of Gadamer, Krüger and Szilasi on Plato (Cf. E. M. Manasse: "Bücher über Platon I," in *Philosophische Rundschau,* 1957), of Dieter Henrich on Kant ("Über die Einheit der Subjektivität", *Philosophische Rundschau,* III, 1955), of Otto Pöggeler on the interpretation of Hegel's *Phenomenology of Mind* (*Hegel–Studien* I).

express in adequate language (i.e., in language as far as possible free from the terminological fixity and rigid conceptual determination characteristic of later developments, themselves based on these beginnings) something that has never been thought and said but which is the mainspring and the necessary presupposition of the metaphysical thought of the West.[66] For this reason, some of Heidegger's most original formulations of basic philosophical concepts occur in writings which are ostensibly devoted to historical interpretation and criticism. In addition, and above all, he has sought to state in his recent writings his own way of thinking—non-representational and non-conceptual—about Being and its truth, and with that as the basis, to reinterpret in an original manner some of the fundamental concepts of European philosophy such as world, man, ground, identity, thought, language, truth and historicity. The essays on "The Problem of Technology", "What is Thinking?", "Building, Dwelling and Thinking", "The Thing" (all in *Lectures and Essays*) are profoundly and daringly original, difficult to render in another language, driving as they do their own original German to the very limit of its expressive and communicative power. And this is no less true of the essays, "The Principle of Identity" and "The Onto-theological structure of metaphysics" (in *Identity and Difference*), the dialogue and essay in *Gelassenheit* (*Serenity*, 1959), the essays on language in *Unterwegs zur Sprache* (*On the Way to Language*, 1959). The verge of obscurity which Heidegger

---

66. In this sense all essential thinking is reminiscent in nature (*Andenken*) and all philosophical inquiry basically historical in character. As Heidegger explains (*Die Frage nach dem Ding*, ff.; E.T., p. 44), this is so because the historical, as different from the past, is something that is still happening, even if to all appearances it has vanished into the past. What appears to us as such, as a happening or movement that is no longer in existence, may well be just a state of rest. The rest-state of happening is not absence of historicity but a basic form of its presence. What is merely past does not exhaust the has-been (*Gewesene*). This is still with us and its mode of being is a peculiar quiescence of happening (*Geschehen*). . . . Rest is only arrested motion, often uncannier than the latter itself. To inquire historically is to set free and to set in motion again the happening that lies resting, frozen and confined, in a question.

might seem to have reached here and in other previous works
(e.g., the essay on Anaximander in *Holzwege*), however, by no
means implies that it has become either a stylistic mannerism
with him or is used as a cloak for obscurantist and mystifying
purposes, for even in such late essays as *Zur Seinsfrage* (*The
Question of Being*), *Was ist das—die Philosophie?* (*What is
Philosophy?*) and the "Dialogue" on Language, Heidegger can
still be as lucid and simple, as free from academic jargon as one
might wish all philosophical writing to be. In these later writings
Heidegger has deliberately renounced the conceptual, grasping,
exact, 'logical' and calculative thinking characteristic of metaphysics, for such thinking, however adequate it may be to the
metaphysical need of keeping a hold on the truth of the essent by
representing and objectifying it, is according to Heidegger, deaf
to the truth of Being. This renunciation is a sacrifice in the true
sense; philosophy, having dreamt out the metaphysical dream
and played out that game to its bitter nihilistic end, here bids
final "farewell to the essent as such, on the way to preserving and
cherishing the favour of Being", a sacrifice in which the might
and majesty of metaphysical thinking are at last given up in
favour of something much more modest and unpretentious and
yet no less difficult and rigorous in its painstaking regard for the
right word. This is what Heidegger refers to variously as 'essential' thinking (*das wesentliche Denken*), a thinking that recalls
(*Andenken*), 'originative' thinking (*das anfängliche Denken*) or
meditative thinking (*das besinnliche Denken*)—an echo of the
grace of Being, man's answer to the soundless voice of Being, a
still attentiveness to the truth of Being, a patient, responsive
putting together in words, and thus bringing into being, of this
truth, so that it might become effective in the lives and thinking
of men. Such thinking is a slow, laborious process and lays no
claim to finality, for it does nothing towards achieving 'results' at
one stroke; at best it is a thinking that prepares the ground (*das
vorbereitende Denken*), so that one day Being itself may reveal
itself in words. It is a thinking that is not *our* doing but is part of

the history of Being (*das seinsgeschichtliche Denken*) and entirely under its governance and disposal, a thinking that hears and seeks to catch a glimpse of what is heard.[67]

II HEIDEGGER'S METHOD

Not only in *Being and Time* and the essays of that phase but also in his later writings, Heidegger's thinking is marked by an acute sensitiveness and attention to points of method, later called the 'way', to the kind of approach and attack demanded by the problem and by an extreme deliberateness and finesse in the use of language. Apart from the second chapter of the Introduction in *Being and Time,* which deals systematically with his use of the phenomenological method, scattered reflections on methodology are to be found all over this work. The very first chapter of the Introduction, dealing with the necessity, the structure and pre-eminence of the question of Being, is of central importance as an explicit statement of the considerations that are to determine and steer the whole course of the inquiry. The 'programmatic' discussion of the task of a 'destruction' of the history of ontology in the next chapter is of equal importance because it directs attention to the 'vertical' dimension of Heidegger's methodology which,

---

67. See *Der Satz vom Grund,* p. 86.

Heidegger often uses the word *das Denken* (Thinking), as qualified in the above manner, to designate his own thought (much as Hegel speaks of *Wissenschaft*), i.e., as the name for thought liberated from its metaphysical shackles and no longer conceived as 'philosophy', as it is on its way to a manifestation of its true nature in Heidegger's own thought. Because such thinking is concerned primarily with the truth of Being, and with that of the essent only from the perspective of the former, it is necessarily historical. As he explains (*Brief über den 'Humanismus',* p. 81), Being is (*es gibt*) as its dispensation or destiny, the history of which finds expression in the great thinkers. Hence, the thinking concerned with the truth of Being is as such historical. There is no such thing as 'systematic' thought and besides that, as illustrating it, a history of past opinions. There is also no such thing, as Hegel believes, as a system of thought which could make the principle of its thinking the principle of history and at the same time take it up into the system. More profoundly conceived, there is the history of Being, integral to which is thinking as the reminiscence (*Andenken*) of this history, a thinking which is brought to pass by this history.

though not entirely lacking in *Being and Time,* plays an increasingly dominating role in his later writings. In *Being and Time,* Heidegger proceeds from the phenomenal and the 'existenziell' to the phenomenological and the 'existenzial', from the facts of experience to the disclosure of the *a priori* conditions of the possibility of experience, from the 'ontic' to the 'ontological'. As a footnote in *Sein und Zeit,* p. 50, suggests, Heidegger conceives at this stage the task of philosophy to be one of scientific *a priori* investigation or research and the actual method followed by him in *Being and Time* may, therefore, aptly be described as the Kantian transcendental method modified and widened under the influence of the more sophisticated discipline of phenomenology and liberalized by an assimilation into it of the 'hermeneutic' procedure of the human sciences (*Geisteswissenschaften*).

Not logical demonstration but understanding (*Verstehen*), the primary mode of being of man in which all knowing and thinking is rooted, is what Heidegger aims at. As he remarks,[68] ontological investigation is one possible type of explication in which something disclosed in understanding is articulated, worked out and appropriated, i.e., in which something is comprehended *as being* this or that. All method, therefore, terminates for Heidegger, not in proof but in an exhibition or disclosure of the underlying phenomenon, in a 'seeing' or 'hearing' of the reality of anything. Hence, the whole treatment of Understanding, Interpretation and Language in *Being and Time*[69] should also be read as a valuable supplement to the discussion of method in the Introduction. The account given here of the nature of possibility and of the projective nature of understanding, the analysis of 'sense,' of the circularity of all understanding and of judgment, the discussion of speech and language—these are valuable not only as part of the analytic of existenz but throw a flood of light on Heidegger's own procedure and on the kind of analysis conducted by him. The same is true of the remarks on

68. *Sein und Zeit,* p. 231 (E.T., p. 275).
69. Division I, chapter 5.

the 'hermeneutic situation',[70] on sense or meaning[71] and on the necessity, which is again and again emphasized, of 'repeating' an earlier analysis on higher levels. Heidegger starts with a merely formally sketched but presupposed idea of existenz and in the light of that describes what is phenomenally evident (facts as experienced and observable). What is thus phenomenally described is then phenomenologically interpreted, i.e., shown, by means of a phenomenological 'construction' or an existenzial 'projection', to be the expression or manifestation of an underlying ontological structure, the 'phenomenon' in the true sense. The primary phenomenon as thus disclosed is for Heidegger not something absolutely 'given' or an eternally, ultimately valid object of an intuitive vision but a construct or project of the understanding, which is through and through 'finite' (*endlich*), as Heidegger has particularly emphasized in *Kant and the Problem of Metaphysics*. Its genuineness and validity must, therefore, be established by referring it back to the facts of experience; it must be again phenomenally verified and shown to be concretely exemplified in experience. This to and fro, circular movement in which the ontic, itself understood in the light of an ontological presupposition, leads to the ontological and back again to the ontic, has its parallel in similar other circular movements simultaneously occurring throughout *Being and Time*. For example, from a particular structure, phenomenologically analysed in the light of an assumed totality, to the whole and back again to the part, until man's ontological structure is grasped in its wholeness; from the inauthentic, described in the light of a presupposed concept of authenticity, to the authentic and back again to the 'everyday' mode of existenz until a clear picture of the way the two modes are related emerges into view; from the preparatory existenzial analysis of man, carried out in the light of a possible temporal interpretation, to the demonstration of the temporal foundations of man's being and back again to a reinterpretation

70. *Sein und Zeit*, p. 232 (E.T., p. 275).
71. *Ibid.*, pp. 151, 323 f. (E.T., pp. 192 f., 370 ff.).

of the existenzial analysis on the temporal level; finally, the
movement, which remains uncompleted in *Being and Time,* from
the vague natural conception of Being to the analysis of man and
his temporal foundations to a clearer concept of Being as essentially temporal in a deeper sense and back again to a re-
interpretation of the results of the existenzial analytic in the light
of this clarified sense of Being. What Heidegger has called "the
thinking of the reversal" has reference to this movement from
'Being and Time' to 'Time and Being'. This coming-to-pass
(*Geschehen*) of the 'reversal' (*die Kehre*), Heidegger says, "is
neither something invented by me, nor does it concern merely my
thought" but is rather a necessity inherent in the very matter
designated by the headings: 'Being and Time' and 'Time and
Being'; "the reversal is in play within the matter itself."[72]

An important methodological digression[73] not only offers a
justification for this necessarily circular character of the whole
inquiry but also brings into focus a characteristic of Heidegger's
procedure which has been widely misunderstood. Man is so
constituted that, clinging obstinately to the superficial and the
outward, he hides from himself, indeed actively resists an attempt to uncover, his ontological depths. Hence, from the point
of view of common sense an ontological interpretation of man,
often reversing the truth of what is generally accepted, is bound
to have the appearance of proceeding by means of constructions
and projections which appear to be forced and which do violence
to our ingrained habits of thought. As Heidegger says,[74] "The
ontological constitution of every essent, and that of man in a pre-
eminent sense, is accessible only in understanding in so far as it is
of the nature of a project. Because understanding . . . is not
merely a kind of knowing but is primarily a basic constitutive
element of existenz, the explicit carrying through of its projective
activity must necessarily be, especially in ontological understand-

---

72. Heidegger's "Preface" in Richardson: *Heidegger,* p. xviii.
73. *Sein und Zeit,* pp. 310–316 (E.T., pp. 358–364).
74. *Kant und das Problem der Metaphysik,* p. 210 (E.T., pp. 240 f.).

ing, of the nature of construction . . . though this does not mean that it should be arbitrary and fanciful." Man's finitude as manifested in his understanding of Being lies, Heidegger says, in his obliviousness, a feature which is neither accidental nor occasional but constant and inevitable. Therefore, "all fundamental ontological construction which aims at the disclosure of the inner possibility of the understanding of Being must, in its project, snatch away from oblivion the content of its projection." That this is true not merely about the ontological interpretation of man but of all interpretation whatsoever is exemplified by Heidegger's own interpretations of past philosophers and of the basic metaphysical concepts in the history of European philosophy. The tendency to veil and cover up his own reality does not characterize only man; ultimately, Being as such tends, while revealing itself, to conceal itself and hold itself back at the same time. The same is true of language, the "shrine of Being", which in speaking keeps back what is its very own, and of the great thinkers whose central thought, the nourishing, invisible source of all they have actually said, remains unuttered. That is why, according to Heidegger, all truth or disclosure of Being by its very nature calls for the exercise of 'violence' or, as in the writings of his later phase, the exercise of a leap of thought and a sensitive, devoted ear, attuned to the true, silent voice of the mystery of Being.

In view of Heidegger's later approach to the history of European thought in terms of the "History of Being", attention may also be drawn to what he says about repetition (*Wiederholung*), tradition (*Uberlieferung*) and destiny (*Geschick*) in connexion with his discussion of historicity. In the analytic of Dasein (*man*) these topics may seem to be of peripheral import but in the later Being-centred phase, these concepts assume an ever growing methodological importance. In fact, the distinguishing feature of the method or way followed by his later thinking has been described by Heidegger himself as a "thinking from the point of view of the destiny of Being" (*Seinsgeschichtliches Denken*), a point of view to which we can attain only through a leap of thought but which brings us to that hidden wellspring of tradition from which, through repetition, we can bring back untold treasures of thought which have failed to enter into this tradition. Brief mention may also be made here of a concept of basic importance which Heidegger has borrowed from Husserl and used i̇ ̇ strikingly original manner throughout the writings of his first ρnase. This is the concept of 'horizon'.[75] Any object or phenomenon is not only knowable as such but is what it is only within a setting, context or perspective which is itself, in the last resort, not of the character of an object or entity of any sort at all. It is only in the light of this horizon or perspective that it can show itself and be thought about and described. Hence, Heidegger always starts with analyses which prepare the context of meaningfulness and open up a perspective within which a particular phenomenon may then be located and rendered visible. How important a role this concept has played in his approach to the main problems of *Being and Time* is richly illustrated, not only by the statement of the aim of the inquiry at the very beginning,[76] but by the whole analysis of 'world', conceived by Heidegger as not itself an entity or essent but as sheer 'horizon', and, perhaps even more so, by the discussion of temporality. In his later writings, the place of 'horizon' is taken, as explained below, by 'region' (*Gegend*) and, place or location (*Ort*) and the approach becomes more explicitly 'topological'.[77]

---

75. On the concept of 'Horizon', see Husserl, *Ideen* I, p. 48 ff; Landgrebe, *Philosophie der Gegenwart*, pp. 66–67; Gadamer, *Wahrheit und Methode*, p. 332; H. Kuhn in *Essays in Memory of Edmund Husserl*, pp. 106–123. Heidegger takes over this concept, transforms it and eventually, along with the 'transcendental' thinking of *Being and Time*, abandons it. For his later criticism of this concept, see *Gelassenheit*, pp. 38 ff. (E.T., pp. 63 ff.).

76. "Our provisional aim is the interpretation of time as the possible horizon for the understanding of Being in general"—*Sein und Zeit*, p. 1 (E.T., p. 19).

77. Heidegger actually speaks of "the topology of Being" in *Aus der Erfahrung des Denkens*, p. 23. Cf. also *Zur Seinsfrage*, p. 32 (E.T., p. 85). It may be pointed out that the Aristotelian concept of *topos*, place or region, was not unknown to Kant. Cf. *Critique of Pure Reason*, A 269, B 325. On this, see Pöggeler's important article entitled "Metaphysik und Seinstopik bei Heidegger" (*Philosophisches Jahrbuch*, 70, 1962); also, *Der Denkweg Martin Heideggers*, pp. 280–299.

"Any genuine method", Heidegger has said,[78] "is based on adequately viewing in advance the basic constitution of the 'object' to be disclosed, or of the domain within which the object lies." So long as the objective aimed at was an 'object' or essent, namely, man, methodological sophistication was quite in place as leading securely to it. But in the second phase of his thought Heidegger realized that no amount of methodological manoevring could build a path leading from beings to Being itself. He also came to realize to a more radical extent the fundamental difference between philosophical thinking as the thinking of Being and 'metaphysical' and scientific thinking about essents. The latter is dominated by the concept of system, of representational system-building through concepts in the quest of certainty, of thinking as a kind of grasping (*Begreifen*) and taking secure possession of its object through conceptualization.[79] In a discussion of the concept of method and its role in modern science and philosophy, Heidegger shows[80] how this concept has developed with the rise of modern philosophy in reaction against the medieval conception of truth (*doctrina*) and of the 'assurance' of salvation through faith. Modern man, rejecting faith in salvation as eternal happiness beyond, conceives it as the free unfoldment of all his creative potentialities in this life. "The problem therefore arises *how* a certainty about his own nature and about the world, sought for by man himself (i.e., pursued by means of his own efforts) for his this-worldly life, can be attained and justified. Whereas in the medieval world the way to salvation and the manner in which truth came to man (*doctrina*) were firmly settled matters, now it was the *search* for the new way that became decisive. The problem of 'method', i.e., the problem of 'striking out a path' for himself, the problem of attaining and justifying a certainty established by man himself comes into prominence. 'Method' is to be understood here not in the 'methodological' sense as a mode of investigation and research but in the meta-

78. *Sein und Zeit,* p. 303 (E.T., p. 350).
79. Cf. *Was heisst Denken?,* pp. 128 f. (E.T., pp. 211 ff.).
80. *Nietzsche,* II, pp. 133 ff.

physical sense of a way of determining the essential character of truth, capable of being grounded by the powers of man himself. . . . The problem before philosophy, liberated from the shackles of revealed Church doctrine, is in what way man can attain, by himself and for himself, to an unshakeable truth. . . ." It is not surprising, Heidegger adds, that Descartes, who first raised this question and answered it with all explicitness and clarity, should have attached supreme importance to the problem of method, a fact evident from the very titles he gave to his principal writings. *Being and Time*, seeking to go beyond the 'metaphysical' preoccupation with what is to a re-opening of the question of the sense of Being itself and aiming at overcoming the subjectivism in which modern philosophy is caught up, still remains embedded in the subjectivistic, man-centred, metaphysical tradition. Going beyond that in his later phase and viewing the development of the metaphysical thinking of the West as itself an epoch in the dispensation of Being (*Seinsgeschick*), Heidegger realized that the whole conception of method is itself a manifestation and an integral part of this subjectivism, that the leap by which alone thought can spring away from the sphere of essents to the dimension of Being must also leave behind the metaphysical concept of method, for in this dimension guidance comes not from man's methodological planning but only from pursuing the ways that open out to an ear that is sensitively and patiently attuned to the unthought and unuttered possibilities latent in the tradition of European philosophical thinking.

This explains why, despite the brilliant and masterly use to which Heidegger had put the Kantian Transcendental Method in his fundamental-ontological inquiries in *Being and Time*, he abandoned it, along with the title 'Ontology', in his later writings. For Kant, as Heidegger understands him, the Being of objects as experienced by a subject consists in their objectivity. The objectivity of objects is an *a priori* determination and condition of the possibility of all experience of objects. Hence the method by which we pass beyond objects to their objectivity, their Being, is called by Kant transcendental. But for Kant this transcendence is rooted in Reason, the faculty of ultimate principles which alone certify and warrant their objectivity to objects of experience. Moreover, the Kantian Reason is only a more stringently formulated version of the Cartesian *ego cogito* and a more elaborately articulated and refined form of that ultimate, all-determining Cartesian ground or condition, the subjectivity of the subject. The transcendental method, seeking to discover the conditions of the possibility of objects and their experience, aims actually at disclosing the ontological structure of essents (conceived by Kant in the narrow, specific sense of objects), i.e., their Being, and for this reason Heidegger seized upon it as ideally appropriate to his own task of penetrating into man's ontological constitution.[81] But since this transcendental procedure is itself possible in the light of a particular conception of Being and is applicable only to a thinking that, starting from essents, moves in the direction of Being and since it is inseparably bound up with the subjectivistic need for the grounding and justifying of everything that is, Heidegger abandoned it when he came to realize later that from beings to Being there is no straight passage but only a leap of thought from one dimension to another. The concept of transcendence, like that of horizon, has its origin in the attempt to represent objects, in view of their Being, and as such is 'metaphysical' in character and inappropriate to an attempt to think of Being as such, to speak of it, not in terms of essents but as and in itself. As Heidegger has remarked, "Horizon and Transcendence are terms conceived from the point of view of objects and of our representation and are determined only in view of these. . . . In this manner, however (i.e., by approaching the Being of anything through these concepts), that which the horizon allows to be what it is, is by no means known as it is in itself."[82]

81. Even in *Being and Time,* however, 'transcendental' is determined in terms of the existenzial ecstatic temporality of *Da-sein* and has nothing to do with the subjective consciousness. Cf. *Einführung in die Metaphysik,* p. 14 (E.T., p. 15).

82. *Gelassenheit,* p. 39 (E.T., p. 64).

Heidegger's later reminiscent, meditative thinking of Being has no ready-made paths laid out before it; yet for this 'preparatory thinking' (*vorbereitendes Denken*), as he calls it, there is still the 'Way'. Not the modern subjectivistically conceived 'method' but the simple idea of a way is what, according to him the Greek *methodos* originally connotes.[83] Here thinking and being 'on the way' are identical so that the way cleared and traversed is not left behind but is taken up into and is one with the movement of thought itself. And it is not a smooth and continuous path but involves passing from one level to another in a leap of thought in which there is neither security nor certainty of arriving at a pre-determined goal but only a tentative, approximately adequate utterance of Being. The way to Being is indeed no path stretching between two distant places, for Being is what is closest to us; on this path, as Heidegger puts it, "We do not aim at advancing further. All that we want is just really to get to where we already are."[84] Explaining in some detail his later attitude to the question of method, Heidegger writes,[85] "The way to knowledge is known in the sciences by the title of 'method' which, particularly in modern science, is no mere instrument in the service of science but has made the latter itself subservient to it. . . . Not only does the method determine the theme but the latter is incorporated into and subordinated to the method. . . . In contradistinction to the procedure of scientific representation, matters stand quite differently in the case of thinking. Here, there is neither method nor theme but only the region or zone (*Gegend*) which dispenses what is thought-worthy and so claims our thinking. Going over the paths of this region, thinking occupies itself with and dwells on the region. Here the way is part of the region, a relationship between the two which, from the point of view of scientific representation, is not only difficult but altogether impossible to see." For meditative thinking, it is the region itself

---

83. See *Der Satz vom Grund*, p. 111.
84. *Unterwegs zur Sprache*, p. 12.
85. *Ibid.*, p. 178.

which as such opens up all access to it, generating and clearing up the paths that lead up to it—the region and the way belong most intimately together. In speaking of this Way, Heidegger has in mind something like the *Tao* of Laotse which, as he puts it,[86] "perhaps hides within itself the mystery of all mysteries relating to a thinking utterance" (i.e., to thinking as inseparable from poetic imagination). Perhaps, Heidegger suggests, even the enigmatic power of the present-day supremacy of method, despite its achievements, itself derives from the fact that these methods are only the backwaters of a large hidden stream, of a Way that opens and strikes out the path for everything, of a Way that is not so much a static thing but the dynamic source of all way-ing, the coming about of all ways.

It should be obvious from the above that for Heidegger the whole conception of thinking itself, as well as of the nature of philosophy, has changed since he wrote *Being and Time,* where he still speaks throughout of conceptualizing, conceptual formulation, 'bringing to a concept' the sense of Being. Later, he was to declare that "the thinking of the future is no longer philosophy",[87] for philosophy aims at conceptualizing, which is a kind of grasping and laying hold of, and at general concepts related together by the purely formal rules of logic, which is only a kind of reckoning or calculating. However useful such grasping and reckoning may be for the sake of achieving certainty in the sphere of essents, they are utterly inadequate when we move in the dimension of Being. Conceptual, representational thinking is itself one way in which the nature of thought, like that of essents and their Being, has been determined through the historical dispensation of Being in the form of European metaphysics. By means of such thinking it is impossible, hence, to think about and enter into the ground and basis, the light of Being—on which metaphysical thinking concerned with the essent as such and in

86. *Ibid.,* p. 198.
87. *Brief über den 'Humanismus',* p. 119.

its totality—stands.[88] This incapacity of conceptual thought, however, does not mean that the only alternative left is a lapse into irrationalism, the mere shadow of rationalism, or into mysticism, "the mere antitype or counterpart of metaphysics."[89] Another kind of thinking, yet in germ and being developed by Heidegger, still remains, for, as he says, "with the end of philosophy, thinking itself does not also come to an end but passes over to another beginning."[90] Such non-conceptual thinking was, in fact, the prevailing character of Greek philosophizing, as Heidegger shows in a penetrating and highly original interpretation and discussion of the terms *noein* and *legein* in Parmenides' sentence (Fragment VI), *chre to legein te noein t' eon emmenai* ("It is necessary to say and to think that the essent is").[91] The conception of thought as embodied in these twin, root terms of the European philosophical tradition, does not yet imply the modern, subjectivistic and 'metaphysical' sense of grasping and clutching. Thinking is here not yet understood "as a grasping, neither as a reaching out to grab what lies in front nor an assault upon it. . . . Thinking is here not conceiving (*Be-greifen*, literally, to have in one's grip, comprehending). At the pinnacle of the initial unfoldment of its nature, thinking knows no concept. . . . This great thinking of the Greek thinkers in its entirety, including that of Aristotle, thinks without concepts", which by no means implies that its thinking is inexact or primitive.[92]

88. Cf. the "Introduction" to *What is Metaphysics?*
89. *Neitzsche II*, p. 28.
90. *Vorträge und Aufsätze*, p. 83.
91. *Was heisst Denken?*, pp. 105–149 (E.T., pp. 170–244).
92. *Ibid.*, p. 128 (E.T., pp. 211 f.).
From Plato onwards, throughout the history of Western metaphysics, thinking has been opposed to Being as its object. Hegel indeed identifies the two but he does this by assimilating Being to Thought, thus carrying modern subjectivism to its highest point. Heidegger, going back to the Pre-Socratics, seeks to recapture the original unity of Being and Thought, which can still be glimpsed in them and to develop a conception of thought in which the latter is seen as an intrinsic aspect of Being itself. Heidegger says in a revealing passage, "In the apparently unimportant distinction between Being and Thought we must discern the fundamental position and attitude of the

As already remarked earlier, Heidegger's thinking, from the very beginning, is 'on the way' to an overcoming of metaphysics; by the time of writing *On the Essence of Truth,* he had seen that this implied giving up the language of essence (*Wesen*), i.e., thinking in terms of essences. (In his later writings, *Wesen* is used in a verbal sense, to denote the process character of Being.) In the terminology of the Platonic, metaphysical tradition, what something is, the 'what' of anything (*to ti estin*) constitutes the nature or essence (the *essentia*) of that thing. The essence as thus understood is, Heidegger says, defined and expressed through what was later called the concept, a representation by means of which we grasp and put at our disposal what something is.[93] As against this, the non-conceptual creative word, instead of enabling us to grasp and lay hold of what is already there before us, instead of serving merely as a means of describing what is present, calls into being. It is evocative of Being; it invokes that presence (*Anwesenheit*), i.e., Being, within which (in the light of which) anything can appear before us as an essent.[94] Even in *Being and Time,* Heidegger was alive to the creative character of true, non-representational thinking which alone is appropriate to Being, as is evident from his whole conception of the projective nature of thought. Later, impressed more and more profoundly with the creative, all-enveloping power of language as the shrine of Being and the dwelling place of man, Heidegger tends to

---

Western spirit against which our attack is really directed. This separation can be overcome only by going back to its *origin,* i.e., in such a way that its original truth is placed within its own limits and established afresh." (*Einführung in die Metaphysik,* p. 89; E.T., pp. 98 f.) The conception of thought underlying traditional logic is based on a prior falling apart of thinking and Being since the time of Plato and to overcome that it is necessary to find our way back to the unity of their intrinsic togetherness. Such overcoming of logic, however, "does not mean an abrogation of thought and the domination of mere feeling; it means a more radical and stricter thinking, a thinking that appertains to Being." (*Ibid.,* p. 94; E.T., p. 103). See also *Identität und Differenz* for Heidegger's account of Being-owned thinking.

93. *Unterwegs zur Sprache,* p. 201.
94. *Ibid.,* p. 227.

reverse the ordinary conception of the relationship between language and thought—instead of taking language as the medium and instrument for the expression of thought, he now describes thinking itself in terms of language and regards the latter as the fountain-head of all creativity. The place of projective understanding is gradually taken by *dichten,* composing in words.[95] Poetic composing (*dichten* in the narrow sense) and thinking, Heidegger says, are the two pre-eminent modes of saying, rooted in the productive, inventive or creative essence of language. As a mode of creative 'saying', therefore, thinking is itself poetic or inventive in character. "All philosophical thinking, and indeed just the most rigorous and prosaic, is in itself poetic and yet it is never poetry", Heidegger says.[96] All thinking, Reason itself, is of the nature of *poiesis* in the sense of inventing, contriving, making up.[97]

In his book on Hölderlin's poetry, Heidegger says, "Poetic composition is the act of instituting (*Stiftung*) by the word and in the word. What is it that is thus established or instituted? . . . Being, which must be opened out, so that the essent may appear. . . . The poet names the gods and names all things in that

95. In the writings of the middle period, projecting and composing are used alternatively. Cf. *Einführung in die Metaphysik,* p. 110 (E.T., p. 121), where Heidegger points out that we come to know what man is not through a learned definition but only by the fact that he creatively comes to grips with the essent, through striving to bring it into Being, i.e., when he provides it with limit and form, i.e., projects something new (not yet present), i.e., composes it originally, poetically (imaginatively) grounds it (". . . . *indem er es in sein Sein zu bringen versucht, d.h. in Grenze und Gestalt stellt, d.h. ein Neues (noch nicht Anwesendes) entwirft, d.h. ursprünglich dichtet, dichterisch gründet"*). Manheim's translation of the sentence fails to bring out the synonymity of *entwerfen* and *dichten* in Heidegger's use, as also the fact that, according to Heidegger, through the imaginative project, we seek to let Being exhibit itself in its truth. There is here no suggestion of "creating original poetry".
Cf. also *Holzwege,* pp. 60–61, where *entwerfen* and *dichten* are used interchangeably.
96. *Nietzsche I,* p. 329.
97. *Ibid.,* pp. 582 ff.

which they are. This naming does not consist merely in something already known being supplied with a name; it is rather that
when the poet speaks the essential word, the essent is by this
meaning nominated as what it is. Thus it becomes known *as*
essent. Poetry is the instituting of Being by means of the word.
. . . Because the Being and essence of things can never be calculated and derived from what is present, they must be freely
created, laid down and given. Such a free act of giving is instituting."[98] In this wide sense of poetry, of a projective saying as
Heidegger also calls it in "The Origin of the Work of Art"[99],
thinking too is projective, poetic or creative. Indeed, he goes even
so far as to say[100], "But thinking is composing, in a deeper sense
than the composition of poetry and song. The thinking of Being
is the original mode of composing (*Dichten*). . . . Thinking is
the utterance of the dictate of the truth of Being. Thinking is the
primordial *dictare*. Thinking is the primal creative composition
(*Urdichtung*), which is prior to all poesy. . . . All composing, in
the wider as well as narrower sense of the poetic, is at bottom a
thinking." And yet this creativity, far from being a property of
man, is itself rooted in his receptivity to the voice of Being, in his
ability to hear the silent chime of the essence of language and in
his dwelling in what Heidegger later calls the *Ereignis*. Going
back, "on his way to language", to the creative word, Heidegger
discovers in it the deeper, root sense of thinking, at a level deeper
than the traditional contrast between poetry and thought.[101]

98. *Erläuterungen zu Hölderlins Dichtung*, p. 38; see also Werner Brock,
Existence and Being, pp. 304–305.
    99. Cf. *Holzwege*, pp. 60–61.
    100. *Ibid.*, p. 303.
    101. As Werner Marx has remarked, "Mankind does remember a time
when, in and through such an immediate saying and singing, the whole of a
meaningful order arose out of the darkness that had shrouded all-that-is. In
and through the mythical song the great and terrifying powers that formed
and ruled the cosmos came to light and shone forth—in the brilliance of the
beautiful and in the terror of the numinous." ("Heidegger's New Conception
of Philosophy", *Social Research*, XXII, 1955.)

Thinking in this sense is identical with creative utterance, though this creativity comes, Heidegger insists, not from the assertive will of man but from his surrender to the voice of Being. Man is capable of speaking the creative word, of thinking, but only in so far as he first listens, and listening, seeks to echo back in words, as a gesture of thankful co-responding, the voice that addresses and claims him as its very own.[102] As in the case of the sense of Being, so also with the nature of thinking and of language in its indivisible unity with the former[103], Heidegger is seeking to arrive at a primordial, ultimate sense on which all their historical manifestations may be seen to be so many variations, specific, concrete forms in which they appear historically, determining and dominating the outlook and nature of man in a particular 'epoch' of Being—a sense, itself not a timeless 'universal' and hence capable only of preconceptual description, implied and presupposed in all these forms but inaccessible in terms of any of them.

Heinrich Ott has called Heidegger "the thinker of thinking (*Denker des Denkens*)." As such a thinker he is well aware of the dangers that thinking has to face. "Three dangers threaten thinking. The good and therefore salutary danger is the neighbourhood of the singing poet. The malignant and therefore sharpest danger is thinking itself. It must think against its own self, which it can do only seldom. The bad and therefore wild and tangled danger is philosophizing."[104]

102. Cf. *What is Called Thinking?*, passim. hr *Vorträge und Aufsätze* (pp. 183 f.) Heidegger remarks about this kind of thinking, "The thinking of Being as such corresponding is a very perplexing, mad affair and, in addition, meagre as to results. But perhaps this way of thinking is yet an indispensable one, a way which does not intend to be a road to salvation and which brings no new wisdom. This way is at the most a field-path, a path across a field, which does not merely talk of renunciation, but has already renounced the claim to be a binding doctrine and a universally valid cultural achievement or intellectual feat." For thinking as co-respondence, see also *Was ist das—die Philosophie?*, pp. 32 ff. (E.T., pp. 69, 71).
103. Thinking is not something, Heidegger would say, that we do with language; it is language that, as it were, does the thinking with us. "It is language that speaks, not man", as he puts it in *Unterwegs zur Sprache*.
104. *Aus der Erfahrung des Denkens*, p. 15.

III HEIDEGGER'S LANGUAGE

As John Wild has remarked,[105] "The importance of Heidegger's book lies not in any systematic reformulations of, or in any subtle distinctions between, received meanings. It lies rather in the development of new uses in a living language for the expression of new insights and new meanings." From what has been said above regarding Heidegger's philosophical aims and approach, it is only to be expected that their novelty and the power

105. "An English Version of Martin Heidegger's *Being and Time*" (*Review of Metaphysics,* XVI, 1962.)
    In this detailed review of the English translation of Heidegger's masterpiece by Macquarrie and Robinson, Professor Wild points out a number of basic difficulties in *Being and Time,* difficulties which he traces back to Heidegger's 'error' in leaving undeveloped and confused the notion of *world* in this work. Despite the penetration of Wild's critical remarks and of his own constructive suggestions, one gets the impression that he is judging this work, firstly, in isolation from the rest of Heidegger's writings and, secondly, from a perspective which is alien to the author's aims as he himself understands them. (An earlier article of Wild's, juxtaposing Heidegger with Merleau-Ponty, gives some idea of what he is looking for in Heidegger. See "Man and His Life-World" in *For Roman Ingarden.*) The fundamental difficulty in the way of understanding Heidegger's thinking, it seems to be confirmed, comes neither from his language nor from the content of his particular thoughts; it arises, rather, from the demand on the reader to shed or at least keep in suspension his own preconceptions and to keep on the track—which is more like walking on a tight rope of which the gradient and direction are constantly shifting than moving along firmly laid out rails—which his thought both builds for itself and follows. As Heidegger has remarked (*Identität und Differenz,* p. 13; E.T., p. 23), "It may happen that when our thinking, set into motion by some particular matter, pursues it, it undergoes a change on the way. In what follows, it is for this reason advisable to pay close attention to the way and not so much to the content." One may also refer to Heidegger's caution about the 'way' in the closing paragraph of the Epilogue to the lecture on "The Thing" in *Vorträge und Aufsätze.*
    It has been maintained here that *Being and Time* is not to be read as a self-contained system but as a work of transition, "on its way" from the metaphysical thinking of the past to a new way of reflecting about Being— and this is true of Heidegger's thinking as a whole. "*Being and Time* means", as he has said (*Einführung in die Metaphysik,* p. 157; E.T., p. 172), ". . . not a book, but a task. What is truly a task is something we do not know and which, in so far as we genuinely know it, that is, *as* a task, we know only in asking."

with which he creates and breaks through into a dimension so long virtually foreign to academic philosophy should be faithfully reflected in his language. The linguistic peculiarities of Heidegger not only constitute a formidable obstacle to his foreign readers but have evoked bewildered and sometimes deprecatory academic comment from German scholars themselves. But these linguistic difficulties are not generated simply by the gnarled Teutonic genius of the German language in general or by some idiosyncratic mannerism, innate love of óbscurantism or craving for notoriety on the part of the author. The manner in which Heidegger handles language, both in the writing of the earlier phase and in those of the later is inseparably bound up with what he has to say and must therefore be taken as an intrinsic part of the method or 'way' of his thinking. He has repeatedly emphasized that in the realm of thought—which is itself part of the wider realm of 'saying'—the first and basic law is the suitability and 'seemliness' (*Schicklichkeit*) of utterance, the precision and conscientiousness (*Sorgfalt*) of speaking, the economy of words.[106] And in his own writings Heidegger demonstrates the utmost care and deliberation in the use of language appropriate to each of the different stages on his 'way' of thought. A brief consideration of this aspect of his thought will therefore be in place here.

Being and Time has not only established itself as an epoch-making classic of contemporary philosophy by virtue of the profound originality of its thoughtcontent, but has also caused quite a stir—as his later writings are doing now—because of its linguistic daring and departures from ordinary German usage. But the boldness and seeming unconventionality with which language is employed by Heidegger, here and in later writings, is intimately determined by the necessities inherent in his thought, as he has himself explained in a passage in *Being and Time*[107] which may here be quoted *in extenso:* "With regard to the lack of pliancy

106. Cf. *Brief über den 'Humanismus'*, pp. 118–119; also *Was ist Metaphysik?*, p. 46 (E.T., p. 391).
107. *Sein und Zeit*, pp. 38–39 (E.T., p. 63).

and the uncouthness of expression in the analyses that follow, we may add the remark that it is one thing to narrate accounts of *essents,* but another to comprehend the essent in its Being. For the latter task we not only lack mostly the words but, above all, 'grammar'. If it is permissible to refer to earlier, on their level incomparable, researches on the analysis of Being, one may compare the ontological sections of Plato's *Parmenides* or the fourth chapter of the Seventh Book of the *Metaphysics* of Aristotle with a narrative piece from Thucydides; one will then see the unprecedented and outrageous character of the formulations which were imposed upon the Greeks by their philosophers. And where (as in our case) the powers are comparatively feebler and where, moreover, the domain of Being to be disclosed is ontologically far more difficult than that which confronted the Greeks, the circumstantiality of concept formation and the heaviness and roughness of expression are bound to increase still further." Again, seeking to disclose the original, authentic phenomenon of temporality behind the veil of the vulgar conception of time, Heidegger says[108], "Finding words by which to define terminologically the primary and authentic phenomena corresponding to the secondary, inauthentic ones, one has to struggle with the same difficulty which grips all ontological terminology. Violence to language is in this field of investigation not arbitrariness but a necessity grounded in the subject-matter itself."

Heidegger's subject-matter is not the realm of essents, to which 'ordinary language' is adequate, but the being of essents and, in *Being and Time,* it is the being of man, to be articulated conceptually in all the rich complexity of its structure. But contrary to the hitherto prevailing view, he conceives man not in terms of substantial categories but in terms of *Existenz.* The 'substance' of man, he asserts, is his existenz, the mode or modes in which man is or exists and his task is to find the language which can adequately deal with the ontological and existenzial sphere of the

108. *Ibid.,* pp. 326–327 (E.T., p. 374).

possible, as against the ontic and the existenziell sphere of actual experience and which can lay bare the phenomenological dimension as against the phenomenal. The traditional categories of metaphysics, according to Heidegger, have been developed in the interest of the Greek quest of the nature of essents as such rather than for purposes of discourse about Being as such; and this categorial language has been determined by a specific sense in which Greeks conceived Being, i.e., as objective presence. In *Being and Time,* Heidegger seeks, accordingly, to forge concepts of an entirely new order, viz., existenzial concepts (or existenzialia) which will not only do justice to man's specific and distinctive mode of being but which will function as basic ontological concepts in the sense that the categorial concepts about objective entities can be shown to be secondary and derivable from them. In this sense Heidegger may be regarded as concerned, not so much with constructing a system of 'thought' as with building up a basic language from which the languages of the systems, metaphysical or theological, may be shown to be ultimately derivable. In the earlier phase Heidegger conceives this as the language of 'fundamental ontology'; in the later, going back into the ground of metaphysics, he seeks to develop a way of talking which carries discourse to a still deeper level and provides the ultimately basic language, the language of the history of Being (*Seinsgeschichte*) and of its destiny and dispensation (*Seinsgeschick*).

Heidegger is thus compelled to fashion a new language, a new idiom, by moulding the largely categorially patterned language of traditional philosophy into a medium for conceptualizing existenzial structures which, since they concern not static entities but modes of man's be-ing, the *that* and the *how* of his *existenz,* are essentially dynamic and of the nature of process. He achieves this, as Erasmus Schöfer has shown in a careful and detailed study of Heidegger's language[109], by coining new word-forms,

---

109. *Die Sprache Heideggers.* The author of this work is a student of linguistic science as developed by Leo Weisgerber on lines indicated by Wilhelm von Humboldt. Schöfer has dealt principally with the language of

largely through converting words of other parts of speech (especially verbs) into substantive forms, though he is by no means exceptional among philosophers in this practice[110]. The philosopher is engaged in the 'higher order' activity of bringing to light and focussing upon relational structures, complex states of affairs and relations and processes expressed by the different parts of speech. These are structural features of experience lying hidden in the grammatical structure of the language we use to talk *about* experience and therefore not noticed usually as really being constitutive elements of experience itself. To be able to talk about them he must isolate, define and conceptualize them, name them and terminologically designate them, without necessarily being guilty, as Ryle seems to think, of the Fido-'Fido' fallacy. To this end Heidegger has coined a whole array of abstract terms, employing circumlocutions, hyphenated phrases, compound terms not in common use, broken up compound words into their component parts and made abstract nouns out of words of almost every other part of speech. These new words serve the purpose of illuminating at one stroke, in the word of Schöfer, a particular phenomenon dug out through the analyses and of gathering it up in one concept. "They sum up, at times awkwardly and in an out-of-the-way manner, the structures and relations first disclosed by a complicated analysis and enable them, by means of the new word, to be grasped and represented as a unified phenomenon."[111] Negatively, these neologisms serve the

---

Being and Time and other writings of that phase, though he has illuminating things to say about the language of the later writings also. Although his approach is linguistic, the author's principal aim is to throw light on Heidegger's thought in its intimate relation to his language and, in particular, to demonstrate that in addition to being an original thinker, he is also one of the few German philosophers (Meister Eckhart and Nietzsche, to whom may be added Hegel) who are also *Sprachschöpfer*, makers of language who have creatively participated in developing the fabric of their mother tongue.

110. Such transformation into nouns is, as Justus Schwarz happily puts it in his essay, *Der Philosoph als Etymologe* (in *Philosophische Studien* I, 1949, quoted by Schöfer), "the trace which philosophical thinking leaves behind in a language."

111. *Die Sprache Heideggers*, p. 71. On Heidegger's word-synthesis and word analysis and the importance of distinguishing the latter from his much-disputed 'etymologizing', see *Ibid.*, pp. 103–115.

purpose of enabling Heidegger to avoid, in conformity with the principal philosophical thesis of the work, traditional terms suggestive of the essentialist 'ontology of the *Vorhanden*', as well as the modern epistemological terminology. Not merely these philosophical 'terms of art' but the grammar which, since the Greeks, has determined the basic structure and form of discourse as also the classification of its constitutive elements, is itself rooted in that ontology and the logic in which it has unfolded itself. The attempt to go beyond it, therefore, necessarily involves at least circumventing these grammatical limitations, until ways of talking are developed in which the grammar has been liberated from its thraldom to logic.[112]

The 'circumstantiality' and 'uncouthness' of expression in *Being and Time*, as also the novel technical vocabulary, is thus meant to force the reader away from the accustomed track of categorial thinking, of thinking in terms of the conceptual framework bequeathed to the Western mind by the Greeks and by the metaphysicians of modern subjectivism. Heidegger's avoidance of traditional terminology, in other words, is deliberately intended to prevent the reader from lapsing into the use of concepts deriving from the substance-centred as well as subject-centred meta-

112. See *Sein und Zeit*, p. 165 (E.T., p. 209). Cf. also *Einführung in die Metaphysik*, p. 40 f. (E.T., pp. 43 f.), where Heidegger refers to the deadness of the traditional grammatical forms which have become mere mechanisms and which constitute a steel net in which language and the study of language have been caught fast. Pointing to the necessity of a real revolution in our relation to language, he says, "It does not at all occur to us that what has been known to us well and so long might be different, that these grammatical forms do not analyse and regulate language from all eternity as if they were something absolute, that they have grown up, on the contrary, out of a very definite interpretation of the Greek and Latin languages", itself based on the fundamental view of Being guiding that interpretation. Heidegger points out further that "the determination of the essence of language, the very inquiry into it, is regulated at all times by the prevailing preconception about the essence or nature of essents and about the meaning of essence. But what essence and Being mean expresses itself only in language. . . . These grammatical forms do not suffice for what we are striving after." What is required, Heidegger suggests, is an essential clarification of the nature of Being in respect of its intrinsic entanglement with the nature of language.

physics of the Western philosophical tradition. This aspect of the
language of *Being and Time* has been well brought out by Hans
Lipps in the course of a penetrating discussion of existential
philosophy.[113] Contrasting Kierkegaard's and Nietzsche's manner of philosophizing with the compelling, stringent conceptuality (*zwingende Begrifflichkeit*) of Heidegger, Lipps has this to
say about the latter's language: "It is just his language at which
people have been scandalized, the alleged far-fetchedness and
forced character of his expressions. But then, one might think of
Aristotle, whose expression *to ti hen einai* too, for example, was
not found by him ready-made in the language[114] and we do
not find fault with him for having made up this expression. . . .
He alone gets stuck in the language of Heidegger who does not
read him the way he needs being read. He requires to be read
literally. This is a way of reading which cannot be taken as a
matter of course, for generally one reads otherwise. Sometimes,
we read with a view to orientation so that we may acquaint ourselves with the thoughts of another. Often we skip even prefer-
ring to read just 'in between'. We content ourselves with getting
just an idea of what the author is driving at. The writer and the
reader meet each other here on a level of average comprehensi-
bility; mostly, things remain half-said, not more being required.
And just in the matter of philosophical discussions, the dimension is usually marked out and established by traditions and
schools, so that one always somehow manages to get along with
terms like 'subject', 'object', 'transcendental', etc. Now, the re-
quirement that Heidegger is to be read 'literally' means just
the opposite of such reading. Not that we have to linger at

113. In an essay entitled, "Pragmatismus und Existenzphilosophie," reprinted in the volume, *Die Wirklichkeit des Menschen,* 1954, pp. 52–54.

114. Heidegger has given, in his use, an unfamiliar sense to a large
number of familiar words. This practice, bold and shocking though it must
appear to contemporaries, has always been a major source of the creative
shaping of language by the great philosophers. To the example from Aristotle mentioned by Lipps here, may be added Plato's use of *ousia* and *idea*
and Aristotle's *kategoria,* equally radical departures from common usage.

words here as in the case of a piece of writing of which the
objective precision motivates a literal reading; here we are required to attend to a word in respect of what, as a *word,* it
'signifies' or conveys. This is something quite different from the
objective, the matter of fact, to denote which words are mostly
employed. Heidegger appeals for a rediscovery of the potency of
words. We must win back the direction in which a word, *of its
own self,* suggests its meaning,—as, for example, the allusiveness
of a word, still word-bound and not objectively fixed, is always
secretly at work in the choice of a word when we are struggling
with the formulation of a thought. It is true that words like 'care'
(*Sorge*), 'disposition' (*Befindlichkeit*) etc. receive here a special
content (*Erfüllung,* filling in of a formal concept by a determinate content of meaning), which is found out above all by following a movement of thought, the adoption of which can only
be appealed for. Here we are not simply referred to an already
given field of objective relations, in and for the articulation of
which language has primarily developed. The unusual and indeed shockingly forced character of the phraseology and of the
way words are compounded is just what keeps us from slipping
into giving to these words 'fulfilments' (*Erfüllungen*) which,
being current and factual, come uppermost to our minds. The
stringent conceptuality of the existenzial analytic is thus something quite different from the exactness of concepts which belong
to a system, for exact means worked out in detail and every
systematic concept can be thus worked out in its implications,
i.e., can be 'realized' *ex definitione.* Through such terms as 'care'
and 'disposition', however, we are arrested and compelled into an
effort at the articulation of what we had already understood
ourselves to be in the depths of our existenz. . . . Nietzsche
said, 'to understand me is a distinction that must be earned.'
Nietzsche and Kierkegaard both sought their reader. Heidegger,
too, seeks him."

In other words, Heidegger deliberately chooses and builds his
terminology and his way of putting things not only for the posi-

tive purpose of disclosing new 'phenomena' but in studied contrast to traditional philosophical vocabulary. The attempt to go beyond metaphysics and comprehend it in its genesis and essence cannot, Heidegger insists,[115] be carried out in the language of metaphysics. The inquiry into the essence of Being expires unless it gives up the language of metaphysics, in which its representational thinking is crystallized. This is so because language is not a means of expression which may be doffed and changed like clothing, as Heidegger puts it, without making any difference to what has been mentioned in it. "It is in language that there manifests itself first of all, and *is*, that which, in our use of keywords, we seem to express only subsequently, making use of expressions which we believe might be discarded at will and substituted by others." Concepts, word-meanings and, primarily, language are not substitutable like 'optical systems' through which we may gaze at a reality existing by itself. Even metaphysical concepts, as Kant saw, are by nature of a different kind than those of science, for that which they grasp and the grasping are here in a basic sense the same. In the realm of the root words of thinking, therefore, it is even less a matter of indifference whether these (metaphysical concepts) are forgotten or whether one goes on using them untested. The attempt to go into the ground of metaphysics and to build afresh implies transforming our way of speaking and a change in our relationship to the nature of language—"inevitably everything here depends on the right way of saying, on that *logos* of which the real nature is beyond the ken of logic and dialectic, themselves offsprings of metaphysics." The utterance of thinking, Heidegger remarks, is not its expression but thinking itself, its movement and its chant.[116] The reader—not excluding the translator! —must there-

115. Cf. *Zur Seinsfrage*, pp. 25 f. (E.T., pp. 71, 73).
116. For examples of the way metaphysical concepts (as embodied in traditional terminology) crop up unawares, see *The Question of Being* and *Zu Einem Vers von Mörike*. The latter, an exchange of letters between Heidegger and Emil Staiger, is valuable for its discussion of 'appearing' and 'shining forth'.

fore be constantly alert and attentive to the precise, literal meaning of almost every word in the text, lest he glide into the usual practice of assimilating the new to the familiar by grasping it in terms of one's own cherished concepts, forgetting that Heidegger's intention is precisely the opposite, that of carrying our thought away from their habitual grooves into another dimension, away from "subject, soul, consciousness, spirit, person, life, man" and from idealism and realism, Reality and the Absolute, away from the traditional epistemological and metaphysical concepts as well as from the conceptual framework of theology. On the other hand, Heidegger wants the reader to concentrate on the positive content of the basic philosophical words, old or new, and give them their full weight. To this end, he sometimes takes a word apart, focussing attention upon the component parts of the word, squeezing out of it all its precise, complex meaning and force (e.g., in his discussions of *Vor-stellen* and *Gegen-stand*); sometimes, as in the later works particularly, he takes recourse to imaginative etymologizing and tries to 'project' or 'compose' the primordial, root meaning of a term, a meaning prior to and underlying the particular meanings a word acquires in actual usage at different times (e.g., the essays on *Logos* and *Aletheia* in *Vorträge und Aufsätze*). As Ortega y Gasset has remarked,[117] "Heidegger pierces through the common and superficial sense of a word and sets it aside. Under pressure he makes the underlying meaning leap up out of the depths. . . . The common word, with Heidegger, suddenly fills up; it fills itself up to the brim, with meaning. . . . It seems to us as if we were surprising a word in its *statu nascendi*." Similarly, Beda Allemann describes[118] Heidegger's procedure as one in which "words are spelt out in respect of their component parts, words which are in themselves transparent but of which the constitutive elements, though open to view, are no longer expressly considered or kept in mind in everyday use."

---

117. "Heidegger und die Sprache der Philosophie", *Universitas*, 7, 1952, quoted in Schöfer, pp. 110, 115.
118. *Hölderlin und Heidegger*, p. 111.

In Heidegger's later writings the tendency, already apparent in *Being and Time,* not merely to coin new word-forms but to break away from the established syntax and grammatical structure of language, comes clearly into evidence. Heidegger has realized that the grammatical rules which govern a language not only render expression possible but, in constituting and giving form to one possibility of expressing and disclosing the nature of things, they can also hinder expression by setting limits to it. With the further realization of the 'metaphysically' determined character of logical, conceptual thinking, there arises a different conception of thinking and, correspondingly, the use of language of which the structure is no longer rigidly governed by logic and grammar. The use of paradox, and fusion of heterogeneous linguistic elements, of thought-circles, of tautology, the *figura etymologica* (e.g., he fights a fight, Nothingness nihilates) and paronomasia—modes of expression common in mystical literature and in Oriental thinking—are clear indications, not so much of the linguistic inventiveness of Heidegger as of the fact that he is labouring to develop a new thought-form, *within* philosophy, which alone is adequate to the thinking of Being. The attempt to think without employing the traditional philosophical concepts, indeed to think non-conceptually, and yet to speak meaningfully and illuminatingly about Being is at the root of these linguistic peculiarities of Heidegger. This, and not any sort of flight into irrationalism and mysticism, may perhaps account for the respect with which Heidegger has recently been referring to the 'thinking' of the German mystic Meister Eckhart and Angelus Silesius, as also for his growing interest in the thought of the far East.[119]

In *Being and Time,* Heidegger's thinking, despite his linguistic innovations and departures, is still within the traditional framework and his language and approach typically academic. Still

119. Characteristically, Heidegger refers to Eckhart (*Vorträge und Aufsätze,* p. 175) as "this master of thinking." Discussing a line from Angelus Silesius, Heidegger remarks, ". . . one is inclined to think that genuine and great mysticism is characterized by the utmost sharpness and depth of thought. And this in fact is the truth. Meister Eckhart testifies to it."

taking language as a neutral 'instrument' of thought and the latter as concept-building, Heidegger constructs a large technical terminology to formulate existenzial concepts. Although even here this terminology is largely derived from his native German, he models, it nevertheless, on philosophical Greek, especially Aristotle,[120] and makes free use of the large 'international' vocabulary of scholarship deriving from Greek and Latin. In the later writings he not only abandons the use of technical terms, along with the representational, rigidly conceptual thinking of the earlier phase, but turns definitely away from the 'foreign' vocabulary of the scholarly tradition, deliberately confining himself to words of pure, simple German descent. Schöfer refers[121] to a conversation (in 1959) between Heidegger and Jean Beaufret, in the course of which Heidegger told the latter that in his experiments with language he endeavoured to approximate to a condition which would correspond to that prevailing before the Latinization of German. The language of the philosophical tradition of the West has been largely moulded by the Greek thinkers and, later, by the Latinized version of Greek terms in medieval times. In German philosophy the influence of Latin terminology can be traced, after the abandonment of Latin as the medium of creative thought, in Kant and the German Idealists. The greatest and most original philosophers of the West have thus been confined in their thinking within a terminological framework inherited, via the Romans, from the Greeks. They have taken it over uncritically and have in consequence remained tied to the Greek way of thinking and of seeing things. But, as Schöfer remarks,[122] "Heidegger, who attempts to think about the nature of Greco-European philosophy, is obliged to dissociate himself from its linguistic mould in order to be able to reflect not in it but about it." Through the elimination of vocabulary deriving from Greek and Latin, Heidegger is able to use a purified language,

120. See Schöfer, p. 282 and elsewhere.
121. *Die Sprache Heideggers*, p. 24.
122. *Ibid.*, p. 11.

rooted in the native dialect, free from the philosophical suggestions clinging around that vocabulary and thus capable of uttering
the truth of Being in ways that were barred to it.

Critics of Heidegger have complained of the rift in the language of *Being and Time* and of the unevenness of its style.
Those parts of the work where Heidegger discusses traditional
doctrines and the views of past philosophers are written in a
discursive, descriptive, abstract, complicated *Akademiker-
deutsch;* others, where he develops his own original thoughts, as
in the analyses of man's modes of being, are analytical, deductive, elaborating. These distinct linguistic levels are present in all
writings of Heidegger but, as Schöfer has pointed out, whereas in
Being and Time they are simply juxtaposed without really fusing
together, in the later writings there comes about a greater coherence and unity in style. The reason for the lack of stylistic and
linguistic unity in the earlier work is to be found in the fact,
already pointed out before, that although *Being and Time* represents a turning-point in the history of philosophy, "it is a work of
transition and bears all the marks of such transition. Both in
content and in language, it represents a transition from the thinking within the framework and language of the history of philosophy (of "the Being of beings") to the sphere of the thinking
and utterance of "Being itself" in the later works."[123] It is only in
these latter that, with the employment of a purely German vocabulary, a unified style and language are possible and actually
attained. In his lecture on Hegel, "the friend of the house", Heidegger describes language—which alone really speaks and not
man—as the treasure house of all that is essential. "Whenever
and in whatever manner man speaks, he speaks only because he
already gives ear to language." This language, the language in
which we are born and which is bequeathed to us, is the mother-
tongue, itself nourished by the dialect out of which it has developed. "The dialect is the mysterious source of every developed

123. *Ibid.,* p. 280.

language. From it stream forth all those precious gifts which the spirit of a language contains in itself. . . . The spirit of language guards and preserves in itself the invisible but all sustaining relationships to God, to world, to men and their doings."[124] Even when the whole conceptual terminology of the European philosophical tradition is renounced, these riches remain, leaving at the disposal of the thinker as yet unactualized possibilities of utterance and, through giving word to what so far has remained unsaid, of letting what has remained hidden so long come to light and manifest itself.

But whether Heidegger writes in the language of the scholarly tradition of Western philosophy or takes recourse to the simple, pure 'mother-tongue', he is never under the illusion that 'ordinary language' can ever deliver its whole secret, surrender all that lies in it and become completely transparent. As he says in a recent lecture,[125] "The difficulty lies in language. Our Occidental languages are, each in its different way, languages of metaphysical thinking. Whether the nature of the Western languages is in itself only metaphysical and hence definitively cast into the mould of ontotheology, or whether these languages can offer other possibilities of saying, which means at the same time of saying and yet leaving unsaid, are questions that must remain open." In a variety of ways, Heidegger has sought to explore creatively the latter alternative, not hesitating to avail himself of the license of linguistic creation generally restricted to poets, delving deep, beyond the purely academic level, into the riches lying buried in the archaic, the literary, the religious and the mystical layers of his native German and drawing into his net the vocabulary of 'German inwardness', as Schöfer calls it, or, as Hans Stoltenberg terms it, the language of the Gothic wisdom of the heart. This, however, by no means implies a lapse into some kind of 'mysticism', and abdication of thinking as such, or that Heidegger is

124. *Hebel der Hausfreund,* p. 10. See also the essay entitled "Sprache und Heimat" (in *Dauer im Wandel,* Burckhardt *Festschrift*).
125. *Identität und Differenz,* p. 72 (E.T., p. 73).

struggling to clothe in words an experience, in itself immediate and ineffable but already given, of which the content is recalcitrant to language. For Heidegger, "The word does not merely name, and so enable us to have in our grasp, our already represented present reality (or essent), it is not merely a means to the depiction of something given. On the contrary, it is the word which first of all bestows Presence, i.e., Being, in which anything appears as an essent."[126] Language here is one with thought, the project of thinking merges into linguistic composing and both together are creative and evocative of genuine novelty, of a new conception of Being, that is, of new Being.

As compared with the writings of the earlier phase, in which language is still in some measure an instrument for the expression of universal meanings, Heidegger's later thinking is much more intimately language-bound. So far-reaching in its consequences for thought is his rejection of the essentialist doctrine—and implied in that, of the conception of meanings as universal essences which may be clothed indifferently in any linguistic symbol— that, in these later writings, what is thought and said becomes inseparable from the individual and unique language and manner of saying it; not only does the thought and the utterance merge into one but the particular language employed and the thought content expressed become indissoluble. Such thinking, like all great poetry, is in a profound sense untranslatable and there is undeniable truth in Karl Löwith's remark[127] that a Whitsun miracle will have to occur, if Heidegger's definition of the love of Being or of the nature of technology were to lend itself to being expressed in English. But this untranslatability, far from being a shortcoming, is not only inevitable but in reality a boon and a challenge to any thinking that concerns itself, not with beings, but with the Being of beings or with Being itself. It compels thought to reflect upon and bring to explicit awareness the spirit of both languages, that of the original and of the trans-

126. *Unterwegs zur Sprache*, p. 227.
127. Cf. *Heidegger—Denker in dürftiger Zeit.*, p. 15.

lation, and to realize more deeply how Being reveals itself uniquely in the spirit of each language. "Through translation", Heidegger says, "the work of thinking is transposed into the spirit and outlook of another language and thus undergoes an inevitable transformation. But the transformation can become fertile because it makes the fundamental way of posing the question appear in a new light."[128]

Ortega y Gasset has given high praise to Heidegger's language as the perfect example of a specifically philosophical style.[129] Yet, Heidegger has himself, in retrospect, repeatedly characterized the language of *Being and Time* as clumsy and uncouth. On his long 'way' to Being, something in itself ultimately simple, Heidegger's unceasing endeavour has been to gather together language in a simplicity of utterance, to eliminate the circumstantiality and heaviness of expression, as also the technical jargon, of the earlier works. He does this by employing, where he develops his own ideas, an essentially German vocabulary. Without restricting himself · to common usage, he exploits the possibilities held out by "the hidden riches of language"[130] thus creatively transforming his mother-tongue itself, in however modest a degree. For, as he says[131], "Thinking draws inconspicuous grooves in language, marks that are even more inconspicuous than those made by the unhurried steps of the peasant walking across a field."

128. Foreword to the French translation of *Was ist Metaphysik?*, quoted in Schöfer.
129. In the essay mentioned in note 117 above.
130. See *Unterwegs zur Sprache*, p. 197.
131. *Brief über den 'Humanismus'*, p. 119.

chapter two

EARLY ESSAYS AND THE "REVERSAL"

Being and Time had as its objective the reopening and elaboration of the question of Being. This involved, as the plan was initially conceived by Heidegger, a double task: firstly, that of giving a temporal interpretation of Dasein and the explication of Time as the transcendental horizon of the question about Being and, secondly, the working out of the main features of a phenomenological destruction of the hisory of ontology in the light of temporality. The published part of *Being and Time* contains only the preparatory fundamental analysis of Dasein, followed by an account of Dasein and temporality, but without the promised third Division of Part I on "Time and Being" in which the inquiry was to proceed in the reverse direction. In the *Letter on Humanism*, Heidegger refers to this 'reversal' (*Kehre*) of the approach from Being and Time to Time and Being as an essential part of the spiralling inquiry into Being and explains why the part dealing with it was withheld from publication along with the rest of the first part of *Being and Time*. As he there says, "Here the whole thing undergoes a reversal. The division in question was withheld because thought failed in giving adequate utterance to this reversal and did not come through with the help of the language of metaphysics. The lecture, *On the Nature of Truth*, thought out and communicated in 1930 but printed only in 1943, gives a certain glimpse into the thinking of the reversal from Being and Time to Time and Being."[1] What this reversal

1. *Brief über den 'Humanismus'* p. 72.

means and what implications it had for the development of Heidegger's thought in its second phase as he has explained it in the *Letter on Humanism,* we shall consider below. The second part of *Being and Time* containing the 'destruction' was never published, also perhaps because of the change of perspective and approach which occurred in Heidegger's thinking in connexion with the 'reversal'. A beginning in this direction, however, was made with the publication in 1929 of *Kant and the Problem of Metaphysics,* and in his later writings Heidegger has constantly returned to this historical destruction, discussing for this purpose the great figures in the history of Western philosophy from the Pre-Socratics to Nietzsche. This aspect of Heidegger's thought will be dealt with in the next chapter. Soon after the publication of *Being and Time,* there appeared Heidegger's much discussed Inaugural Lecture, *What is Metaphysics?* and, in the same year (1929) an essay, *On The Nature of Ground.* Another essay, entitled *On the Nature of Truth,* was also conceived in this period and made public in the form of lectures, though not published, after repeated revision, until 1943. These essays give some idea of the way Heidegger sought to approach the problem of Being in the first phase of his thought and exhibit both the unity and the integral character of his thinking as well as its inner dynamism and mobility. Because of their intrinsic importance and also because they prepare the way for the development of Heidegger's thought in the second phase, a brief account of these is first given here.[2]

I THE EARLY ESSAYS

What is Metaphysics? is concerned not with the expounding of any thesis about metaphysics but with the unfoldment, elaboration and solution of a metaphysical problem—the problem of Transcendence which is here taken as being identical with the prob-

2. Ampler analyses of these essays, as also of *Kant und das Problem der Metaphysik* and *Die Selbstbehauptung der deutschen Universität* will be found in Richardson, *Heidegger.*

lem of Nothingness. The various sciences, Heidegger begins by
pointing out, are engaged in investigating the different fields of
essents; the pursuit of science means that a particular essent,
man, breaks into the totality of what is in such a manner that
essents manifest themselves as and how they are, becoming,
through the in-break of science, *what* they are. But in its mode of
relationship, its attitude and in the way of its breaking into,
science is concerned solely with what is, the essent, and nothing
beyond it. Science has no use for this Nothing beyond what is and
turns away from this Nothing as from "a horror and a phan-
tasm."[3] What, Heidegger asks, is this Nothing beyond essents? To
define Nothingness is impossible, for that would be to treat it as
itself an essent. Nor can it be derived from negation, a form of
logical judgment, for negation presupposes the Nothing which is
"more fundamental than the 'not' and negation." Despite the
formal impossibility of an inquiry into Nothingness, however, we
may still attempt, Heidegger asserts, to determine whether it is at
all 'given' in experience and how it is encountered and recognized
as such on the basis of a preconceptual familiarity with it implied
in our everyday use of 'is not'. Nothingness is the complete negation of the totality of essents not merely in the formal sense of
negating in imagination the idea of such totality, but in reality.
This totality, though never cognitively in our grasp, is what we
find ourselves placed in the midst of and of which we always
have some awareness. The totality of what is is disclosed in our
moods and feelings and among these the attunement of anxiety is
distinctive in that it brings us face to face with Nothing itself.
This is an event in Dasein which, though rare and fleeting, is of
fundamental importance (being the ontic manifestation of what,
in the ontological sense is always implicitly there), for it transforms man into his *Da-sein*. Anxiety reveals the Nothing, not as
an essent, not as an object, not as something detached from the

3. On the feasibility of an inquiry into Nothing, see *Einführung in die
Metaphysik*, pp. 18–22 (E.T., pp. 19–24).

totality of essents but as at one with this totality as it slips away
from us. The encounter with Nothingness in anxiety does not
mean that the totality of essents is either annihilated or negated
in judgment. The essence of the Nothing consists rather in a total
relegation to the vanishing totality of essents—Nothingness re-
pels Dasein, referring it back to the totality as it slips away
(*abweisende Verweisung*). This is a nihilation which discloses
the totality for the first time in its sheer otherness to Nothing.
"The essence of the primordially nihilating Nothing lies in the
fact that it alone brings Dasein face to face with what is as such,"
for the primordial disclosure of Nothingness alone renders possible the revelation of beings. To be *Da-sein* means to be suspended and held within Nothingness and this means being beyond, transcending, the totality of essents, a transcendence which
alone renders self-hood and freedom also possible. This Nothing
is not an entity but an event, a nihilating which occurs in the
Being of beings.[4] Because mostly we are lost in essents and held
fast to them, we are ordinarily not aware of Nothing which yet
unceasingly nihilates, manifesting itself in the guise of judgments
of negation. This, however, is neither the sole nor even the chief
mode of nihilation manifesting itself in Dasein—the harshness of
opposition and the violence of loathing, the pain of refusal, the
mercilessness of an interdict and the bitterness of renunciation

4. Cf. *Brief über den 'Humanismus,'* p. 113: "Because nihilation is
present in Being itself (which is not a given property of and discoverable in
essents), therefore we can never observe it as something given and adhering
to essents." It is equally impossible, Heidegger points out here, to drive
Nothing from no-saying. Because the Nothing never appears as an object, it
is falsely concluded that it must have its origin in the no-saying of a subject.
Such a conclusion is, of course, only a manifestation of modern subjectivity.
"Nihilating is in Being itself and by no means in the Dasein of men, in so far
as this (Dasein) is conceived as the subjectivity of the *ego cogito*. . . .
Being nihilates—as Being. That is why in the Absolute Idealism of Hegel
and Schelling, Nothing appears as the negativity of negation in the nature of
Being. The latter, however, is then conceived as unconditioned will, in the
sense of absolute actuality, which wills itself in the form of the will of
knowing and of love. In this will, Being still lies hidden as the Will to
Power."

are more abysmal and oppressive, Heidegger says, than the mere adequacy of rational negation. Dasein's suspension in Nothingness makes man the stand-in (*Platzhalter*) for Nothing and at the same time constitutes his transcendence, his metaphysical character, by virtue of which Dasein goes beyond what is, the totality of essents. Classical metaphysics as well as Christian dogma had their own conception of the Nothing, each implying a view of Being, according to which Nothing was the conceptual opposite of what truly is, that is, its negation. According to Heidegger's analysis, Nothing ceases to be the vague opposite of what is and reveals itself as integral to the Being of essents. Being and Nothing belong together, not because they are at one in their indeterminateness and immediacy, as Hegel thought, but because Being itself is essentially finite and reveals itself only in the transcendence of Dasein suspended in Nothingness.[5]

The problem of Nothing thus embraces the whole of metaphysics as concerned with the question of Being, at the same time forcing us to face the problem of the origin of negation, that

5. In the 'Postscript' of 1943, Heidegger explicitly states that Nothing which "never and nowhere is, unveils itself as that which is distinguished from all essents, i.e., what we call Being." Only the essent, but not Being is accessible to science, for the latter is neither an existing quality of essents nor capable of being conceived and established objectively. "This, the sheer other to all essents is what is not, the non-entity." Instead of dismissing Nothing as the merely nugatory we should try, Heidegger says, "to experience in Nothing the vastness of that which gives every essent the warrant to be. This is Being itself. Without Being, whose unfathomable but still not unfolded essence is vouchsafed us by Nothing in essential dread, everything that is would remain in a state of Beinglessness. But then, even this, regarded as abandonment by Being (*Seinsverlassenheit*), is not sheer Nothing, assuming that it is of the truth of Being, that there never is Being without the essent, that there never is an essent without Being. . . . Nothing as the other to what is is the veil of Being."

In the earlier editions of this essay, Heidegger had said, "There is indeed Being without the essent. . . .", whereas in later editions this reads, "Being never is without essents. . . ." The emendation was noted and commented upon by Max Müller (*Existenzphilosophie in geistigen Leben der Gegenwart*, 2nd edition, pp. 45–46) and discussed by Schulz "Über den philosophiegeschichtlichen Ort Martin Heideggers", *Philosophische Rundschau*, I (1954), pp. 65–93, 211–232. See also Richardson's discussion of what he calls "the case of the altered epilogue." (*Heidegger*, pp. 563–565.)

is, to a decision as to the legitimacy of the rule of 'logic' in metaphysics. Science itself, it has been shown, is rendered possible as the investigation of essents by the overtness of Nothing, i.e., by Dasein's going beyond essents in their totality. Because Nothing manifests itself in the very depths of man, he is struck with wonder that things are and how and why they are, and so gives birth to science. Philosophizing itself is possible only as a leap that launches us into the Nothingness which sets us free from the idols we all carry with us and to which we all cling, making us return again and again to the fundamental question of metaphysics: "Why are there essents at all, rather than Nothing?"[6]

In *Kant and the Problem of Metaphysics* also, Heidegger speaks[7] of Nothingness as the transcendental horizon of the disclosure of essents in the course of his discussion of the Tran-

6. For a full discussion of the significance of the question, "Why are there essents rather than nothing?", see *an Introduction to Metaphysics,* Chapter I. Heidegger explains here how this is the basic question of metaphysics, the foremost of all questions in respect of comprehensiveness, depth and primordial character. To take the leap of asking this question, with its recoil upon itself, is to philosophize. The question not only asks for the ground of what is but, by confronting the essent with the alternative of Nothingness, deprives it of its obviousness and renders it questionable in its totality.

In the "Introduction" to *What is Metaphysics?*, Heidegger expresses surprise that it has never occurred to his critics to consider why a lecture seeking to think the truth of Being by way of the Nothing and thence to the nature of metaphysics, should claim that this is the basic question of metaphysics. Why does this attempt to think of Being by way of the Nothing return in the end to a question concerning the essent again, asking 'why?' in the traditional causal manner of metaphysics, very much as the metaphysician Leibniz, in his *Principles of Nature and Grace,* asked, 'why is there anything rather than nothing?' Is the question at the end of the lecture a metaphysical question, like that of Leibniz, about the surpeme cause of everything that is? As Heidegger explains, the question here is asked in an entirely different sense for, not being concerned with essents and their first cause, it starts with that which is not an essent, i.e., Nothing, which is the sole theme of the lecture. From a point of view that has passed beyond metaphysics to its own ground, i.e., from the point of view of the truth of Being itself, to raise this question is to ask, "How is it that essents take precedence everywhere and lay claim to every 'is', while that which is not an essent, the Nothing—which in this sense is Being itself—remains forgotten?"

7. Pp. 113–115 (E.T., pp. 125–128).

scendental Deduction: it is the projection into Nothing, which is not to be conceived as a *nihil absolutum*, that constitutes the transcendental condition of the possibility of objects in general. The transcendental, non-empirical object or X of which Kant speaks[8] is not an essent and yet a 'something', i.e., according to Heidegger, Nothing conceived as pure horizon within which essents can appear and be known. Heidegger explicitly states that anxiety and Nothingness are discussed by him solely with a view to elucidating the possibility of an understanding of Being, adding that "the Being of beings can be understood at all only if in the roots of its nature Dasein holds itself suspended in Nothingness—therein lies the deepest finitude of transcendence."[9]

What is Metaphysics? formulates a solution of the problem of transcendence, showing how going beyond the essent occurs in the very essence of Dasein, and concludes that this going beyond is metaphysics itself. But, as Heidegger says in the 'Postscript' the main question—what is metaphysics?—remains unanswered because the question itself goes beyond metaphysics in the traditional sense, arising as it does from a thinking which is already on the way to an overcoming of metaphysics but which is compelled, by the very nature of the case, to speak the language of what it seeks to overcome. Traditional metaphysics is concerned with the truth about essents and seeks to determine what essents are by way of conceptualizing the beingness (*Seiendheit*) of

8. *Critique of Pure Reason,* A 108 and A 235 ff, B 294 ff.
9. P. 214. J. P. Sartre has discussed Heidegger's view of Nothing and compared it with Hegel's (*Being and Nothingness,* pp. 16–20). In *Nietzsche* (vol. I, p. 73), Heidegger himself points out how German Idealism, conceiving Being as will, also had the daring to think of the negative as comprehended in Being. A penetrating examination of the conception of finitude in the philosophy of Heidegger will be found in Henri Birault's article, "Heidegger et la pensée de la finitude" (*Revue Internationale de Philosophie,* No. 52). Birault, following Kojeve's interpretation of Hegel, refers to the similarities between Hegel and Heidegger as philosophers of finitude, seeking to interpret human existence in finitistic and atheistic terms. Birault also gives a historical account of the concept of finitude and negativity differentiating Heidegger's conception of *Endlichkeit* from the views of Plato and Sartre and from the Christian doctrine.

what is. It inquires into the truth about beings in the light of the truth of Being, which is the ground on which it functions and which provides the horizon within which it moves, but which remains unknown and unfathomable to itself. To ask, "What is metaphysics?", in so far as it involves asking what its own ground is, is thus already to rise beyond metaphysics, while yet remaining partly caught up in it.

Closely linked with this implicit motivation (i.e., a realization of the questionability of metaphysics) behind the lecture is the attack against the primacy of logic in metaphysics, for its helplessness in face of the problem of Nothing. As Heidegger suggests in the 'Postscript', the thinking of Being—"essential thinking", as not only concerned with Being but as itself an occurrence of Being—which only follows the thinking whose forms and rules constitute 'logic' cannot remain faithful to the law of its own truth. " 'Logic' is only *one* of the possible explications of the nature of thinking and one which, as its name shows, is based on the experience of Being as attained in Greek thought. The suspicion cast upon 'logic' . . . arises from a knowledge of that thinking which has its source not in the observation of the objectivity of essents but in the experience of the truth of Being." The exactest thinking, Heidegger adds, is never the most stringent thinking, for the former merely subserves the reckoning of and with essents whereas the latter seeks strenuously to keep in view the essential nature of its subject matter.[10] As against such 'calculative thought', the thinking that is primarily determined by what is the other to essents is called by Heidegger 'essential thinking'.

Written in the same year as *What is Metaphysics?* the essay, *On the Nature of Ground (Vom Wesen des Grundes)* discusses the problem of *arche* and tries to show how the metaphysical quest for an ultimate ground of things—and the scientific quest

10. For a critical discussion of Heidegger's attack on logic and an elucidation of the sense in which it should be understood, cf. Walter Bröcker's article, "Heidegger und die Logik" in *Philosophische Rundschau*, I (1953–54), pp. 48–56

for the causes of things—springs from the very nature of Dasein's existenz as constituted by Transcendence. The concept of *arche* or Ground is a central concept of metaphysics and its analysis goes back to the *Metaphysics* of Aristotle, 1013a–1014a, where three types of ground are distinguished, viz., the ground of the 'what', of the 'that' and of the truth of anything. The principle of ground or sufficient reason as enunciated by Leibniz (*nihil est sine ratione*, there is nothing without a reason or ground), Heidegger points out, does not throw any light on what ground itself is; in its positive formulation (*omne ens habet rationem*), it speaks of the essent, saying that everything that is must have a ground but says nothing about the nature of ground as such. Leibniz's discussion of the origin of this principle (in *Primae veritates*) makes it evident, however, that propositional truth always needs 'grounding' and shows how the concept of truth is intrinsically linked up with that of ground. A consideration of truth in the ontic sense (the pre-predicative manifestness of essents, in which propositional truth is rooted) as well as in the ontological (the overtness of Being which renders ontic truth itself possible) shows the same inner connexion and suggests, further, that basic to both truth and ground is Dasein's transcendence, which alone renders these possible. Ontic truth and ontological truth are concerned, Heidegger says, with the essent in its Being and with the Being of essents respectively. "They are intrinsically bound up with each other because of their relationship with the distinction between Being and beings (Ontological Difference). Along with the emergence of this distinction, and based on it, there appears truth in this bifurcated form." Since Dasein, with the comprehension of Being inherent in it, relates itself to essents, the ability to make this distinction (i.e., the factual occurrence of the Ontological Difference) must be grounded in an essential character of Dasein.[11] This ground,

11. In the Foreword to the 3rd edition (1949) of this essay, Heidegger says that both *Vom Wesen des Grundes* and *Was ist Metaphysik?* were written in 1928 and remarks on the link connecting the two as follows:

Heidegger says, lies in its transcendence and it is, therefore, in
the domain of transcendence that an elucidation of the nature of
ground or *arche* must be sought. As existenz, Dasein is inherently
transcending, going beyond the essent as such, beyond everything that is, including itself. "With the fact of *Da-sein* this rising
up beyond is already there," as Heidegger says. That *towards*
which the transcendence occurs is the world, which is itself no
essent but a constitutive element in the structure of transcendence (for which reason the world-concept must be regarded as
a transcendental one). Dasein's transcendence is thus constituted
by its being-in-the-world, not in the sense that it factually exists
in the world but in the sense that its very existence as Dasein
depends upon its being ontologically constituted as being-in-the-
world. Dasein's existenz as transcending renders it possible that
essents should manifest themselves by "entering into a world".
"Only when in the totality of essents one essent emerges as
Dasein, there comes the hour and the day of the essent's entry
into a world (*Welteingang*). Only with this primordial occurrence of transcendence, when an essent of the nature of being-in-
the-world breaks into the totality of essents, there arises the possibility of essents manifesting themselves."

It is in the context of Dasein's transcendence as being-in-the-
world that Heidegger now proceeds to elucidate the nature of
ground. As an existenzial, the world is the totality of the 'for the

---

"The latter reflects on the Nothing, the former mentions the Ontological
Difference. The Nothing is the 'not' of essents and is thus Being as understood from the point of view of the essent. The Ontological Difference is the
'not' between the essent and Being. But just as the 'not' of essents is not
sheer nothing, so also the Difference as the 'not' between the essent and
Being is not a mere *ens rationis,* a mere construct of the understanding that
distinguishes." The 'not' of the Nothing and the 'not' of the Difference,
though not one, are yet connected together in the sameness of the essence of
the Being of essents. The two essays seek, without explicit awareness of it, to
bring into view this sameness' as a problem for further reflection.

As will be evident to the reader, Heidegger's exploration of the sense of
Being and his critical inquiry into the ground of metaphysics both revolve
round the "Ontological Difference", which is thus a basic concept in his
philosophy.

sake of' (*Umwillen,* the *ou heneka* of Aristotle) or the ends of Dasein. In willing these ends, i.e., in projecting himself on possibilities of his own self, man goes beyond himself, thereby becoming a self. The willing, however, which projects forward this 'for the sake of' and is its basis, is not an act of will in the usual sense, for all such acts themselves presuppose transcendence. As the primary projection of the 'for the sake of', it is freedom itself. When, in consequence of transcendence, freedom holds projected before it, as its correlate, the 'for the sake of', there comes about world—"The world dispenses itself and 'worlds' (*weltet*)." Freedom is thus the ground of the world, in a transcendental sense.

This interpretation of freedom as based on transcendence, Heidegger points out, goes deeper than the Kantian determination of freedom as spontaneity (in the sense of causing itself), for freedom is not just one sort of ground but the source of ground in general. "Freedom is freedom in relation to ground," a relation which Heidegger calls grounding. Rooted in the freedom of transcendence, grounding manifests itself in three modes: instituting or founding (*Stiften*); providing a basis or rooting (*Boden-nehmen*); establishing or justifying (*Be-gründen*). Grounding in the first sense is the projection of the 'for the sake of', the free, transcendental act of letting a world dispense itself the world-project (*Weltentwurf*). But man's reaching up beyond in the project of a world implies, at the same time, finding himself in the midst of essents, attuned to them and wrapped up in them (*Eingenommenheit vom Seienden*). By virtue of being taken up with essents, Dasein secures a ground to stand upon, becomes rooted in essents. This is grounding in the second sense. Establishing himself in the midst of essents, man thus sets up a world, projecting possibilities of his own self. Thirdly, Dasein relates itself to essents (the 'intentionality' of Dasein), not being merely in the midst of them or in a world. Grounding in the above two senses renders such intentionality possible, giving rise, at the same time, to grounding as establishing or justifying.

Grounding in this sense is necessarily bound up with the manifestness of essents as its transcendental condition and it renders ontic truth possible. With such grounding there comes into being the problem of 'why?' But the transcendental possibility of the 'why?' lies in the fact that all why-asking presupposes a pre conceptual comprehension of Being (what, how, that and not) without which no 'why?' would be possible. This primary comprehension of Being, therefore, "contains the first and last primordial answer for all questioning" and constitutes thus the ultimate grounding (as establishing or justification). This is transcendental grounding in the sense of ontological truth, for it lays bare the ontological constitution of what is. And because ontic truth (manifestness of essents as and how they are) is based ontological truth, all disclosure and discovery of essents must in its way be concerned with grounding, must seek to find out causes, to prove and validate itself. Grounding, as manifested in the three senses of Ground, viz., possibility (projection of world), basis or fundament (being taken up with essents) and justification (ontological grounding of essents), has thus its origin in Dasein's transcendence, i.e., in the finite three-fold freedom to ground (corresponding to the three modes of grounding); it alone renders possible, in its unity, that whole—essents in their totality—within which Dasein can exist. As to the question whether the three modes of grounding have any common feature which links them together in a basic unity, Heidegger only throws out a hint here that each of these, in its own way, springs from the concern (Sorge) for perdurability and continuance, which in turn is possible only as temporality.[12]

The Principle of Ground or Sufficient Reason says that every essent has its ground. The above account of the nature of ground explains why this is so.[13] Because of the prior comprehension of

12. Since Heidegger's lectures on Schelling have not so far been published, it is difficult to know to what extent his own views on freedom and ground are derived from Schelling and directly or indirectly via Schelling from Jakob Boehme's concept of Ungrund.

13. In this essay, Heidegger discusses the Principle of Ground as saying something of the essent only (viz., that every essent has a ground) and as

Being already present in all our dealings with essents, Being is, to start with, of the nature of grounding. "Because 'ground' is an essential transcendental feature of Being in general, therefore the Principle of Sufficient Reason applies to essents. And ground is

---

uniformative about the nature of Ground itself. In a full-scale study devoted to this principle much later (*Der Satz vom Grund*, 1957), Heidegger realized that he had been too hasty in arriving at the above conclusion. As he says there (pp. 84–85), "That account, though correct, led to confusion, firstly, in respect of the possible ways and openings suggested by the Principle of Ground for dealing with the particular problem of the nature of Ground and, secondly and above all, in respect of the basic question (i.e., the question of Being) which has inspired all (my) thinking, and towards the service of which that essay was also a contribution." All grounding comes from Being and it is by virtue of its grounding character that beings always have a ground.

Beginning with the Greek concepts of *arche* and *aition*, ground has been variously conceived in the history of thought as *ratio, causa,* principle, justification and condition of possibility. The word denotes the basis, the *fundus,* on which something rests. Ground (principle) and Reason are translations of the Latin *ratio*—a translation which also bifurcates the undifferentiated *ratio* into the two-fold sense of Reason (*Vernunft*) and ground or cause. *Ratio* itself is the translation of the Greek *logos*, containing within itself the implicit double sense of Being as presence and as ground, both together in their unity with speech. The literal meaning of the term *Logos,* according to Heidegger, originally refers to Being and Ground in one without, however, distinguishing between the two and hence without also an awareness of the unity which they form together. Because of this unity of Being and Ground, the conception of Being as Ground, remained implicit; later thought, seeking to represent Ground, 'displaced' it to the essent, as belonging to that rather than to Being. Really speaking, it is to Being that ground and grounding belong; Being and Ground are the same in the sense of belonging together in a unity of essence, not fusing together in bare identity but held apart in their togetherness. But so long as *logos* is interpreted in terms of the later *ratio* and *Vernunft* this is bound to remain hidden. As the source of all grounding, Being itself is without ground and to speak of it as self-grounding would be to treat it as if it were itself an essent. Being itself rests, not on anything that can be described in terms of ground, reason or cause but in the mystery of play (*Spiel*), that highest and profoundest play of which Heraclitus speaks, the play of *aion,* of world as the dispensation of Being, in the later language of Heidegger. Implicit in the way Being revealed itself to the Greeks is the conception of Ground, which became explicit later in the European attitude to essents and in the definition of man as the rational animal; it has culminated in the complete domination of our lives by the Principle of Sufficient Reason in the form of the omnipotence of technology in the Atomic age of today. "Is this the last word that can be said about Being," Heidegger asks in conclusion, "that it is Ground?" Does the nature of Being not need deeper reflection and a more adequate formulation?

implied in the nature of Being because Being (not beings) is
there only for a transcendence," a transcendence that is triply
grounding in the above manner. Freedom, finite because in
projecting certain possibilities it deprives itself of others, is thus
the source of the principle of ground. "Freedom is the ground of
Ground," not as itself one of the modes distinguished above but
as their transcendental unity. In this sense, however, this ground
is the abyss (*Ab-grund*) of Dasein; in projecting world, man
rises up beyond essents and beyond himself and through such
rising up knows himself as this abyss, finite in his thrownness and
in his world-project, finite in his transcendence and in his freedom to ground, finite and, therefore, a being that goes into remote distances (*ein Wesen der Ferne*), for "only through such
primeval moving beyond to the distant, which he accomplishes in
transcending all that is, can he achieve the true nearness to
things."

In all the writings of the first phase, Heidegger seeks to approach the problem of Being through the comprehension of
Being inherent in Dasein, through an analysis of man's capacity
to go beyond himself and beyond essents as such. The problem
of transcendence is thus central to this approach. *Being and
Time,* as Heidegger points out in *Vom Wesen des Grundes*[14],
has no other aim than to offer a concrete demonstration of a
project of transcendence with a view to the attainment of the
'transcendental horizon of the inquiry into Being', the preparation of the ground on which the problem of Being may be
raised. An elucidation of the nature of transcendence was attempted there in order to win a horizon within which the concept
of Being could be philosophically grounded and ontologically
interpreted. *Was ist Metaphysik?* approaches the problem of
transcendence by way of an inquiry into Nothingness understood
as the other to what is. In *Vom Wesen des Grundes* also the
nature of ground is discussed, much more explicitly, in terms of

14. P. 39, Note (E.T., p. 97, note).

transcendence, for as Heidegger says there, "It is only through transcendence that the essent as essent can come to light and it constitutes, therefore, a pre-eminent domain for the discussion of all problems concerning the Being of essents." This essay does not merely discuss the nature of ground in the context of transcendence but also aims, through this discussion, at elucidating the nature of transcendence itself.[15]

Heidegger defines transcendence as the ground of the Ontological Difference; it is by virtue of his transcendence that man can distinguish between Being and beings and so relate himself to essents in the light of his comprehension of Being. In transcendence, Dasein goes out beyond all essents as such, including itself, reaching up to world, which is part of the structure of transcendence, of Dasein's being-in-the-world, itself. In order to clarify further the conception of transcendence, Heidegger enters into a discussion of the concept of world.[16] Further, transcendence is dealt with here as the basis of the freedom through which Dasein's project of the world is rendered possible. As manifesting itself in freedom, Dasein's transcendence is the source of the three-fold grounding. Man, as thrown, establishes himself in the midst of essents, at the same time setting up a world through the limited projection of his possibilities—both by virtue of his transcendence, which also renders possible the intentionality of his relationship with essents. Transcendence

15. As Heidegger points out (p. 37; E.T., p. 93), the first express mention of transcendence occurs in Plato's doctrine of the *agathon* as *epekeina tes ousias*, "beyond Being", in the *Republic* (vi, 509B). The *agathon* is conceived by Plato as the primordial ground of the possibility of truth, understanding and Being as connected together in the unified conception of the ultimate end, the *ou heneko* or the 'for the sake of'. In later tradition, however, the emphasis on the separate existence of Ideas in a celestial region, the *hyperouranios topos*, has tended to overshadow the transcendental conception of the *agathon*. For Heidegger's interpretation of the Idea of the Good, also see *Platons Lehre von der Wahrheit* and *Nietzsche II*, pp. 223–228.

16. *Vom Wesen des Grundes*, pp. 21–33 (E.T., pp. 47–80). This supplements the elaborate analysis of this concept in *Being and Time*.

conceived as the source of the three-fold grounding is thus what being-in-the-world means.

In *Kant und das Problem der Metaphysik*, Heidegger is naturally very much concerned with the problem of transcendence. The central problem of the *Critique of Pure Reason* is the problem of the possibility of ontological knowledge: How can finite human Dasein go beyond what is, transcending the essent which it has not only not itself created but on which it is dependent for its very existence as Dasein? This is the problem of the nature and basis of the transcendence involved in the prior comprehension of Being within Dasein. Essents can present themselves to Dasein only if it is already capable of this pre-ontological comprehension of Being and is 'turned towards' and open to what may confront it. This primary 'turning towards' and 'letting things confront' it, which alone can bring into being a horizon, an area of free-play (*Spielraum*) for essents to manifest themselves in, constitutes the transcendence of Dasein. Such transcendence is called by Heidegger Dasein's "holding itself suspended in Nothingness," for the 'object in general' of the *a priori* 'turning towards' is no essent but a Nothing (i.e., Being itself as the other to 'what is'). The main purpose of the Transcendental Deduction, in both its forms, is thus, according to Heidegger, to demonstrate the possibility of transcendence, a transcendence which is essentially finite in character, and to elucidate its complex structure as constituted by pure understanding and pure intuition, with the synthesis of the pure imagination playing the dominant mediating role. The pure imagination, i.e., the 'transcendental Schematism', in fact constitutes, according to Heidegger, the basis and indeed the very essence of the finitude of Dasein's transcendence. And since the Schematism, as Heidegger interprets Kant, necessarily operates with pure images of Time, it is temporality that ultimately renders transcendence possible, as *Being and Time* seeks to demonstrate. Kant's highest principle of all synthetic judgments, that "the conditions of the *possibility of experience* in general are likewise conditions of the *possibility of the objects of experience,*" expresses, according to Heidegger, the basic unity of the full structure of transcendence or ontological knowledge. This consists, not in the knowledge of essents, but in the prior projection of a horizon (the X or object in general; the Nothing as Heidegger calls it) within which essents may be encountered in the light of an *a priori* project of their Being. In place of the traditional "proud name of an ontology" which presumes to supply *a priori* synthetic knowledge of things in general, Kant substitutes a 'transcendental' philosophy which is content to investigate the nature of man's finite transcendence, i.e., of the subjectivity of the human subject in all his finitude. This is also Heidegger's aim in his first 'fundamental ontological' phase, though with the explicitly recognized objective of re-awakening the problem of Being and of conceptualizing the nature of Being as it enters into man's pre-ontological comprehension by virtue of his transcendence.

On the Nature of Truth (*Vom Wesen der Wahrheit*) marks a significant advance in Heidegger's thinking and points forward to the second phase of his thought after the reversal (*Kehre*). It will, therefore, be appropriate to deal with it here briefly. In *Being and Time,* the relevance of the notion of truth to the problem of Being was barely hinted at; *Vom Wesen des Grundes* made it more explicit how the problem of truth was closely involved in any discussion of transcendence, ground and Being. The present essay, dealing with truth not merely from the point of view of Dasein's overtness, his discovering character and the discoveredness of essents, but with truth in its own essence, leads, through the compulsion of its own inner logic, from the metaphysical view of truth as concerned with essents as a whole to a deeper conception of truth as an occurrence in Being itself, from the truth of essents in their totality to the truth of Being.[17]

17. A clear exposition of this essay is given, along with an English translation, by Werner Brock (*Existence and Being,* pp. 142–183; 319–351). Like some of Brock's other renderings, however, his translation of a 'key-term', as he calls it, like *das Seiende im Ganzen* by "the things that are within the *whole"* does not make sense.

As Heidegger explains (*Nietzsche I,* p. 277), the phrase "essents in their totality" is used by him to denote all that is not sheer nothing: Nature,

Heidegger begins with an examination of the conventional view of truth as agreement or correspondence. Whether truth is understood as the truth of things (*Sachwahrheit*), in which a thing really is what it is taken to be, or as propositional truth (*Satzwahrheit*) based on the former, in both senses it means agreement or correctness—*veritas est adaequatio rei et intellectus*. According to the medieval theological conception, the truth of (created) things consists in their conformity with an idea in the divine intellect and therefore the truth of the thoughts and propositions of the human intellect, i.e., their conformity with things, has its ultimate sanction in the divine intellect. In later philosophy the Creator is replaced by Reason but the basic conception remains the same, giving rise to the impression that the determination of the nature of truth has nothing to do with the problem of Being. This way of conceiving the nature of truth is taken for granted and the nature of untruth, failure to agree, is simply dismissed as falling outside truth in its essence, for untruth is the very opposite of truth. When, however, propositional truth is understood, in the Greek sense, as the correspondence (*homoiosis*) of a statement (*logos*) with a thing (*pragma*), the question arises as to the inner possibility of such correspondence. In order that a proposition should correspond with a thing or state of affairs, the two should be in some respect similar, as these two are not. The possibility of comparing them must therefore be sought in the way a proposition is 'about' the thing. The proposition is related to the thing by way of representation, it represents (*Vor-stellen*, lit. placing in front of, presenting) the thing *so as* it is. "The representative statement speaks of the thing

---

inanimate and living; history and its manifestations and those who fashion and carry it; God, the gods and half-gods. And it includes what is in becoming, what is originating and what is passing away; appearance, semblance, delusion and falsity; even nothingness as the limit of this whole of what is.

A. de Waelhens and W. Biemel have provided a very helpful commentary on this essay in their article, "Heideggers Schrift 'Vom Wesen der Wahrheit'" (*Symposion—Jahrbuch für Philosophie*, III, 1952).

represented, stating it to be *such as* it is. This 'such—as' (*so—
wie*) applies to the representation and what it represents." To
represent something means here, as Heidegger explains, letting
something stand over against us as an object (*Gegenstand,* lit.
what stands opposite).[18] "What thus stands opposite to us must,
as thus placed, come to us traversing an area of openness (or an
open 'towardness'—*ein offenes Entgegen*) and yet stand in itself
as a thing, manifesting itself as an invariable entity. This manifestation of the thing, by traversing an open 'towardness', is accomplished within an area of overtness, which is not itself
created by the representation but is only taken over and occupied
by it as a realm of relationships." All the activities and relationships of man occur in an area of overtness, standing within which
he relates himself to essents manifesting themselves in it. Making
a statement about an essent, by representing it and giving it the
status of an object is at the same time to submit to the require-
ment of representing it *so as* it is in the statement made. Such a
statement is true in the sense of being correct, for it has taken the
essent as manifest in the area of overtness as its measure, being
itself based on a relationship of overtness to the essent. A statement can be true in this sense only because the speaker, open to
what manifests itself as an essent, has freely accepted it as a
binding criterion. Hence, Heidegger concludes, the essence of
truth lies in freedom, for it is the freedom of man's openness on
which truth in the sense of correctness is grounded.

It may be objected that to ground truth, allegedly something
eternal, independent of man and above him, on freedom is to de-
base it, and turn it into a property of the human being, into
something subjective and arbitrary. This, Heidegger declares, is a
prejudice which can be dissipated, provided we are ready to alter
our manner of thinking about freedom and the nature of man.
Once we do this and try to grasp the essential connection between freedom and truth we shall be led to a realization of the

18. For a detailed discussion of *Entgegenstehenlassen* see *Kant und das
Problem der Metaphysik,* pp. 69–82 (E.T., pp. 74–89).

hidden ground of man's own nature, itself rooted in a more profoundly conceived truth. Freedom, which has been described
here as freedom for what is manifest in an area of overtness, is
what lets a particular essent be the essent that it is. "Freedom is
the letting-be of essents," it is to yield oneself to the essent, to
accede to what is manifest and to its overtness, conceived by the
Greeks as *aletheia* or unconcealedness. Letting-be, i.e., freedom,
is in itself exposing, ek-sistent; it is exposing oneself to the uncoveredness of essents. It is through such ek-sistent yielding and
letting oneself into the uncoveredness of the essent as such that
this uncoveredness, the overtness of what is manifest, i.e., the *Da*,
is itself maintained as such. Freedom, as identical with such ek-
sistenz and letting-be, is not a property possessed by man but, on
the contrary, itself 'possesses' man as his *Da-sein* and renders
man's historicity itself possible.[19] Truth is that unconcealedness
of the essent through which an overtness comes to prevail, an
overtness within which all man's attitudes and activities then
operate.

When man does not let the essent be what it is, illusion and
untruth arise. But since ek-sistent freedom as the essence of truth
is not a property of man, who is, as *Da-sein*, himself 'owned' by
it, untruth cannot arise merely due to the incapacity and negligence of man. Untruth must come from the essence of truth itself
and hence any inquiry into the nature of truth which aims at
reaching the core of the problem must show how untruth also has
its origin in the essence of truth. Through his attuned ek-sistenz
man is let into the uncoveredness of the essent in its totality—
which is not just the sum of the known essents—and all his
behaviour vibrates with this manifestness of the essent in its
totality. Yet this whole eludes his grasp and cannot be understood in terms of manifest essents, remaining something indeterminate and indeterminable, though itself determining everything.
What is in totality remains hidden and it is just the letting-

19. See also *Vorträge und Aufsätze*, pp. 32–33.

be which, in letting each particular essent be and so manifest itself, at the same time covers up, hides, essents as a whole. "Letting things be is in itself also a concealment." Da-sein's ek-sistent freedom thus simultaneously both reveals (particular essents) and conceals (essents in their totality). This concealment is a keeping back, a non-revelation and hence un-truth in the authentic sense. "The hiddenness of essents in their totality, the authentic un-truth, is older than all manifestness of this or that essent, more primordial than the letting-be itself," the mystery that attaches to the essent as such and pervades the *Da-sein* of man. In letting things be, ek-sistent *Da-sein* keeps this hiddenness itself hidden. The essence of truth thus comprises within itself its own dis-essence (*Unwesen*) in the form of un-truth—a paradox pointing to the unexplored dimension of the truth, not of beings but of Being.[20]

Holding fast to what is practicable and controllable, man bars from himself an awareness of this concealment of the hidden and this ground-phenomenon of Dasein is lost in oblivion. What is thus forgotten, however, is not abolished out of existence by being forgotten but rather acquires a mysterious presence of its own. Denied all access to it, man falls back on his own resources and abandons himself to the realm of the practicable, planning and scheming and taking himself as the measure of all things. Oblivious of the essent in its totality and its concealment, man clings to his own measures for his self-assurance. Dasein not only ek-sists but at the same in-sists, sticking obstinately to the multiplicity of essents and to what it can practically do with them. The ek-sistent turning away from the mystery of concealment and the in-sistent turning towards the practicable, one in

20. As Heidegger explains (*Nietzsche II*, p. 362), this statement is not a formal general proposition belonging to an essentialistic ontology in which 'essence' is represented metaphysically, appearing as 'Idea' in its historically decisive form. The statement, meaning the word 'essence' (*Wesen*) in a verbal sense (be-ing), is about Being itself in regard to the way It, Being, is. How Being is, consists in the 'staying out' (*Ausbleiben*) or withdrawal of its own self.

origin and essence, constitute that aberration (*Irre*, going astray, confusion) into which man does not just incidentally lapse but within which, in-sisting ek-sistently, he always already stands. Aberration, erring, is part of *Da-sein's* inner constitution. "In the uncovering of particular essents, the concealment of the hidden whole of essents has its way and, as the oblivion of this concealment, it takes the form of aberration or loss of bearings." All the ways in which man falls into error are due to this but so also is his ability, in his very faltering and fumbling, to shed error by experiencing his aberration as aberration. In his in-sistent ek-sistenz man is particularly subject, even in his oblivion, to the sway of the mystery of concealment and to the pressure of this aberration, being afflicted by the compulsion of both. Truth in its full nature, comprehending its own opposite or dis-essence within itself, holds man under the sway of this affliction, this need, which makes him turn his gaze again towards the mystery and ask what the essent in its totality is, what the Being of essents is.

In tracing the inner possibility of propositional truth back to the ek-sistent freedom of letting-be as its ground and suggesting that this ground itself has its essential origin in concealment and erring, Heidegger's aim was to show that the nature of truth is not an empty and abstract generality but is strangely complex in its structure. A reflection on this leads beyond the confines of our accustomed conceptions regarding the nature or essence of anything, beyond the problem of the essence of truth into the problem of the truth of essence (*Wesen*), i.e., that of Being itself. In fact, as Heidegger adds in a concluding note appended later, the problem of the essence of truth was prompted by the question about the truth of essence or Being.[21] But the attempt to answer the latter question cannot succeed, and could not be carried through, without abandoning the language and approach

21. *Vom Wesen der Wahrheit*, p. 26. The first two paragraphs of this note were added in the second ed. (1949) and are not included in Brock's translation.

of traditional metaphysics and effecting a reversal in the mode of thinking. "The question about the essence of truth has its answer in the statement: the essence of truth is the truth of essence" (*Wesen,* to be taken as a verb, i.e., in the sense of be-ing). But to say this, and to show how the nature of truth is inseparably bound up with the truth of Being needs a complete alteration of perspective and a change in the way Being reveals itself to us. "The answer to the question of the essence of truth is the utterance of a reversal within the history of Being," an utterance for which the metaphysical terminology of 'essence' (*Wesen*) is no longer adequate.[22] In the present lecture the crucial question

22. Arguing against the concept of essence as something invariable, Heidegger says (*Nietzsche I,* pp. 173–174) that the nature or essence (*Wesen*) of something is traditionally taken as the universal which is common to many particulars. But the fact that the essence of anything is in certain contexts—not always—what is common to many particulars is a consequence of the essence and not its intrinsic character. The identification of essence with the property of universality has blocked the way into the all-important problem of truth for centuries. Particular truths are different from each other and are many; but the essence is universal and, as valid for many, one. This universal, i.e., what is valid for the many in question is, however, then taken as the universal validity in an absolute sense. Universality now means, not what is valid for these particulars but what is in itself and in general and for ever valid, the immutable, the eternal, the timeless. This is how the principle of the immutability of essence, and so of the essence of truth, arises. This principle, Heidegger asserts, is logically correct but metaphysically false. From the point of view of the particular 'cases' of truth, the essence of truth consists of what is common to the many and as such one and identical. But from this it does not by any means follow that the essence in itself cannot change. For, admitting that the essence of truth changes, the changed essence can, despite the change, still be the essence which is valid for the many. What persists through the change is the immutable within the essence which, as such, is ever changing. This, Heidegger claims, is an affirmation of the essential character of the essence, of its inexhaustibility and of its real self-hood and identity, in sharp contrast with the vacuous identity of sameness, as which alone the unity of the essence can be conceived so long as it is taken merely as a universal. From the point of view of traditional logic, the conception of a changeable essence is bound to be judged as leading to sheer relativism. But this objection against the changeability of essence is valid only under a preconceived notion of unity and identity and of what is called the Absolute; it stands and falls with it and with the validity of the conception of essence as what is valid for many.

For an account of Heidegger's conception of Identity, see the essay in *Identität und Differenz.* Essence (*Wesen*) in the sense of *essentia* is,

regarding the meaning (*Sinn*), i.e., the overtness or the truth of Being and not merely of beings, is deliberately left undeveloped, Heidegger says, and "the thinking proceeds to all appearances on the lines of metaphysics. Yet in its decisive steps, which lead from truth as correctness to ek-sistent freedom and from this to truth as concealment and error, it accomplishes a change in the direction of the enquiry which involves the *overcoming* of metaphysics."

II THE REVERSAL OF THOUGHT AND THE *LETTER ON HUMANISM*

The principal aim of *Being and Time* was to re-awaken the problem of Being in the fundamental sense in which it had lapsed into obscurity in the Western metaphysical tradition since Plato and Aristotle. In the necessarily 'representational' thinking of this tradition the essent is indeed investigated in regard to its Being, but Being itself, its meaning and the way it unfolds and reveals itself, i.e., its truth, is taken for granted and presupposed. At the very start of this tradition Being was understood in the sense of objective presence and this conception of Being, oriented to what is objective and simply given (*vorhanden*) and to the temporal mode of the present, itself never became a problem. Hence the sense of Being, what Being itself is, has remained

---

according to him, the 'metaphysical' interpretation, based on its concern with the 'what' of essents, of the more fundamental *wesen*, be-ing, taken as a verb.

Cf. also *Vorträge und Aufsätze*, pp. 37–39, where *Wesen* is explained in terms of *waehren* (to last) and *gewähren* (grant, vouchsafe). *Wesen*, taken as a verb, is the same as 'to last, to continue', but it can never be established, Heidegger asserts, that enduring can only rest on the Platonic *idea* or on *essentia* in any of its forms, nor that the enduring is merely what goes on without cease. "Only what is vouchsafed endures. What has its origin in early times and so endures is the vouchsafing (i.e., that which grants)." Every dispensation (*Geschick*) of disclosure into which man is cast comes from this source of all vouchsafing. Elsewhere (*Unterwegs zur Sprache*, p. 201), Heidegger adds that *wesen* does not merely mean to last and endure but rather to come on and be present and, while enduring, to concern us, provide us with a way, to reach out to us and sustain us.

buried in oblivion as the Unthought (*das Ungedachte,* that which has never been subjected to thinking) of the Western metaphysical tradition. *Being and Time* re-opens the question, bringing it for the first time in the history of Western philosophy (as Heidegger himself claims) into the focus of explicit inquiry. The sense² of Being is to be disclosed through an elucidation of the comprehension of Being that is part of Dasein's ontological constitution. This is achieved in *Being and Time* by exhibiting, by means of the preparatory analytic of Dasein, the conditions of the possibility of such comprehension within Dasein itself. This is followed by an explication of the true character of temporality (as against the vulgar conception of time as an unceasing flow of 'nows', in terms of which Being was hitherto understood) and of the temporal structure of Dasein. A path has been laid out to lead the inquiry right up to Time as the 'transcendental horizon' within which and through which Dasein's understanding of its own Being functions—entirely from within Dasein itself and in terms of Dasein's own overtness and comprehension of Being. The question that still remains to be answered is whether a path can also be built that may lead from primary Time to the sense of Being itself.

The whole inquiry, conducted in the manner of traditional, transcendental metaphysics and conceived as universal phenomenological ontology, based on the hermeneutic of Dasein, was nevertheless inspired by a sense of the inadequacy of traditional metaphysics and was calculated to discredit it. The aim of replacing it by a Fundamental Ontology also inspired *Kant and the Problem of Metaphysics* and the essays discussed above in which fundamental metaphysical concepts such as those of Nothing, Ground, Transcendence and Truth were discussed so as to lead, beyond the limits of traditional metaphysics, into the fundamental ontological dimension, i.e., to the problem of Being itself. The first essay—*What is Metaphysics?*—showed that if we seek, from within Dasein itself, to pass from the overtness inherent in it to Being (which, as Heidegger says in *Being and Time,* is sheer transcendence) we have to stop short at Nothing, for that is what reveals itself as Dasein's transcendence. This was also the conclusion of the book on Kant. The essay on the nature of Ground also made it evident that the conception of freedom, based on Dasein's transcendence as the source of all grounding, leads to the discovery that this freedom itself is the 'abyss' of Dasein, with its source in the 'not' between beings and Being, the Ontological Difference. The essay on the essence of Truth, lastly, led to the brink of the problem of Being, to the problem of the truth of Being as the nodal problem on which everything hinges and where the direction of the inquiry must turn round so that Being is no longer approached by way of Dasein but proceeds from the truth of Being to the nature of man. This is the reversal to which Heidegger's thought was led by the necessity inherent in its own movement.[23] What prevented its being carried into effect was the language of traditional metaphysics; it was metaphysics itself. *Being and Time,* seeking to go beyond it, was itself seen to be in the grip of the subjectivity characteristic of metaphysical thought

23. The Reversal is meant to be understood in a historical sense, i.e., not as a personal event (a conversion) in Heidegger's life, nor even as a revolution in 'his' philosophy, but as a happening in the history of Western thought itself. From this point of view, Heidegger's philosophy represents that historic movement, augured by Hölderlin and anticipated by Nietzsche, in which the Western philosophical tradition, having brought to the surface all its inherent possibilities, suffers a 'peripety', annuls itself and passes over into another beginning. The present century, it may be pointed out (as Heidegger has), is marked by a similar reversal in the history of science, such that its inherent will to universal and total objectivization of what is has culminated in utter 'unobjectifiability'—man's onslaught on the essent has brought science to the point of the essent's counter-attack against man, to a point where what is has become utterly incapable of being represented and conceived—where it can only be calculated. The developments which have occurred in contemporary Anglo-Saxon philosophy as the present writer interprets them, show a similar trend. Ludwig Wittgenstein, the other 'extreme' (as Erich Heller calls him) of contemporary thought, is the 'locus' of the dissolution and transformation of traditional metaphysics into something deeper and more basic. Like *Being and Time,* the *Tractatus* may be said to mark the consummation and close of a whole epoch and the *Philosophische Untersuchungen,* like the works of Heidegger in the second phase, the inauguration of a new one. Common to both Heidegger and Wittgenstein is their recognition of language as the fundamental reality for thought.

and of its concern with the truth of essents. It was therefore powerless to lead to the truth of Being. It was not possible to think adequately about Being, on the basis of the primary temporality as it had emerged at the end of the inquiry into Being and Time, by means of the methodology and the conceptual framework of *Being and Time* as initially planned. The chapter which was to deal with "Time and Being" and in which Being was to be thought about in terms of primary temporality, along with numerous problems which were postponed earlier for treatment in this chapter, was dropped.[24]

The whole project had to be abandoned as incapable of being carried through, as a path that could indeed bring us to the verge of the problem and give a glimpse of its real nature but which, by its very nature, was incapable of leading *into* the heart of the main objective, that is, the sense or truth of Being itself. Before the inquiry could proceed further on its goal it was necessary to have a closer look at the credentials of metaphysics, to go down into its roots and thus to shed the remaining vestiges of its hold on the inquiry. As Heidegger remarks in the 'Introduction' added in 1949 to *What is Metaphysics?*, "A thinking that seeks to reflect on the truth of Being, but which is itself rooted in the age-long habit of representing the essent as such, itself gets entangled in such representation. Under these circumstances, both by way of a preliminary reflection as well as in order to lead on to the transition from representational thinking to the thinking that recalls, nothing becomes more important than raising the ques-

24. The following are some of the topics to which Heidegger promises, at various places in *Sein und Zeit,* to return in the omitted chapter: a consideration of the forgetting of world in European thought (p. 100); the new conception of *logos* (p. 160); the development of the idea of Phenomenology (p. 357), of Ontology (p. 230) and of Science (p. 357); the elucidation of the connexion between Being and Truth (p. 357); the discussion of language (p. 349); the 'as' in thinking of something as something and the nature of the copula (p. 360); the concrete working out of the structure of world (p. 316) and of everydayness (p. 372); the relation between space and time (p. 368) and the being of time (p. 406). The entire existential analysis is to be repeated in the framework of a thorough consideration of the concept of Being (pp. 333 and 436).

tion: what is metaphysics?" When one penetrates, as Heidegger does in this 'Introduction' into the ground of metaphysics, the foundation it stands upon, it becomes evident that metaphysical thinking is only concerned with the truth of the essent as essent. In its representation of what is, it has the latter focally in its sight. But this sight itself is dependent on the light of Being, which as such remains beyond the range of metaphysical thinking. Every interpretation of the essent occurs on the basis of an illumination of Being, its unconcealedness. "But whether and how it manifests itself in and as metaphysics, remains obscure. Being in its revelatory essence, i.e., in its truth, remains unconsidered. . . . The truth of Being may thus be called the ground (of metaphysics)." A thinking, therefore, that sets out in quest of the ground of metaphysics, the truth of Being itself, instead of merely representing the essent as essent, has, Heidegger says, in a way given up metaphysics, which can no longer retain the first place in a thinking concerned with the truth of Being. From the point of view of metaphysics, such thinking goes back into the ground of metaphysics. But, as Heidegger here only suggests, what still appears from this point of view as ground is presumably something different, as yet unformulated, when considered in itself.

Although operating with a prior conception of Being, metaphysics does not discuss Being itself, "for it does not reflect on Being in its truth, nor on truth as unconcealedness, nor the latter in its essence." This essence of truth is beyond the reach of the representational thinking of metaphysics and has remained concealed from it during its long history from Anaximander to Nietzsche. Throughout this history, Heidegger points out, confusion has prevailed in its statements about Being, for though metaphysics speaks of Being, what it really means is sometimes the essent as essent and sometimes essents in their totality. What is at stake in this quest for the truth of Being is the "nearness and remoteness" of that from which philosophy itself, as the representation of the essent as such, derives. This is the occurrence, brought about by Being itself, of the original relationship of Being with the nature of man, a consummation to which metaphysics has itself become the barrier. Metaphysical thinking, which is projected, set up, by an essent as such, i.e., man in his will to grasp Being in the network of his concepts, is basically representational in nature and must be supplemented, Heidegger asserts, by a kind of thinking "which is brought to pass by Being itself and, therefore, subserves Being."

The realization of this incapacity of metaphysical thought to go back into its own ground, the truth of Being, and to think about the Unthought of this truth, is what prevented the promised third Division of *Being and Time* from appearing. The reversal promised there was rendered impracticable by this reversal in Heidegger's own way of thinking. But this 'turn' in thinking was itself, in turn, brought about by Heidegger's ceaseless effort to think about *that* reversal, the reversal from 'Being and Time' to 'Time and Being'. A "change in thinking", a total shift of perspective, prevented the carrying through of the plan of *Being and Time* on its own terms and according to its methods. The nature of this change, which was only hinted at in some essays on the poetry of Hölderlin, was indicated explicitly, after a long period of silence following the publication of *Being and Time* and the early essays, in the *Letter on Humanism* (1947), though it was not until the publication of the two-volume *Nietzsche* (1961) that a full view of the way of thought travelled by Heidegger during the period of transition (1930–1946) became available. This change, Heidegger explains in the *Letter,* is "not an alteration in the standpoint of *Being and Time* but is a change through which the thinking attempted there at last emerges into its location in the dimension out of which the experience (or awareness) behind *Being and Time,* the experience of the oblivion of Being, developed." This change is thus not a break in the voyage of Heidegger's thought nor an abandonment of one goal for another. Even in its radical shift of perspective and alteration in style and approach in the second phase, Heidegger's thought remains loyal to its one and only objective, following it as "a star fixed in the heavens."[25]

What is the nature and scope of this change? It is a change, first, in the basic mood, a change of attitude towards the whole quest. In his early work on Duns Scotus, Heidegger expresses his determination to effect a "break-through into the true Reality and the real Truth".[26] This Promethean, aggressive attitude, in

25. *Aus der Erfahrung des Denkens,* p. 7. The 'change in thinking' from the *Being and Time* phase to the later, rather abruptly and briefly announced in the *Letter on Humanism* after a long period of silence, caused widespread bewilderment among scholars and has given rise to conflicting interpretations of the character of this change. It has been criticized by some as a departure from the sober rationality and scientific attitude of the early phase, as an abandonment of the path of scholarly inquiry and a lapse into mysticism and as a break-down and failure of thought as initially planned in *Being and Time.* Others insist that there is at least a break in the movement of thought such that there is no bridge leading from the first to the second phase. Still others, in closer sympathy with the 'way' of Heidegger's thought, see the 'reversal' as implicit in *Being and Time* itself. Karl Löwith, in his widely read and influential *Heidegger—Denker in dürftiger Zeit* (1st ed. 1953), is vehemently critical. In his remarkable discussion of the significance of *Was ist Metaphysik?* (in Über den philosophiegeschichtlichen Ort Martin Heideggers," op. cit.), Walter Schulz has shown how the way of Heidegger's thought inherently leads through the 'reversal', of which the first step is the passage from beings to Nothing and the second, more difficult than the first, from Nothing to Being. Heidegger was able to take this step, Schulz remarks, because he has remained loyal to his own starting-point in *Being and Time.* Pöggeler (in "Sein als Ereignis" and in his book, *Der Denkweg Martin Heideggers*) also convincingly brings out the unity of Heidegger's way. Fridolin Wiplinger, in his elaborate exposition of Heidegger's philosophy from the perspective of the problem of truth (*Wahrheit und Geschichtlichkeit,* 1961), even characterizes Heidegger's thought as itself a "thinking of the Reversal".

Replying to Richardson's question regarding the occurrence of the 'reversal' in his thinking of Being (Richardson, *Heidegger,* pp. xvii–xxiii), Heidegger quotes from his lecture course of 1937–38, showing how his thinking was occupied with the 'reversal' (i.e., with the question of 'Time and Being' as already contemplated in *Being and Time*) even a decade before the appearance of the *Letter on Humanism.* As he points out here, the Reversal is in play within the matter thought about in *Being and Time* itself, demanded by it, and not something invented by himself or merely an affair concerning his thinking. He remarks further that the 'happening' of the Reversal 'is' Being (*Sein*) as such and it can be thought only *from* the Reversal. He refers in this connexion to a lecture delivered in 1962, entitled, "Zeit und Sein" ("Time and Being"), first published in *L'endurance de la pensée* (Paris, 1968).

26. Quoted by Pöggeler in "Sein als Ereignis," op. cit., p. 602.

which man thinks of himself as destined to take truth and reality
by storm, as it were, pervades all Heidegger's early writings.[27]
This attitude of man's self-assertion (*Selbstbehauptung*), however, is not to be understood as peculiar and personal to Heidegger in the early phase; it is rather an attitude inseparably
bound up with the whole of the Western metaphysical quest, at
least since the rise of modern subjectivism with the philosophy of
Descartes and not absent among the Greeks. In its modern form
it is crystallized in the conception of the human spirit (*Geist*) as
intellectual will, of which a classical expression may be found in
Hegel's Inaugural Lecture at Berlin University: "The courage of
truth, the faith in the power of the spirit, is the primary condition
of philosophy. Man, since he is spirit, can and should respect
himself as worthy of the highest; he cannot think too highly of
the greatness and power of his spirit and with that faith there can
be nothing so unyielding and hard as not to open itself to him.
The nature of the Universe, hidden and closed to start with, has
no power to withstand the boldness of man's search for knowledge; it must open itself before him and disclose to his eyes its
riches and its depths, offering them for his gratification."[28] In
lectures delivered in 1935 at the University of Freiburg,[29] Heidegger, too, describes spirit or *Geist* as "a fundamental knowing
resolve toward the essence of Being" and as "the mobilization of
the powers of the essent as such and as a whole" and speaks of
the debilitation or emasculation of the spirit characteristic of the

27. And yet Heidegger has already, even in the *Being and Time* phase,
gone equally beyond Greek Prometheanism and Hegelian Absolutism, as
shown by the key role played by the concept of 'letting' (*Lassen*) in the
writings even of this period. Heidegger recognized in an *Introduction to
Metaphysics* that "the relationship to Being is one of letting-be", that all
willing is grounded in letting-be (p. 17). The whole of the essay, "On the
Nature of Truth" is a plea for the notion of 'letting'.

28. Commenting on this passage (*Der Satz vom Grund*, p. 145), Heidegger says that it would be wrong and ungenerous to take these words as a
piece of presumptuousness on the part of the person of the thinker in face of
the Absolute; it is, on the contrary, expressive of a readiness to respond to
the demand placed upon thought by Being manifesting itself in the form of
the absolute concept.

29. *An Introduction to Metaphysics*, p. 41.

modern age, quoting with approval the definition of spirit given
by him in his address, in 1933, on "The Self-assertion of the
German University". In "The Origin of the Work of Art" (1935),
he says, still within the grip of the language of metaphysics:
"Knowing, which is a willing and willing, which is a knowing, is
the ecstatic entry of the existing man (i.e., Dasein) into the
unhiddenness of Being."[30] The way Dasein understands itself
and its relationship to Being before the 'reversal' is, as Walter
Schulz puts it,[31] the self-assertion of Dasein in its impotence and
finitude, a kind of 'heroic nihilism', incarnated in the figure of
Prometheus, to whom Heidegger refers as the first of the philosophers in his address of 1933.

Around 1935, this mood (*Stimmung*) changes. There is an
abdication of this will, of this self-assertion in the face of Being.
The study of Nietzsche, with whom Heidegger intensively occupied himself, by way of lectures delivered during 1936–40, seems
to have brought home to him the devastating, shattering realization that Nietzsche's philosophy of the Will-to-power was only
the nihilistic culmination of something inherent in the very
nature of the metaphysical tradition of the West as it had developed from Plato onwards. The realization that in his own philosophy, deliberately seeking to 'overcome' metaphysics, this will,
this nihilistic canker, was still a powerful driving force, standing
between him and Being—the goal of his entire quest—seems to
have led to the collapse of this will and to a complete surrender

30. *Holzwege*, p. 35. In fairness to Heidegger it must be added that even
before writing this essay—in fact, since the inception of *Being and Time*
itself—he was 'on the way' to a deeper conception of willing and had
realized that man's relationship to Being can only be one of 'letting'. As
against the interpretation, generally accepted, of the reversal offered here,
Heidegger would, therefore, be quite justified from the point of view of his
basic *intentions* to insist, as he does insist, on the continuity of his thought.
Cf. the "Zusatz" to the Reclam edition (1960) of *Der Ursprung des
Kunstwerkes,* where Heidegger discusses the apparent contradiction in this
essay between 'positing' (willing) and 'letting'. See also *Nietzsche* and
Gelassenheit for Heidegger's unceasing preoccuption with the problem of
Will and its interpretation in terms of Being.
31. *Op. cit.*, p. 89.

to the 'Voice of Being.' It is of this supreme renunciation of the
metaphysical will by thought that he speaks in the *Feldweg:*
"Renunciation does not take. Renunciation gives. It gives the
inexhaustible power of the simple." This is the sacrifice, the offering of thankfulness and homage for the grace of Being, of which
Heidegger speaks in the 'Postscript' to *What is Metaphysics?* This
is not a failure of the courage to think but an acknowledgement
that it flows, not from the assertive will of man but through a
demand of Being itself.[32] The dominant mood now is not anxiety
in the face of Nothingness but one of tranquil detachment.[33]

In the second place, there is a change in the conception of the
task of philosophical thinking, its nature and its purpose. Not
only is 'metaphysics', as consituting the core of such thinking,
abandoned as a game that has finally been played out, but even
the Fundamental Ontology of *Being and Time* is dropped as a
possible discipline.[34] The term 'philosophy' itself becomes sus-
pect; as Heidegger says,[35] "the thinking of the future is no longer

32. *Aus der Erfahrung des Denkens,* p. 9.
33. Cf. *Gelassenheit,* 1960.
34. Heidegger asserts (*Brief über den 'Humanismus',* p. 109) that already in *Being and Time,* he was attempting to "think ahead" into truth of
Being and so was in quest of a fundament for ontology. "That thinking,
because of its concern with the other question (i.e., the truth of Being), had
from the very first emerged clear of the 'Ontology' of metaphysics (including
that of Kant). 'Ontology', however, whether transcendental or pre-critical, is
open to criticism, not because it thinks about the Being of essents and, in
addition, forces Being into a concept, but because it does not think the truth
of Being and therefore fails to recognize that there is a kind of thinking that
is more stringent than conceptual thinking. Seeking to think forward into the
truth of Being, thinking (i.e., in *Being and Time*), because of the difficulty
of a first coming through, speaks very little of that wholly different dimension. The language is not yet true to itself, in so far as it has not yet
succeeded in giving up the absurd intention of being 'science' and 'research',
while holding on to the valuable help of phenomenological seeing. In order,
however, to make this venture of thought within the prevailing philosophy
distinguishable and at the same time intelligible, it was possible to speak
only in the horizon of the prevailing (mode of thought) and by using the
terminology current in it. Since then, I have realized that just these terms
were bound to lead, directly and unavoidably, to confusion." Cf. also *Einführung in die Metaphysik,* p. 31 (E.T., p. 34).
35. *Brief über den 'Humanismus',* p. 119.

philosophy because it aims at thinking on a level deeper than metaphysics, which term also means the same." This thinking, Heidegger continues, without intending to discard the name of "love of wisdom" and become, as Hegel desired, wisdom itself in the shape of absolute knowledge, is on its way to "a descent into the poverty of its preliminary, provisional nature." Thinking is no longer conceived as an activity centred in man and reaching out towards Being. "Thinking unfolds and realizes the relationship of Being with the nature of man. It does not itself produce this relationship. . . . All efficacy rests in Being, flowing down from there towards the essent. Thinking, in turn, lets itself be claimed by Being, in order to give utterance to the truth of Being."[36] To realize the essential nature of thinking and thus make it in practice what it truly is, it is essential that we liberate ourselves from the technical interpretation of thought, a way of understanding the nature of thought going back to Plato and Aristotle, for whom thinking was a *techne,* the activity of deliberation in the service of doing (*praxis*) and making something (*poiesis*), also characterized as *theoria.* In this technical interpretation of thinking, sanctioned by 'logic', which also emerged at this time, Being as the true element within which thought moves and has its sustenance is sacrificed. Thinking expires, like fish out of water, when it abandons its element, for it is this element which enables thinking to be what it is. "To put it simply, thinking is thinking of Being, where the 'of' has a double meaning. Thinking is of Being in so far as, being brought to pass by Being, it belongs to Being. At the same time it is thinking of Being in so far as, belonging to Being, it listens to Being."[37] It is Being which constitutes that "silent power of the possible" which enables, renders possible, thinking, bestowing upon it its own proper essence.

A thinking which concerns itself with the truth of Being and is therefore no longer representational, cannot, like metaphysics, occupy itself with the construction of concepts. But the aban-

36. *Ibid.,* p. 53.
37. *Ibid.,* p. 57.

donment of conceptual thought, i.e., of philosophy in the traditional sense is not an abdication of thinking as such. Liberated
from the fixity of concepts and the straight-jacket of logic, thinking for the first time comes into possession of its own essential
nature as "a thinking that recalls" (*Andenken*), by immersing
itself in the historical revelation of Being as it speaks through the
language of the ancient philosophers and of poets, ancient and
modern, in whom it has found utterance. Such thinking is, therefore, inherently historical in character. As Heidegger says[38], the
mystery of reminiscent thinking (*An-denken*) lies in the fact that
in such thinking, as it peers down into what has been, this 'has
been' itself comes back to us from the opposite direction, comes
towards us as a task set for us by the future; "suddenly, thinking,
as remembrance of the past, is compelled to think of what has
been as something that has yet to unfold itself." This is the task
of thinking and expressing in words that which still lies as the
Unthought (*das Ungedachte*) in what has been already thought
in the past.

The language and the terminology which has been developed
by metaphysical thinking through the ages is utterly powerless to
enable us to reflect on its own foundation, on the truth of Being
itself, and give it utterance in words. But, as Heidegger says,
"The one and only thing that is of supreme concern is that the
truth of Being should find utterance and that thinking should
find the proper language for that". *Being and Time* was on the
way to this but, as a pioneering attempt, it was still held fast in
the tradition and language of metaphysics. The inadequacy of
this language and the need to find a more suitable way of expressing the truth of Being, i.e., what Being means, seems to have led
Heidegger to immerse himself in the poetry of Hölderlin and to
occupy himself, afresh and more intensively, with the nature of
language.[39] Language is regarded now not so much as a mani-

38. *Erläuterungen zu Hölderlins Dichtung*, p. 94.
39. As Heidegger, however, remarks in his "Preface" to Richardson,
Heidegger (p. xxiii), the multi-fold thinking of Being requires not a new
language but a transformed relationship to the nature of the old.

festation of the overtness of Dasein as rather the locus and vehicle of the self-revelation of Being itself. "Language is the house of Being," a house in which man, too, has his dwelling. It is here that Being is to be sought for and found through the patient creative effort of raising in words a temple in which Being may shine forth in its truth. Language is 'brought to pass' by Being, a house put together by Being, ek-sisting within which man is aware of Being and of his relationship with it. In its concern for the words in which Being itself may 'come to word' and enshrine itself, thinking thus stands in the neighbourhood of poetizing or composing (*Dichten*). In his essay on "Hölderlin and the Nature of Poetry," Heidegger says,[40] "The poet names the gods and he names all things in respect of what they are. This naming does not merely consist in bestowing a name on something that is already known; the poet, in uttering the essential word, rather nominates the essent to be, for the first time, what it is through this naming. Thus it becomes known *as* an essent. Poetry is the verbal instituting (*Stiftung*, founding, setting up) of Being." The nature of language and, as rooted in that, the relationship between thinking and composing (*Dichten*) is a topic to which Heidegger returns again and again in his later writings.

In the course of the analytic of Dasein in *Being and Time*, Heidegger says, time and again, that this analysis is provisional and incomplete and will have to be carried out all over again, in respect of each of the main features of Dasein emerging from the analysis, in the light of a clarified idea of Being. This is what he does in his treatment of man after the reversal. The direction of the inquiry is now no longer from man to Being but from Being to man, who is now interpreted in terms, or in the light of, Being.[41] In the 'Introduction' to *What is Metaphysics?*, Heidegger

40. *Erläuterungen zu Hölderlins Dichtung*, p. 38 (E.T., pp. 304 f.).

41. In the phrase "from man to Being" (as referring to the procedure in *Being and Time*), 'man' should be understood in the sense of the being of man, i.e., as Dasein. The phrase should not be taken to imply that in that work Heidegger aims at deriving the concept of Being from some type of anthropology or philosophy of man developed in isolation from the question

explains why man had to be taken as the point of departure in *Being and Time*, despite the fact that even that work had as its ultimate aim "to lead our thinking on the way on which it may find the relationship between the truth of Being and the nature of man, to open up a path for our thinking on which it may expressly ponder upon Being itself in its truth." No express reference to the oblivion of Being could be made in *Being and Time* because it had still to be demonstrated. "A realization of the true nature of such oblivion led to the crucial conjecture that the conception of the unconcealedness (i.e., truth) of Being requires that the relationship of Being to the essence of man be conceived wholly as a feature of Being itself, rather than of man. But this conjecture, though already entertained, could not be raised explicitly as a problem in *Being and Time* until the determination of man's essence was first extricated from the traditional subjectivistic and rationalistic approaches."[42] From the changed perspective in thinking after the reversal, man is regarded "no longer as the master of what is. Man is the shepherd of Being."[43]

Replying to Jean Beaufret's suggestion of a revival of humanism and to his interpretation of *Being and Time*, with its

---

of Being. As Heidegger remarks in *Was heisst Denken?* (pp. 73–74; E.T., pp. 79 f.), "Every philosophical, i.e., thinking, doctrine of the nature of man is *in itself already* a doctrine of the Being of the things that are. Every doctrine of Being is *in itself already* a doctrine of the nature of man. But neither of the two can be arrived at by a mere reversal of the other, through a dialectical manoeuvre. . . . *No* way of thinking, including that of metaphysical thinking, starts from the nature of man, passing over thence to Being or, the other way round, starting from Being, returns thence to the nature of man. Every way of thinking moves rather within the whole nexus, within the totality of the relationship between Being and the human essence, otherwise it is no thinking." The difference between the approach in *Being and Time* and that after the *Kehre* is, concisely expressed, that between approaching the question of Being from the point of view of the Being of a being (in this case, human being) and interpreting the latter in terms of a new conception of Being itself. However deep it may go, a consideration of the Being of the essent still moves within 'metaphysics'; from there to Being itself there is no smooth passage but only a leap of thought.

42. *Was ist Metaphysik?*, p. 12.
43. *Brief über den 'Humanismus'*, p. 90.

analysis of human nature, as the document of a humanistic, man-centred philosophy, Heidegger discusses the metaphysical roots of humanism as it has developed since Roman times. All humanism, including the humanistic interpretation of man as a rational animal or as person, he says, is as such based on a pre-existent and presupposed metaphysical doctrine about the totality of what is. "Every determination of the nature of man which takes for granted a view of the essent, without inquiring into the truth of Being, is consciously or unconsciously, metaphysical. . . . Humanism, in determining the humanity of man, not only fails to inquire into the relation of Being to man but is even a hindrance in the way of such inquiry."[44] Metaphysics, oblivious of man in his relationship to Being, fails to take notice of the simple fact that man comes into possession of his true nature only in so far as he is responsive to the claim of Being. Man stands in the clearing or light of Being and in this consists his ek-sistenz; the 'there' (*Da*) of Da-sein is this clearing of Being, where he stands in the proximity or nearness (*Nähe*) of Being. This is a nearness in which man is not externally related *to* something other, but is itself the dimension of Being, from which all 'nearness' in the ordinary sense flows. Man, as man, has his dwelling in the neighbourhood of Being.[45] Thrown into existence by Being itself, man ek-sists so as to guard the truth of Being, cherish and make it manifest by giving it utterance in words. It is in this sense that man is the shepherd of Being. Man's 'project' of Being is not generated by his fancy or self-will but is brought about by Being itself. And the historicity that characterizes Dasein is itself the manifestation of a temporality that inheres in Being primarily,

44. *Ibid.*, p. 64.
45. *Ibid.*, p. 84. As Heidegger remarks, this 'nearness' is the clearing of the 'there' in which man dwells as ek-sisting. The nearness of Being, the 'there' of Dasein, is called 'Home' in his address on Hölderlin's elegy, "Homecoming". The homelessness of modern man, Heidegger says, was realized by Nietzsche but he could not find any other way out of it, stuck up as he was within metaphysics, than a mere inversion of metaphysics. Hölderlin's was a profounder insight into the real character of man's homecoming into his own essence, the nearness to Being.

entering into Dasein because of its intimate involvement in the history of Being itself (*Seinsgeschichte*). Thus, what principally concerns Heidegger, as it emerges more clearly in the second phase of his thought, is not so much man, as Sartre and his followers thought, as the 'nature' or essence of man. This is not itself something 'human' but is wholly determined by Being. Hence any description of man in his essence can only be in terms of the way Being has entered into relationship with man, i.e., in terms of man's *Da-sein*.[46]

Heidegger admits that in the *Being and Time* period, when new ground was to be broken and a start made towards a dimension of thought counter to that of metaphysics, his language and thought had to retain a foothold on metaphysics. Being, approached through Dasein, had to be described in terms hallowed by the metaphysical tradition, e.g., transcendence and ground. In the phase after the '*Kehre*', Heidegger is extremely careful of the language he employs in speaking of Being and tries to eliminate every trace of metaphysically tinged expressions. In order to guard against the misunderstanding of his own use of the term "Being" (*Sein*) in the sense sanctioned by tradition, he sometimes spells it as "*Seyn*" in the 19th century manner, sometimes writing it with a cross over it (*Sein* crossed out) and even going so far as to suggest the abandonment of the term altogether.

---

46. Aligning himself with the school of Heidegger interpretation represented by G. Krüger and K. Löwith, Laszlo Versényi has severely criticised Heidegger for his alleged "nonhumanism" in his well-written study, *Heidegger, Being and Truth* (Yale, 1965). Entrenched securely behind a neoclassical position, he showers what he thinks are deadly barbs against Heidegger. Versényi knows, and presents briefly, the letter of Heidegger's texts very well indeed. Nevertheless, he is so completely out of sympathy with the spirit and the central direction of this philosopher's *questioning* that his criticisms appear to be aimed against a Heidegger of his own imagining. This is another confirmation of the "almost insurmountable difficulty in making oneself understood" about which Heidegger speaks in his letter to Richardson (*Heidegger*, p. viii). Surely, something has gone seriously wrong in the way Versényi introduces (p. 135, with frequent repetitions on later pages) the reference to "*das ganz Andere*" in *Unterwegs zur Sprache*, p. 128, and converts it into the "that which is Wholly Other" of "a negative theology and mysticism"!

With this there goes a radical change of style and of the vocabulary. The trappings of erudition, the weight of learning and the gestures of scholarship fall away, without prejudice to an unceasing concern with what has been thought in the past. As against the thickness and intensity of the earlier writing, there appears an artful simplicity and freshness of style in the later works, but without loss of expressive power. The thinking becomes evocative and poetical but is none the less pointed and steered by the inner logic of its movement. Correspondingly, the vocabulary also alters and the formidable apparatus of technical terminology is dropped in favour of the natural resources of a language rich with the associations of its own literary heritage. Instead of coining technical terms with well-defined 'logical powers' and thereby achieving conceptual articulation, Heidegger seeks now to lay bare, and to utilize for thought, the richness of meaning hidden in common words, words which have been worn out and denuded of their force by ordinary usage. While the 'definition' of a term empties it of all but the bare minimum of meaning, the 'topological' interpretation (*Eröterung*) of basic words, with which Heidegger now engages himself, enables us to have a glimpse of the entire expanse of meaning-fulness out of which the single word speaks to us. By disclosing to our view the 'region' in which the word has its genesis, he enables us to draw from it meanings which have remained obscure and so far un-uttered by it. This is the simple explanation of the 'verbal jugglery', the 'play with words' and the 'forced etymologizing' of which Heidegger is often accused.[47]

The Western metaphysical tradition culminates in the subjectivism of modern philosophy, bearing, in its end-phase, Nihilistic

47. In order to bring out the specific character of "topological thinking", Pöggeler distinguishes three different ways of understanding a matter: *Erklären, Erläutern* and *Erörtern*. The last, Pöggeler says, constitutes the Logos of Heidegger's thinking and is an approach he traces back to the ancient discipline of Topics, the *ars inveniendi*. cf. his review of books by Viehweg and by Hennis—note 3, above; also his review of books by Viehweg and by Hennis in *Philosophischer Literatranzeiger*, XVIII, 4 (1965).

fruits in the thinking of Nietzsche. *Being and Time* is an attempt to shake off the hold of this tradition, for it is based on an uncritically assumed conception of Being. But as a first attempt it succeeds only partially in its manner of posing the question, in its approach to it and in its language. Attempting to step out of the sphere of subjectivity, it still proceeds from man (and the understanding of Being immanent in him) to Being, with undiminished trust, characteristic of metaphysics, in a methodology that can lead securely to port. But once it was realized that the impulse behind the thinking in *Being and Time* was one that inevitably led toward an overcoming of metaphysics by going back into its foundation, the truth of Being itself, it became equally obvious that this could not be achieved through the language and the methodological devices at the disposal of metaphysics. And where the language of tradition could not be avoided, new meanings had to be given to, though not arbitrarily imposed upon, some of the basic philosophical terms in that language.

By the time the *Letter on Humanism* was written, Heidegger had emerged clear of the vestiges of the metaphysical approach, with full consciousness of the necessity behind the change in the manner of posing the question and conducting the inquiry. Without having traversed the path taken by *Being and Time* and the early essays, the explicit realization of the need for a new approach and a new way of speaking would never have come. The impulse and the basic philosophical experience behind his thought, in the first as in the second phase, is the same.[48] The 'way' taken by Heidegger's thinking, probing forward and moving occasionally into blind 'forest-trails', is continuous and pushes ahead towards its one and only goal, the utterance of the truth of

48. Qualifying the clear-cut distinction Richardson makes between Heidegger I and Heidegger II (i.e., between the earlier and the later phases of his thought), Heidegger remarks ("Preface" to Richardson's *Heidegger,* p. XXIII) that this distinction is justified only if it is steadily borne in mind that only by way of what is thought in I is it possible to have access to what is to be thought in II, but that I becomes possible only if it is contained in II.

Being. At different stations or halting places on this way, he has sought to formulate the truth of Being in what appeared to him the most adequate fashion, which in retrospect he has sometimes thought to be clumsy. As he has said recently,[49] "I have abandoned an earlier standpoint, not so that I might adopt a different one in its place, but because even that earlier standpoint was a halting-place in a thinking that is on its way. The way is what is enduring in thought." That is why Heidegger, even after having moved beyond *Being and Time* in the sense indicated above, can say in the *Letter on Humanism* that the thinking which attempted to take a few steps forward in that work has not even today gone beyond *Being and Time*. That is why he comes back, again and again, to this work in his later writings, re-interpreting its basic concepts in terms of his advance along each milestone in the journey of his thought, insistently reminding the reader of the continuity of his thought and the singleness of his purpose. His writings after the reversal are both a criticism and a commentary on *Being and Time*. "Perhaps," Heidegger remarks,[50] "the basic short-coming of the book *Being and Time* is that in it I have ventured out too far too soon." The treatment of most of the topics dealt with there is not only explicitly provisional but opens out vistas which are explored and investigated more adequately only in Heidegger's subsequent writings.

49. *Unterwegs zur Sprache*, p. 98.
50. *Ibid.*, p. 93.

chapter three

HEIDEGGER AND THE WESTERN METAPHYSICAL TRADITION

I HEIDEGGER'S APPROACH TO PAST THOUGHT

All philosophical thinking, according to Heidegger, moves within the intellectual horizon opened up by a tradition. It may seek to enlarge this horizon and may attempt a critical reconstruction of that tradition by bringing into view something that has been ignored and bypassed by it. But no thinker, however original he may be, can lift himself out of the tradition that sustains him and from which the driving power and the manner of his questioning is derived. Man's knowledge of what is and his understanding of what it means to 'be' never sheds its linkage with the 'here' and the 'now', never reaches up into the *topos hyperouranios*, the heavenly region of the pure, the timeless and the Absolute. In the sense in which Heidegger raises the question of Being, the question could be raised only within the framework of the Western philosophical tradition as founded by the early Greek thinkers and only at a point in the history of that tradition where it terminates in the philosophy of Nietzsche. The question of Being is thus essentially and intrinsically a historical one, requiring both a critical, regressive analysis or "destruction" of the history of ontology as well as a reconstruction of that history in the light of the deeper and more original understanding of Being and of man in his relationship to Being acquired in the course of the inquiry. The phenomenological destruction promised for the second (unpublished) part of *Being and Time* —a task of which the nature and necessity is explained by Heidegger in Section 6 of that work—is an integral part of the question of Being, having the positive aim of acquiring a new perspective on the entire history of European thought and reconstructing it from the point of view of what has remained in it unsaid and unactualized.

This question is historical, further, in the sense that, as Heidegger insists, the historical destiny of Western man is bound up with the asking or failure to ask, with the manner of asking and answering, this question. Not to be content with gaining knowledge of the essent as such but, going beyond that, to inquire into the Being of essents or into Being as such may seem like verbal idolatry. Being cannot be grasped like a being and is as impalpable as Nothingness. Is it then, Heidegger asks, just an empty word, unreal vapour and an error, as Nietzsche says?[1] In his *An Introduction to Metaphysics* he seeks to demonstrate that Being is neither a mere word nor empty abstraction but, with its richness of content and dynamism, holds in itself the spiritual destiny of the West. In the first place, we can meaningfully talk and think about Being because we (i.e., Western thinkers) stand within a tradition which has taken its birth with the question about Being and of which the unfoldment has been determined by this origin. Secondly, a glance at the spiritual impoverishment of present-day Western man and at the bleakness and benightedness of his world—in Heidegger's words, "the darkening of the world, the flight of the gods, the depredation of the earth, the standardization of man, the supremacy of the mediocre"—it becomes obvious that the word 'Being' has an empty sound for us only because we have for long fallen out of Being and because

1. For a contemporary echo of Nietzsche's verdict, see the amusing "Discussion" between Marjorie Grene and Stuart Hampshire in *Encounter,* April, 1958, arising out of a review of Marjorie Grene's book on Heidegger by Hampshire. She "heartily" agrees with her critic that Heidegger's ontology "is indeed empty and arrogant nonsense."

our relationship to our tradition and to language has been disturbed and disrupted. What the Western world is today, it has come to be in consequence of its metaphysical foundations in early Greek thought, of the way Being revealed itself in it and of its subsequent withdrawal from the sight of Western man. To ask "What is Being?" or "Why are there essents rather than nothing?" is, therefore, not just a question of merely academic interest, remote from man's basic concerns, a professional luxury confined to the chosen few. As a philosophical question, it has arisen rather from a thinking that breaks the paths and opens the perspectives of the knowledge in which and by which a people comprehends and fulfils itself historically and culturally, of that knowledge which kindles and threatens and necessitates all questioning and valuing.[2]

Nor is this a question that concerns only the self-realization of single individuals seeking to attain philosophical truth in personal experience. Heidegger is not interested at all either in proving universally valid, eternal and changeless verities or in an experience that is only personal and private or, for that matter, in any sort of experience in the psychological, subjective sense. His is the quest of the *koinon* (Heraclitus), the common, the suprapersonal, of the concepts, the language and the presuppositions which provide, determine and mould the intellectual horizon and the historical destiny of a whole people; it is the quest for the ultimate metaphysical or spiritual foundations on which the Western man's life is grounded, for the way Being has revealed itself to him and withdrawn itself from him and in so doing has shaped his nature and destiny from Greek times to the present day. The question of Being thus is not a mere intellectual pastime but one in which man's entire historical existence is involved. Nor does it seek to provide an ontology in the traditional style, much less to assess critically the past mistakes of ontology. "We are

2. *Einführung in die Metaphysik*, p. 8 (E.T., p. 9).

concerned," Heidegger says,[3] "with something quite different, to restore man's historical existence—and that always includes our own future existence in the totality of the history allotted to us—to the power of Being which has to be opened up again by man for himself by going back to the origin." The question of Being, far from being merely verbal, amounts to a reflection on the genesis of our *hidden history*, it is a question that points to the hidden ground of our historical existence and on the answer to which our future historical existence depends.[4] As in the case of Nietzsche, Heidegger's thinking is inspired by a passionate concern for the present, for what *is* in the world of the present, for what man, fated by Being, has made of himself and his world today, for the way he dwells in it and for the basic attitudes which dominate his way of seeing things and comprehending them. The present technological era, with its emasculation of the spirit and its restless craving for mastery over everything that is, is one in which man has become utterly blind to the Being of things and to the disclosure of all reality in them other than their calculability and amenability to manipulative control. The desiccation and hollowness of man's world today, with all weight gone out of things, and the corresponding loss of man's ability truly to dwell in it as in a home, is a consequence, Heidegger declares, of the whole Western past which has worked itself out in the present and is its living foundation. Nietzsche saw the Western spiritual horizon threatened with Nihilism—that "un-

3. *Ibid.*, p. 32 (E.T., p. 34).

As Werner Marx says (Cf. "Heidegger's New Conception of Philosophy", *Social Research*, 1955; see also *Heidegger und die Tradition*, passim), Heidegger' philosophy is the quest of a second, new beginning. "Today when we say of any particular thing, that 'it is' or 'is not', that 'it is' or is only 'becoming', that 'it is true, genuine' or only 'sham' or when we say that man is 'in truth' or 'in error', we are still thinking under the influence of the first conception of the 'essence of Being and Man' as poetically composed by these first thinkers. In this sense the Pre-Socratics set a 'beginning', and a 'first beginning'. The ultimate aim of Heidegger's 'new conception of philosophy' during his second phase is to attain a 'second beginning'—to compose anew the Essence of Being and the Essence of Man."

4. *Einführung in die Metaphysik*, pp. 70, 71 (E.T., pp. 77, 79).

canniest of all guests, standing at the door"—and following upon him, Heidegger, with an even deeper insight into the hidden forces behind Western intellectual history and a more thorough familiarity with it, sees in the eclipse of Being today the relentless sway of total Nihilism, the completion of a process that has been at work at least since the time of Plato.

The question of Being is hence directly determined by the history and the present state of the human spirit on earth. "The asking of this question is immediately and fundamentally linked up with the crucial historical question of coming to a decision. . . . What history here means, however, is not so much the past, for that is just what does not happen any longer; much less is it the merely contemporary, which also does not happen but is only a passing event, comes and goes by. History as happening is the acting and being acted upon in and right through the *present*, determined from out of the future and taking over what has been. Our asking of the basic metaphysical question is historical because it opens up the happening (*Geschehen*) of human existence in its essential relationships, i.e., to essents as such in their totality, in respect of possibilities and futures never inquired into and because at the same time it binds it back to its beginnings in the living past, thus sharpening it and giving it weight in the present. In this questioning our Dasein is summoned to its history in the full sense of the word, called to it and to decision in it. . . . The basic point of view and attitude of the questioning is itself historical, standing and holding itself in what is happening, inquiring out of this and for the sake of this."[5] The immediate urgency of raising the question of Being comes from the fact that Being has become for us a mere word and floating mist, a fact which is not just a psychological characteristic of present-day man but one in the midst of which we stand, a state of our existence, the mode in which we are ourselves constituted in relation to Being. "The emptiness of the word 'Being', the total

5. *Ibid.*, pp. 33–34 (E.T., pp. 35–37).

vanishing of its appellative force" (as Manheim happily translates) is a manifestation of that perverse and false relationship to language characterizing man today and which is itself rooted in our disrupted relationship to Being as such. Since the destiny of language itself, as Heidegger says, is grounded in the particular relationship of a people to Being in any age, even the basic words of our language no longer speak to us with their full force and with the weight of the tradition which they not only embody but of which they are themselves the wellspring.

The above considerations explain why Heidegger has ceaselessly attempted to come to grips—more strenuously than perhaps any other original philosopher—not only with the central doctrines of the great European philosophers but with the entire course of the history of Western philosophy as a whole, trying to arrive at a complete view of its inner nature and dynamism, much as only Hegel had done before him, from the perspective of the question of Being.[6] But he interprets this history not in terms of the thought that has found explicit utterance in it but from the point of view of the unexpressed presuppositions underlying it, of what has remained unsaid in it. This general principle of interpretation, laying no claim to 'scientific' history, is employed by him in the interpretation of individual philosophers, of the larger movement of philosophical history and of the basic philosophical words and concepts coming down from the early Greek origins of Western thought. Already in *Kant und das Problem der Metaphysik,* Heidegger explicitly adopts the method of

6. This concern with the historical tradition and with the Greek world whose foundations still sustain the Western world is inspired by Heidegger's passionate concern for the future destiny of man on earth and for man's regeneration through a new relationship to Being. As he remarks, "Just because we have ventured upon the great and long task of pulling down a world grown old and of rebuilding really and truly anew, i.e. historically, we must know the tradition. We must know more, i.e. in a manner more stringent and binding than all ages and times of upheaval before us. Only the most radical historical knowledge can make us alive to the extraordinary character of our tasks and preserve us from a new wave of mere restoration and uncreative imitation." *Ibid.,* p. 96 (E.T., p. 106).

interpreting past philosophers, not in terms of what they have actually said but, through a consideration of the latter, to lay bare what is implicitly presupposed in it. Every philosopher, in explicitly formulating his thoughts, leaves unexpressed the driving idea at work implicitly in his formulations and the task of *philosophical* interpretation, as opposed to that of purely historical scholarship, is to bring this to light by a creative project of thought. "Real exegesis," in Heidegger's words, "must show what does not stand in the words and is nevertheless said. To accomplish this the interpretation must use force. The essential thing is to be sought where scientific interpretation has nothing more to find, branding as unscientific everything that transcends its own preserve."[7] Explaining the procedure adopted by him in his own much-disputed interpretation of the *Critique of Pure Reason,* Heidegger says,[8] "Now, if an interpretation merely reproduces what Kant has explicitly said, it is, from the very outset, no interpretation in the proper sense. The task before a proper interpretation is to bring expressly into view that which Kant, in his attempt to provide a foundation for metaphysics, has managed to disclose, over and above what he has explicitly formulated, but which, nevertheless, is something that Kant himself could not possibly go on to state. In all philosophical knowledge the decisive thing is not what is said in so many words but what is brought into view, through what is said, as that which still remains unsaid. . . . But, of course, in order to wrest from what the words say that which is implicitly intended in them, every interpretation must necessarily use force. Such force, however, cannot be just rambling caprice. The power of an illuminating idea must drive and guide the exposition. Only by virtue of this can an interpretation venture upon the ever audacious undertaking of putting one's trust in the hidden inner passion of a work, in order thus to be led into the unsaid in it and be constrained to

---

7. *Ibid.,* p. 124 (E.T., p. 136).
8. *Kant und das Problem der Metaphysik,* pp. 182 f. (E.T., pp. 206 f.).

say that. And that is also the way in which the guiding idea itself emerges into clarity in all its power."[9]

Such interpretation aims at re-opening a basic problem at a point where historically a particular formulation and answer has been given to it, at 'repeating' the problem so as to disclose in it possibilities which have not yet been actualized. 'By the repetition of a basic problem we understand the opening up of its original possibilities, hidden so long, by the elaboration of which it is transformed and so alone preserved in its substance as a problem. To preserve a problem means to hold it free and living in respect of those inner forces which render it possible as a problem in its very roots.' The possible, according to Heidegger, is the wellspring of all actualized thinking and a repetition aims at retracing the path taken by the actual back to its source in the possible, in order to capture it in its moment of birth, as it were, and to see if the possible, the potential and the implicit, offers other ways in which it may be actualized in thought. Only when, starting from the present, we succeed in reaching, step by step, back to the beginnings of the historical unfoldment of the whole of European thought, to the wellspring of the possible, shall we be in a position to see that as one actualized possibility, leaving still others at the disposal of thought. Only thus will it be possible to make another beginning in thought and thus enable a renewal and regeneration of the present. As Heidegger remarks,[10]

---

9. See also *Einführung in die Metaphysik*, p. 134 (E.T., p. 147 f.), where, referring to the already "proverbial far-fetched and one-sided character of the Heideggerian method of exegesis," Heidegger remarks, "Nevertheless, we may and, indeed, must ask here: which interpretation is the true one? Is it the one that simply takes over the perspective into which it happens to find itself already and because it presents itself as familiar and obvious, or is it rather the interpretation which questions the customary perspective in its very roots, because it could be, and in fact is so, that this line of vision does not lead to what needs being seen?" The latter kind of exegesis, Heidegger adds, needs a leap that is possible only if we really *ask* a question and through such questioning first create our perspectives. "But then, this is done not in a rambling, capricious way nor by clinging to a system taken as a norm, but in and out of historical necessity, out of the exigency of our historical existence."

10. *Ibid.*, pp. 29 f. (E.T., p. 32).

"To ask the question about Being means nothing less than to recapitulate (*wieder-holen*) the beginning of our historical-spiritual existence, in order to transform it into a new beginning. This is possible. It is in fact the authentic pattern of historicity, for all history takes its start in a fundamental happening. But we do not repeat a beginning by reducing it to something past and now known, which we may simply affect and ape. The beginning must be begun again, *more radically*, with all the strangeness, the darkness, the insecurity that attend a true beginning. Repetition as we understand it is anything but an improved continuation of what has been up till now by means of the same old methods."

Heidegger's attitude toward history and his interpretation of the historical course of Western philosophy may be brought into sharp focus by contrasting it with the way Hegel has interpreted that history. For Hegel, the history of Western philosophy is not just a succession of diverse views and doctrines, one giving place to another, without any inner connexion between them, but represents the process, in itself coherent, uniform and necessary, of the progress of the spirit towards complete consciousness of itself.[11] Philosophy as the self-development of the spirit towards absolute knowledge is identical with the history of philosophy; the latter is only the externalized form of the inner dialectic of pure thought itself, its various epochs representing the dialectical

11. In Heidegger's Being-centred thought, the place of this is taken by the dispensation or destiny (*Geschick*) of Being. Explaining the role of the individual thinker and the suprapersonal character of the history of thought, Heidegger says in *Der Satz vom Grund* (pp. 144–146), that of all that is difficult to grasp in this world, what is most difficult to grasp, because it lies closest to us inasmuch as we ourselves are that, is the idea that the history of thought rests on the dispensation of Being. This history is not the story of the personal views of individual thinkers thinking original thoughts but of the way thinkers respond to the claim of Being itself. We all stand in the clearing of Being, in the area of openness and light brought about by the way Being dispenses itself, in its own withdrawal, to us. But we do not just stand round unconcerned in this clearing; we stand in it as appropriated by the claim of Being, owned and charged by Being and in its service. The thinker is charged and endowed with the gift appropriate to the task of putting into words the Being of what is, of building and forming in the clearing of Being, of taking care of Being.

unfoldment of one and the same truth at progressively fuller stages of its evolution. "No other philosopher *before* Hegel," Heidegger remarks,[12] "has attained to such a fundamental point of view in philosophy which both enables and requires philosophical thinking to move within its history and at the same time makes this movement identical with philosophy itself." The first stage in this process is represented by Greek thought, with which philosophy proper begins and which is the stage of thesis. Thought, at this stage, emerges into pure objectivity, into the universal as such, but because not yet referred to a subject and mediated by it, this is also the stage of abstraction. The beginning, the first emergence of thought, Hegel says, is necessarily the most abstract; it is the simplest and the poorest or emptiest and so the earliest philosophers are the poorest of all. In this stage, Being or the Real as the abstract universal and pure objectivity is, as Heidegger puts it,[13] *not yet* determined and *not yet* mediated through the dialectical movement of the spirit's absolute subjectivity and hence, for Hegel, the philosophy of the Greeks is still in the stage of this 'not yet' and satisfying, as he says, only to a limited extent. The next higher stage, that of antithesis, begins with Descartes in whose philosophy the subject is posited and recognized *as* subject for the first time, thus enabling the objectivity of the previous stage to be grasped explicitly as objectivity. From the point of view of the last stage as represented by his own philosophy, Hegel quite appropriately says of Descartes, "With him we really enter into a philosophy that stands on its own . . . Here, we may say, we are at home and can, like the sailor at the end of a long voyage on a stormy sea, cry, 'Land!' " The third and highest stage, that of synthesis, in which the two earlier stages are annulled, conserved and taken up (*aufgehoben*, in the three-fold sense of *tollere, conservare* and *elevare*) is reached in Hegel's own System of Speculative Ideal-

---

12. "Hegel und die Griechen," in *Die Gegenwart der Griechen im Neueren Denken, Festschrift für Hans-Georg Gadamer,* p. 44.
    13. *Ibid.,* p. 52.

ism, "containing within itself everything that the labour of thousands of years has produced, the consummation and final result of all that has gone before," as he says in his *Lectures on the History of Philosophy*. This is the crowning stage of the concrete universal in which the Spirit, rich with its own self-unfolding process, comes to itself explicitly in the absolute certainty of itself as the absolute, fully self-conscious subject. As Heidegger points out,[14] Hegel sees the nature of history in the light of Being conceived as absolute subjectivity and judging the course of philosophy before its culmination in the Spirit's absolute certainty of self-consciousness in his own system, finds in it only a movement from the less developed to the more.[15]

For Hegel as for Heidegger, thought is concerned with something that is in itself historical in the sense of a happening (*Geschehen*). According to Hegel, thought's concern is with Being as self-thinking thought, which comes to itself only in the process of its speculative development and the happening is understood as one whose process character is determined by the dialectic of Being.[16] Heidegger not only does not accept the subjectivistic interpretation of Being as thought but rejects the view that particular philosophies and epochs of philosophy emerge one from another in the sense of the necessity of a dialectical process,[17] thus differing from Hegel on both these points.

14. *Ibid.*, p. 54.
15. Referring to Hegel's approach to history, Heidegger says (*Brief über den 'Humanismus'*, pp. 81 f.), "The happening of history occurs as, and arises from, the destiny (dispensation) of the truth of Being, in which Being gives itself and, in giving itself, also withdraws itself. Nevertheless, Hegel's conception of history as the development of the 'Spirit' is not untrue. It is also not partly right and partly wrong. It is as much true as metaphysics, which in Hegel's system achieves for the first time an expression of its absolutely conceived essence. Along with its inversion by Marx and Nietzsche, absolute metaphysics is part of the history of the truth of Being. What is generated by that is not touched or disposed of by refutations of any sort. It can only be taken in and assimilated by retrieving its truth so that it is conceived more deeply, as embedded in Being itself and is withdrawn from the sphere of merely human views."
16. Cf. *Identität und Differenz*, p. 40 (E. T., p. 45).
17. Cf. *Was ist das—die Philosophie?*, p. 29 (E.T., p. 63).

Heidegger also differs from Hegel in his estimate of the early thinking of a historical tradition. "The basic error," he says,[18] "lies in the belief that history begins with the primitive and backward, the clumsy and weak. The opposite is true. The beginning is the uncanniest and mightiest. What comes after is not development but shallowness and diffusion, the failure to hold on to the beginning, rendering it ineffective and harmless and exaggerating it into a caricature. . . ." Discussing the Anaximander fragment,[19] he asks, "With what claim does the earliest address itself to us, presumably the latest of the late-comers of philosophy? . . . Does the chronological and historical remoteness of the utterance conceal in itself a historical nearness of what it leaves unsaid and which speaks, beyond the present, into coming time? . . . May it not be that what is early outstrips the late, the earliest outstripping the latest most of all?

Summarizing the main points of divergence between himself and Hegel, Heidegger says,[20] "For Hegel, the concern of thinking is with Being in respect of essents as they are appropriated by thought (*Gedachtheit*) in and as absolute thinking. For us, the object of thinking is the same, Being, but Being in respect of its difference from beings. To put it more pointedly, for Hegel the matter of thinking is the thought (*Gedanke*) as the absolute notion. For us, the object of thinking is, provisionally expressed, the difference as difference." Further, for Hegel as well as Heidegger, the criterion for a dialogue with the historical heritage is the penetration into the power of the thinking of earlier thinkers. But whereas Hegel finds the specific power of thinkers in what has been thought by them, in so far as it can be taken up (*aufgehoben*, in its three-fold sense) as a specific stage in the dialectic of absolute thinking, Heidegger seeks for this power not in what has already been thought, but rather in what is yet unthought

18. *Einführung in die Metaphysik,* p. 119 (E.T., p. 130).
19. *Holzwege,* p. 300.
20. "Die Onto-theo-logische Verfassung der Metaphysik," in *Identität und Differenz,* pp. 42 f. (E.T., p. 47).

and from which what has been thought receives its essential character and scope. To the more popular question whether there is any 'progress' in philosophy, Heidegger has a characteristic answer: Philosophy, in so far as it is mindful of its nature, does not move forward at all. She steps into her place and marks time so that she may ceaselessly think of one and the same thing. Moving forward, that is, away from this place, is an error that follows thinking, like a shadow thrown by thinking itself.[21] Admitting that it is what has already been thought that makes for the not-yet-thought, which comes up ever afresh in its plenitude, Heidegger continues, "The criterion of the unthought does not lead to the incorporation of what has been thought previously into still higher levels of development and systematization surpassing it, but demands that the heritage of thought be liberated in respect of what still lies in reserve in its 'has been' (*Geswesenes*). It is this which holds tradition initially in its sway and is prior to it, though without being thought about expressly and as the originative source." Finally, for Hegel the dialogue with the preceding history of philosophy has the character of annulment (in the three-fold sense of *Aufhebung*), whereas for Heidegger it is of the nature of taking the step back (*der Schritt zurück*). "The annulment leads into the surmounting, gathering-together sphere of absolutely posited truth in the sense of the completely developed certitude of self-knowing knowledge, while the step back opens the realm, hitherto overlooked, with reference to which the essence of truth first of all becomes something that deserves thought." The step back, Heidegger explains, does not mean taking an isolated step in thought but a particular manner of thought's movement and a long way. "In so far as the step back determines the character of our dialogue with the history of Occidental thought, it leads our thinking in a way beyond what has hitherto been thought in philosophy. Thinking steps back before what concerns it, i.e., Being, and thus brings what

21. *Brief über den 'Humanismus'*, p. 81.

has been thought into a confrontation (*Gegenüber*) in which we have a view of the whole of this history and that, too, in respect of what constitutes the wellspring of this entire thinking, for it is the wellspring that alone provides the domain in which this thinking abides. This is, in contrast to Hegel, not a problem coming down to us already posed, but is rather something that has remained throughout unasked in the entire course of this history of thinking . . . , the difference between Being and beings."[22] The difference of essent and Being, itself unnoticed and unnoticeable by metaphysics, is the realm within which metaphysics, i.e., Occidental thinking in the totality of its essence, can be what in fact it is. Hence, Heidegger concludes, the step back is the step that leads out of metaphysics into the essence of metaphysics, into the source and ground of its essential constitution; the step back, taking us out of the charmed circle of metaphysical thinking, alone gives the necessary distance and perspective from which one can contemplate its essential nature and meditate on the 'ontological difference' on which, as on its unthought ground, it rests.

The continuous re-appropriation of a living tradition depends upon its re-interpretation from age to age. But every age necessarily interprets the past from its own dominant perspective and in terms of its own conceptual framework and language, thus transforming what it receives from the past in the very process of assimilating it. In seeking to go back—and recapture in its purity (and yet creatively, from the present perspective, in our case the perspective of the *question* of Being)—to the thinking of an age in which the foundations of this tradition were laid, we have, therefore, in a sense to reverse the process by which the original significance of the central concepts, and the sense of the basic words in which they were embodied, has been obscured by the strata of new meanings imposed upon them by later interpretation. In addition, the utmost care must be exercised to avoid

22. "Die Onto-theo-logische Verfassung der Metaphysik," in *Identität und Differenz,* p. 46.

interpreting earlier thinking in terms of later concepts which have evolved from them; though these alone have become historically effective, yet they only constitute one possible interpretation that might be given to the central concepts of the earlier thinkers. As Heidegger has said,[23] all later thinking that seeks a dialogue with the earlier must inevitably reach out to it from its own place in history, if it is at all to bring the silence of early thought into an utterance; but this need not necessarily imply projecting later conceptions into them, so long as care is taken to enter, in an expressly inquiring spirit, into the field of vision and hearing of early thinking. No previous thinker, Heidegger asserts, has been able to reach back to the beginning of Western philosophy and to recapture its true character *as* a beginning. As he remarks, "Neither Nietzsche nor any other thinker before him—not even, and in particular, he who, before Nietzsche, for the first time thought philosophically about the *history* of philosophy, viz. Hegel—penetrate into the first beginnings; they rather see the beginning as coloured by, and in the light of, what was already a falling away from the beginning and its stagnation: in the light of the Platonic philosophy."[24]

Such re-interpretation and mis-interpretation, transformation and falsification has occurred repeatedly not only in the course of the transmission of ideas from one period of history to another but also continuously, within the same period, as between its different phases. In its most dramatic form, however, the process can be seen at work in the historically 'fateful' translations by which Greek concepts were taken over into Latin and, later, into the vernaculars. In his quest for the unimpaired revelatory power of ancient words, Heidegger has frequently drawn attention to the havoc wrought by this translation of the Greek philosophical language into Latin, a language embodying the wholly different medieval spirit and outlook—an occurrence, Heidegger points out, by no means accidental and harmless but the first stage in

23. *Vorträge und Aufsätze*, pp. 238 f.
24. *Nietzsche I*, p. 469.

the process by which we are cut off and alienated from the original essence of Greek philosophy. The translation into Latin of the Greek *physis* as *natura,* of *ousia* as *substantia,* of *logos* as *ratio,* for example, does indeed convey something of the sense embodied in the Greek terms but, as Heidegger again and again shows in his discussions of these and other terms, the Latin 'equivalents' equally stand between ourselves and what the Greek terms say, hiding from our view their original sense and obstructing entry into the genuine Greek vision and way of thinking.[25] Such translations, of course, like all milestones in the history of thought, are not just examples of capricious and avoidable misinterpretation but constitute the very stuff of a continuous historical tradition. As Heidegger has remarked,[26] in the case of important and effective translations, "the translation is not only interpretation but is tradition, an integral part of our philosophical heritage. As tradition it belongs to the innermost movement of history . . . An important translation corresponds, in a particular epoch of the destiny (*Geschick*) of Being, to the way in which a language, destined by Being, speaks." That is why every attempt to recapture the unuttered meaning of past thinking requires a creative leap of thought and a new, all-embracing perspective, based on disillusioned, critical awareness of the present, an ear for the message of the past and a passionate concern for our future destiny.[27]

25. See *An Introduction to Metaphysics.*
26. *Der Satz vom Grund,* p. 164.
27. On Heidegger's approach to the history of philosophy, cf. W. Szilasi, *Interpretation und Geschichte der Philosophie* (in *Martin Heideggers Einfluss auf die Wissenschaften,* by Astrada, etc.) Helmuth Plessner compares (*Offene Problemgeschichte,* in *Nicolai Hartmann, der Denker und sein Werk*) Heidegger's approach with that of Hartmann. Werner Marx (*Heidegger und die Tradition*) discusses critically Heidegger's new determination of Being in relation to the traditional conception as represented by Aristotle and Hegel. For excellent summaries of Heidegger's interpretation of the Western philosophers, cf. P. Fürstenau, *Heidegger—das Gefüge seines Denkens,* pp. 101–168 and Kanthack, *Das Denken Martin Heideggers.* See also Richardson, *Heidegger,* pp. 301–382, for a presentation of Heidegger's views on Plato, Aristotle, Descartes, Hegel and Nietzsche.

II THE GREEK THINKERS

Greek thought begins with reflection on Being, not merely in the sense of the totality of what is (*ta onta*) but with an awareness of the Being (*einai*) of all that is, of the essent in its Being. That the Being of essents claimed the thinking of the early Greeks, says Heidegger, actually is the beginning of the Occident as a historical reality and the hidden source from which its destiny springs.[28] Being (*eon, on*) revealed itself to the early Greek thinkers, the founders of the Western philosophical tradition, as *ousia*, which means, according to Heidegger, not substance as the Latin translation of this term interprets it, but constant presence (*Anwesenheit*).[29] In the light of this way of understanding Being, never explicitly considered by them, they apprehended the totality of essents as *physis*, that which emerges, unfolds itself, enters into and remains in manifestness. The central question of their inquiry, and thenceforward the main theme of Western philosophy, is concerned with the totality of essents conceived as *physis*. It is metaphysics in the sense that it is not about particular essents but about the essent as such, i.e., in respect of its Being, going *beyond* essents to their Being in order, in the light of that, to understand the nature of what is. In a basic sense, as Heidegger remarks,[30] metaphysics is physics, *episteme physike*. The Greeks inquired into the Being of essents,

28. *Vorträge und Aufsätze*, p. 227.
29. Heidegger has devoted a long essay to Anaximander of Samos in which he gives an elaborate interpretation of the oldest philosophical utterance of Western thought ("Der Spruch des Anaximander" in *Holzwege*). Discussing the word *chreon* ('necessity' in the usual translation; Heidegger renders it as need or use—*Brauch*), he shows that already with Anaximander, an awareness of the Being of what is and of the distinction between Being and beings had flashed out. "*To chreon* is the oldest name in which thinking gives utterance to the Being of essents, in which also the nature of the relationship between Being as presence and essents (what is, as present) finds the first expression, a relationship that springs from the nature of Being itself. *To chreon,* anticipating the *logos* of Heraclitus, expresses the way Being itself *is* as the relation with essents.
30. *Vom Wesen und Begriff der Physis*, p. 9.

into the truth of what is, and in this they were guided by the light of a particular conception of Being, of what it means to be, viz. the sense of Being as presence. They inquired into the Being of beings but they never asked what Being itself meant and therefore could not be aware of the particular sense of Being presupposed in their own thinking about essents as such. The history of Western philosophy, except for its earliest pre-Socratic period, is a history of 'metaphysical' thinking, i.e., thinking about the Being of essents (not about Being itself) and it begins with the oblivion of Being as such and of *its* truth. The oblivion of Being is the oblivion of the difference of Being from beings which is implied in all inquiry about the Being of essents. In uncovering itself in the essent, Being withdraws itself as such and, along with that, conceals its difference from the essent. The difference breaks out in Anaximander, in Parmenides, in Heraclitus, a lightning-flash in the illumination of which their thinking takes its birth; but the difference does not reveal itself *as* the difference and so remains unnamed and unthought. The history of Being begins with the oblivion of Being, of Being's own nature and of its difference from the essent.[31]

All reflection on the Being of what is, however, is itself carried on in the light of an implicit conception of Being which derives not from man but is something that comes *to* him as the destiny that holds his thinking in its grip, depending on the way Being illuminates itself in him, on the way Being dispenses and reveals itself to man. As Heidegger explains,[32] in every age Being itself is understood in a determinate sense, disclosing itself in some aspect. But all understanding, as a basic mode of disclosure, must itself move in a determinate line of vision (*Blickbahn*), a perspective which must have opened out in advance. The determinate understanding of Being moves in a predetermined perspective, not itself made by man but in which man finds himself immersed, a dispensation of Being itself, as Heidegger later

31. *Holzwege*, p. 336.
32. *Einführung in die Metaphysik*, p. 89 (E.T., p. 99).

calls it. Not even the Greeks did or could, due to reasons inherent in the case and not because of any human deficiency, bring this perspective to light. The history of the way man has understood and interpreted the Being of essents in their totality is, therefore, rooted in the different ways in which Being itself has, from age to age, revealed itself variously to man, in the history of Being (*Seinsgeschichte*), as Heidegger calls it. The history of Being, which is the history of the self-bestowal of Being (*Seinsgeschick*) to man and has thus an intrinsic reference to man as the seat of its illumination, is in the West the history of the way Being reveals and bestows itself in and through its own withdrawal from man. In revealing itself as the light in which essents enter into overtness, it withdraws its own essence into itself; without such revelation man could never have asked what Heidegger calls the 'leading question' (*Leitfrage*) of philosophy, the question about the Being of essents, and without this withdrawal man would not have become alienated from Being as such and, forgetting the 'fundamental question' (*Grundfrage*) of philosophy, the question about Being as such, abandoned himself to the essent as such. Being only reveals and gives itself to man as its own withdrawal and man's oblivion of Being is actually the abandonment of man by Being. The history of philosophy is the history of man's attempt to understand what is. But this understanding is itself the way Being reveals itself in Dasein and is rooted in man's relationship to Being. As Heidegger asserts, "the relationship of Being to beings can come only from Being and can have its basis only in the nature of Being"[33]. The history of man's thinking of Being is thus a manifestation of the history of Being itself. And since the former is in the main a history of the way man has thought about the essent as such and as a whole, disregarding Being itself, the latter is conceived by Heidegger as the history of the self-concealment of Being. The history of philosophy, as Heidegger reads it, is thus itself grounded in the

33. *Holzwege*, p. 334.

invisible, deeper history of Being and though exhibiting, on the surface, development and advance in thinking (i.e., on the level of our knowledge of and control over essents as such), it is at best a history of the progressive withdrawal of Being from man's vision and so of man's growing alienation from Being.

Traditionally, Being is contrasted with Becoming, with Seeming, with Thought and with the Ought, fateful distinctions already latent in early Greek thought.[34] As against Becoming, Being is permanence; as against Appearance, it is the enduring prototype, the self-same; as against Thought, it is the object, what lies in front; as against the Ought, it is that which is presented to us as something to be realized. All these determinations of Being, through what the Greeks distinguished from it, at bottom mean the same; constancy of presence (*Anwesenheit*), with the notions of "contemporaneity and presence, of constancy and stability, sojourn and occurrence" included in it.[35] An examination of these contrasting pairs, however, shows that in each case Being and what is opposed to it belong intimately and inseparably together in a deeper sense, that these distinctions have emerged historically from a conception of Being in which they were originally at one with, and implicit within, Being itself. Parmenides conceived Being in sharp contrast with Becoming, thus explicitly bringing out the character of the former as the sheer fullness, gathered in itself, of the permanent, untouched by restlessness and change. Heraclitus says at bottom the same.

Being and appearance are also bound together into an original unity on the basis of which they were then distinguished from one another; the power of coming forth and abiding, *physis*, which for the Greeks constituted the Being of all that is, is at the

34. The following account of Heidegger's interpretation of early Greek philosophy is based on *Einführung in die Metaphysik*, Chap. IV. For an elaborate account of Heidegger's treatment of Parmenides and Heraclitus, see the book by G. J. Seidel mentioned on p. 50, note, above. Seidel has also an excellent chapter on "The Meaning of Language for Heidegger".
35. See *Was heisst Denken?* 143 ff. (E.T., pp. 235–238) for further discussion of the Greek conception of Being as presence.

same time a shining forth, appearing and standing out of hidden-ness (*aletheia*). To be an essent is to come to light, to present and display itself; but what appears always has the possibility of appearing as what in truth it is not, of being mere appearance and illusion. As Heidegger puts it, where there is unconcealment of essents there is always the possibility of semblance and, con-versely, where the essent has stood, unshaken and for long, in a certain semblance, this appearance can shatter and fall away, revealing the essent in its naked truth. Seeming and semblance are for the Greeks not subjective and imaginary but are inherent in the essent and hence, as Heidegger puts it, "they were per-petually compelled to wrest Being from appearance and preserve it against appearance . . . in the ceaseless struggle between Being and Seeming they wrested Being from the essent, bringing permanence and unconcealment to the essent."[36] As against the later falling apart of Being and Seeming with Plato, the great age of Greece was a unique creative self-assertion amid the confusion of the complex struggle between the two powers of Being and Seeming. Seeming belongs to Being itself as appearing and be-cause of this the early Greek thinkers, Parmenides in particular, devoted their main effort to the task of rescuing Being from Seeming by distinguishing it from the latter and from non-Being —it is with this distinction that, as Heidegger says, Western man's historical existence begins. The inner unity of Being and appearance has found concise expression in Heraclitus' saying: *physis kryptesthai philei*, i.e., Being, as physis (coming forth out of hiddenness) in itself tends to self-concealment, to a relapse into that. Being and Seeming are locked together, intrinsically, in the unity of *polemos*, of perpetual war. Becoming too, like seem-ing, is not sheer nothing and therefore, though opposed to Being in the sense of what stands out in permanent sameness, is yet comprehended in Being in the larger sense.

The differentiation between Being and Thought also springs

36. *Einführung in die Metaphysik,* p. 80 (E.T., p. 89).

from an original, inner belonging together of the two, an initial unity which itself, as Being in the profounder sense, as it were, requires its own differentiation. Logic, the science of 'thought', cannot itself explain the nature and origin of this separation because logic itself arose on the basis of this separation, after Plato's interpretation of Being as *idea* had already turned Being into an 'object' of knowledge. It can be shown, Heidegger claims, that in early Greek philosophy Being (as *physis*) and thought (as *logos*) were conceived as intrinsically belonging together, provided that we understand *logos* also in a deeper, more original sense, keeping out its later misinterpretation in terms of thinking as a subjective process, of reason, of judgment, of the Christian doctrine. Originally, *logos* meant, according to Heidegger, gathering or collection, having the sense of both collecting and collectedness; it was the primal gathering principle. "*Logos* signifies here neither meaning nor word, nor doctrine, nor the spirit of the latter but the permanent, self-abiding, original collection of gathered-togetherness. . . . *Logos* is the permanent gathering together, the self-contained togetherness of the essent, i.e., Being."[37] *Physis* and *logos* together constitute a unity and in that sense are the same. What is is in itself gathered presence, holding together what tends to come apart; so conceived, Being is at the same time radiance and harmony, the supreme beauty.[38]

In order to show how this original unity of *physis* and *logos* is

---

37. *Ibid*, p. 98 (E.T., p. 108).
38. Heidegger has also dealt at length with his interpretation of *logos* and *legein* in an independent essay in *Vorträge und Aufsätze*. Discarding all later interpretations of *logos* as "ratio, as word, as cosmic order, as the logical and the necessity in thought, as meaning, as reason," as derivative he goes back to its original meaning: laying down, collecting and gathering, and as such, speech. *Logos,* as Heidegger explains it (p. 227), is the gathering principle, the *Hen panta* (all is one) of Heraclitus. "The *logos* names that which gathers together all that is present (i.e. the essent) in its presence (i.e. Being), laying it out in such gathering. The Logos names that within which the presence of the present takes place. . . . In the thinking of Heraclitus the Being (presence) of essents manifests itself as the Logos, the gleaning, gathering laying out (*lesende Lege*)." Heidegger also shows here how, for the first time, Heraclitus determines the nature of man in terms of his belongingness to Being.

eventually broken up, Heidegger offers his own interpretation of the well-known line of Parmenides, *to gar auto noein estin te kai einai* ("thinking and being are the same" in the usual translation, no less un-Greek, Heidegger says, than the misinterpretation of *logos*) as also of his saying, *chre to legein te noein t'eon emmenai* (ordinarily translated as "It is necessary to say and to think that the essent is").[39] To understand the real meaning of *noein*, he insists, we must carefully refrain from projecting into it the modern conception of thinking as the activity of a subject, with Being as its correlate, and from interpreting it in Kantian or Hegelian terms. We should understand *noein* in the sense of *vernehmen* (to apprehend), in the double signification of taking up, accepting, letting what appears come up and of hearing a witness, questioning him and so determining.[40] Being, in the sense of *physis* or emergence into unhiddenness, and *noein* are the same in the sense of inherently belonging together; where unhiddenness occurs and Being prevails, there occurs also, as necessarily implied in it, apprehension. Further, such apprehension, far from being a power exercised by man as subject, is itself possible to man because he himself is part of Being (*physis*) and so shares in the apprehending (*noein*) that is intrinsic to Being. The being of man himself is determined by the inner unity and togetherness of *physis* and *noein*. Apprehension, Heidegger says, is here not a faculty belonging to man, with his nature already defined; apprehension is rather a happening, sharing in which alone man enters into history as an essent, appears, that is, in the literal sense, comes into being. Apprehension is not a mode of activity which man possesses as an attribute; on the contrary, man himself is a function of apprehension. What the saying of

39. For a detailed discussion of this line, see *Was heisst Denken?*, pp. 106–117 (E.T., pp. 172–193); also see the essay, "Moira" (in *Vorträge und Aufsätze*). For Parmenides also the nature of man and his relationship to Being comes from Being itself.

40. See also *Was heisst Denken?*, p. 125 (E.T., p. 203), where *noein* is rendered as 'being mindful of' or 'taking care of'.

Parmenides expresses is thus a definition of the essence of man in terms of the truth of Being.

For the early Greeks, man stands in an intimate bond with Being, deriving his own nature from that bond and existing as the locus of the self-disclosure of Being. At the same time, needed and necessitated by Being itself, he seeks to wrest the truth of Being, to make Being itself shine forth and appear by bringing it to a stand in the permanency of well-defined form, through knowledge and art, by embodying, rendering manifest and realizing Being *in* the essent (*ins-Werk-setzen,* as e.g., when the artist incorporates the truth of Being in a 'work' of art) through the exercise of force against the order of *physis* or *dike*.[41] Knowing as apprehension (*noein*) is not mere passive reception but is an act of violence, a marching out to engage the essent in the battle for Being. Within Being itself, conceived as *physis* and *logos,* there is inherent the possibility and the necessity of *logos* (i.e., *noein* as a gathering together or *legein*) differentiating itself from *logos* in the sense of the togetherness, the gathered character, of Being itself. *Logos* acquires the sense of a gathering together that makes manifest, occurring in and through man, and, as the gathering and apprehending of the being of essents, it becomes a feature of the constitutive essence of man and no longer an element in Being itself. Further, man's break-through into Being, but for the sake of Being and in its service, in knowledge and art, is at the same time a break-through into language. Language, giving form to the essent and opening it up in its being, is a collecting, gathering together and so disclosing, *logos.* It brings the essent into openness, delimitation and permanence;

---

41. For an elaboration of the Greek tragic conception of man, as the *deinotaton,* the uncanny agent of acts of violence, see Heidegger's interpretation of the first chorus song in the *Antigone* of Sophocles in *An Introduction to Metaphysics,* where he speaks of "the creative man, who marches out into the un-said, who breaks into the un-thought, enforces what has never happened, makes what has never been seen to appear." See also "Der Ursprung des Kunstwerkes" in *Holzwege,* for an elucidation of the concept of setting into a work (*Sich-ins-Werk-Setzen*).

in primordial speech the Being of the essent is opened up in the texture of its gatheredness and maintained and preserved as such. Himself gathered together within the structure of Being, standing and acting in *logos* as gatheredness, man (as a function of *noein* or apprehension) is the gatherer charged with the task of preserving and fulfilling primarily through language (poetic creation and thought), the disclosure of Being, of guarding such disclosure against seeming and closure. *Logos* and *physis* thus split apart, facing each other as it were, but still forming a harmonious whole, the differentiation still in the service of Being. As yet this does not mean any breaking away of *logos* from Being, nor imply that *logos* stands opposed to Being in such a way as to stand in judgment (as Reason) on Being, determining and regulating what is to count as the Being of essents.

The secession of *logos* occurs, Heidegger points out, when it abandons its original essence, when Being is interpreted differently and its *physis* character is lost from view. The slow and long history of this transformation, in the midst of which Western man has long been standing, culminates in the domination of thinking as *ratio* over the Being of what is and the determination of man's essence in terms of Reason. The initial differentiation of *logos* and *physis* was followed by the breaking away of *logos* from the original unity and ultimately to its being elevated to a position of supremacy through the philosophy of Plato and Aristotle. Plato conceives Being as *idea* or *eidos,* an interpretation which then dominates the whole course of Western philosophy right up to Hegel, with whom the first phase of Western thought, as Heidegger calls it, comes to its definitive close. Idea or *eidos* means the look, the view presented by anything that confronts us, its visage. In such presentation the thing stands before us, is present, i.e., *is* in the Greek sense; this is *physis* immobilized and held fast in the *aspect* presented by it. In the visage that it shows, the essent, that which is present (*Anwesende*), presents itself in its what and how, its *ousia,* which signifies at the same time the presence (*Anwesenheit*) of what is present as well as the latter in respect of its 'what'. The subsequent distinction between *existentia* and *essentia* is based on the Greek understanding of Being as constancy of presence and the Platonic interpretation of the latter as *idea*. *Idea* understood as presence, Heidegger points out, includes in itself the sense both of emerging into unhiddenness (simple *estin*) and of the *what* of the emergence (*ti estin*) and its correlate the *that* (*oti estin*). The interpretation of Being as *idea* follows from the conception of Being as *physis* (emerging and appearing), but with Plato the *idea*, instead of being recognized as the derivative that it is, usurped the position of *physis* as the sole and proper meaning of Being. What happened was nothing less than a betrayal of the original Greek insight. Being and apprehension, what is seen and seeing, belong together in one whole, but from this it does not follow that being seen alone can determine and constitute the presence (Being) of the thing seen or that Being should be conceived in terms of apprehension alone and defined as that which is apprehended by the intellect. In the interpretation of Being as *idea*, Heidegger says, not only is a consequence of the initial conception of the nature of Being twisted and elevated to the status of that nature itself but the falsification is once again misinterpreted. Being is not only understood in the sense of *idea* (whatness or quiddity), but the latter is exalted as the real essent (*ontos on*) above the whole realm of essents, which is now degraded into the *me on*, the unreal and the imperfect, having only a share in Being (*methexis*), an imperfect copy of the ideal prototype. A chasm (*chorismos*) opens up between the *idea* as what really is and the essent as what in reality is not. The meaning of appearing, too, is transformed; it has no longer the sense of emerging or showing itself but becomes *mere* appearance, seeming—*on* and *phainomenon* fall apart. The meaning of truth, which was at the beginning the *aletheia* or unhiddenness of *physis*, also undergoes a change. Truth is understood now as the adequation (*homoiosis*) of the disclosure of essents to the ideal pattern, the idea, i.e., as the correctness of seeing, of apprehension in the sense of representation. The transformation of Being from *physis* to *idea* has been decisive, Heidegger claims, in giving to the history of the Occident its essential character and mould. In his essay on Plato's doctrine of truth, Heidegger brings out the Unthought in Plato's thinking through a detailed discussion of the Allegory of the Cave in the *Republic*, Book VIII. What remains unthought here, according to him, is a transformation in the conception of truth from unhiddenness to correctness of perception or knowing, from *a-letheia* to *orthotes*. The original Greek sense of truth as a wresting away from hiddenness is indeed present in the Allegory, but it is dominated and overshadowed by another conception of truth which comes into prominence. *Aletheia* comes under the domination, the yoke, of the *idea*, as Heidegger puts it, and truth as unhiddenness recedes into the background. In consequence, not only the character but also the locus of truth changes. "As unhiddenness it is still the basic feature of essents themselves. As correctness of 'seeing', it becomes a character of man's attitude toward essents,"[42] i.e., a property of knowing. This change in the nature of truth goes hand in hand with the determination of the Being (*presence*) of essents as *idea*, so that presence is no longer regarded as the emergence of the hidden into unhiddenness, as it was in the beginning, but as *idea*, itself determining truth and rendering it possible. Plato's thought results, Heidegger says, from the change in the nature of truth, a change which manifests itself as the history of metaphysics, of which the final culmination begins in the thinking of Nietzsche.[43]

With the changed interpretation of *physis* there goes a corresponding transformation in the meaning of *logos.*. *Logos* as gathering renders essents manifest; language is that through which the *legein* or gathering and manifesting of this *logos* occurs. But when attention is focussed on the task of guarding authentic discourse against mere repetitive talk emptied of its

42. *Platons Lehre von der Wahrheit*, p. 42.
43. Cf. also the illuminating discussion of Plato's theory of art in *Nietzsche I*, Chapter I and comments on Plato scattered throughout the work.

revelatory power, the former comes to be identified with *logos* itself and becomes the locus of truth.[44] *Logos* as gathering was initially identical with the occurrence of unhiddenness (truth) and rooted in it, but now, in the sense of statement, it becomes itself the seat of truth in the sense of correctness. Originally, truth as unhiddenness was a feature of the essent and governed by gathering but now it becomes a property of *logos* (statement) not only thus shifting its locus but also changing its character from primordial unhiddenness of the essent to the correctness of statement. *Logos* thus detaches itself from its initial unity with *physis* and becomes, as statement, the arbiter of what is to count as Being, unfolding, in course, into the discipline of ontology and the doctrine of categories. The Principle of Contradiction, declaring that when two statements contradict each other, what they are about cannot *be*, embodies and illustrates this changed conception of the relationship between *physis* and *logos*. Further, since *logos* as statement is itself an objectively existing entity, it can be employed as an instrument to gain and secure truth as correctness, as an *organon*. With this final transformation of *logos* into a tool, "there arrives the hour of the birth of Logic." Ever since Aristotle, Logic, born complete in most essentials, has remained the authoritative and standard perspective for the interpretation of Being, right down to Kant and Hegel. The only thing that remains, Heidegger acidly remarks, is now "to lift it off its hinges" and effect radical changes in its very foundations.

The transformation of *physis* and *logos* and consequently of their relation to one another is a fallingoff from the first beginning. As Heidegger says, "The philosophy of the Greeks conquered the Western world not on the strength of what it was in its original beginning but through what it had become towards

44. As Heidegger points out in a discussion of the *homo mensura* doctrine of Protagoras (*Holzwege*, pp. 94 ff.; also *Nietzsche II*, pp. 135 ff.), the change in the interpretation of what is, including man, came about as a result of the Platonic struggle against the Sophists and, in that sense, in dependence upon them.

the end of this beginning,"[45] an end which came to its final culmination with Hegel in the last century. The inner ground of the transformation of *physis* and *logos* into idea and statement lies in the change in the nature of truth from unhiddenness to correctness. The original essence of truth could not be retained and preserved and there was a "collapse of unhiddenness", of the area opened out for the appearing of the essent; from the debris 'idea' and 'statement', *ousia* and *kategoria,* were salvaged, as Heidegger puts it, each existing as an objective entity, disjoined from the other and connectable only by a relation having itself the character of an objective entity. Ever since, philosophy has laboured to explain and render plausible the relation between judgment (thought) and Being by all sorts of ingenious theories, in vain, because without reopening the root-question of Being itself. The definitive interpretation of Being itself that emerges, in consequence of all this, is crystallized in the word *ousia,* Being in the sense of constant presence, simple givenness (*Vorhandenheit*). According to this conception of Being, henceforth to dominate European thought, only what always is, the *aei on,* counts as really being. This conception, along with the consequent interpretation of Being as *idea* also paves the way for the separation between Being and the Ought. Once Being is conceived as idea, itself in a way an essent, it no longer has its potency and its power to render something possible within itself, but becomes subordinate to something above it, to the Idea of the Good (*idea tou agathou*) which, therefore, as Plato says, stands beyond Being (*epekeina tes ousias*).[46] It is this Idea of Ideas, the Good, that endows Being (as *idea*) with the power to function as prototype. The Ought thus separates itself from Being, from within Being itself, and sets itself above it. The change in the conception of truth and the consequent interpretation of Being (presence) as *idea* converts as it were Being itself

---

45. *Einführung in die Metaphysik,* p. 144 (E.T., p. 158).
46. On *agathon,* see *Vom Wesen des Grundes,* pp. 37–38; *Platons Lehre von der Wahrheit,* pp. 36–40; also *Nietzsche II,* pp. 223–233.

into an essent and the highest Idea, the Good, appears as the highest essent, the supersensible first cause of the existence and appearance of all sensible essents, called by Plato and, following him, by Aristotle, the divine (*to theion*). Since Plato's interpretation of Being as *idea*, Heidegger says,[47] all thinking about the Being of essents has been metaphysical and metaphysics itself theological or, as in a later formulation, ontology, theology and logic in one, ontotheologic. With Plato, thinking becomes 'philosophy', i.e., representational thinking, which catches only the essent in its net, or thinking in concepts, which is aimed, with its grasping and grabbing, with its calculative character, at attaining mastery over the essent. A new epoch of Being begins, not yet infected with subjectivism and still moving within the basic Greek experience, it is true, but nevertheless destined to cast its nihilistic shadow over the entire course of Western philosophy up to Nietzsche, with whom 'philosophy' runs out its course, opening out the possibility, and the necessity, of a new beginning.

In Aristotle's conception of *energeia* as the Being (*ousia*, presence) of essents, there was indeed a flash of the original spirit of Greek thought. *Energeia* in Aristotle means, according to Heidegger, coming or being brought into unhiddenness and presence and enduring so in an accomplished piece of work, a meaning which was totally lost with the Latin translation of this term into *actualitas* and its eventual transformation into Reality and Objectivity.[48]

The ontology of the *Vorhanden* (the simply given), in the language of *Being and Time*, with its conception of Being as constant presence, itself contains within it the seeds of the differentiation, and eventually of the dissension, of Becoming, Seem-

---

47. *Platons Lehre von der Wahrheit*, p. 48.
48. See also the next chapter for Aristotle's doctrine of *energeia*. As already remarked, in Heidegger's writings scattered discussions of Aristotle are to be found all over. Except for a commentary on Aristotle's *Physics* B 1 (*Vom Wesen und Begriff der Physis*) dealing with the Aristotelian concepts of *physis, ousia* and *kinesis,* nothing by way of a systematic treatment has, however, been published. Hence the meagre treatment of Aristotle here.

ing, Thinking and the Ought from Being. The original unity of Being as *physis* in its intimate relation to Truth, as unhiddenness and comprehending within itself the relationship to the essence of man, flashing out for a brief historical moment in early Greek thought, could not be sustained, with consequences which have been working themselves out in the shape of the history of Western philosophy.[49] The ground for this lies, Heidegger says, in the magnitude of the beginning and in the nature of a beginning as such. "As a beginning, the beginning must in a sense leave itself behind, thus necessarily hiding itself (though this self-concealment is not nothing). A beginning can never directly preserve its power as a beginning and the only way to preserve its force and safeguard its continuation is to repeat the beginning, draw it out once again (*wieder-holen*), in its originative character, in a still deeper sense,"[50] i.e., by explicitly bringing out what has remained unthought in it. That is why, in his quest for a new conception of Being, Heidegger goes back to the earliest Greek thinkers who had a glimpse of the Being of essents (*physis*) as the unity of the various elements that later fell apart and renders explicit their unuttered but presupposed conception of Being itself—Being as constant presence (*Anwesenheit, ousia*). It is this way of understanding Being, i.e., the determination of the meaning and content of the infinitive 'to be' in terms of the present 'is' and not the other way round, that led to the separation of Becoming, Seeming, Thinking and the Ought from Being, though they are themselves not sheer nothing. "But if, in these distinctions, all that is opposed to Being is *not* nothing, then it is *itself essent,* ultimately even more so (since Being itself gets its determination in opposition to them) than what the narrow conception of Being regards as essent. But then, in which sense of

---

49. Already by the time of Aristotle, *physis* had come to denote a particular region of essents, distinguished from the sphere of *ethos* and *logos* and no longer having the broad meaning of the totality of essents. See *Holzwege,* p. 298.

50. *Einführung in die Metaphysik,* pp. 145 f. (E.T., p. 160).

Being are Becoming, Seeming, Thought and the Ought essent? In
no case in the sense of Being from which they are distinguished."[51]
The Greek understanding of Being, dominating the whole
course of Western philosophy, is, Heidegger concludes, too narrow and does not suffice to name everything that 'is'. It is oblivious of the one and only distinction that counts, the distinction
between Being and beings, and so generates, through this oblivion, the entire unfoldment of the subsequent tradition of 'metaphysical' thinking. For this reason, Being must once again be
experienced anew in its very fundament and in all the breadth of
its possible nature. The Being which they (these distinctions)
encircle must itself be transformed into the encompassing circle
and ground of all essents, not excluding the 'terrible power of
negativity' (Hegel), the Nothing. And such re-thinking of Being
must take cognizance of the fact, itself hidden from the Greeks
and from subsequent philosophy, that from the very beginning
the perspective governing the disclosure of Being was Time
(Being, presence, the 'is'), though time as understood, in its
turn, in the light of that narrow interpretation of Being as simple
givenness (*Vorhandenheit*), as a succession of given nows.

With the arrival of Christianity, the highest essent, the Divine
(*to theion*), became God the Creator and the Being of essents as
a whole was understood to lie in its createdness by God. The
leading question of philosophy, viz. the question of what the
essent is in its totality, appears as having been conclusively
answered, the question itself being thus done away with and
that, too, on an authority far superior to the chance opinions and
delusions of men, as Heidegger puts it.[52] "Biblical revelation
which, according to its own assertion, rests on divine inspiration,
teaches that all that is, is created by a personal creator God and
is sustained and ruled by Him. Through revealed truth, pro-
claimed by the Church doctrine as absolutely binding, the question as to what the essent is has become superfluous. The Being
of the essent consists in its being created by God (*omne ens est*

51. *Ibid.*, p. 155 (E.T., p. 170).
52. *Nietzsche I*, p. 131.

ens creatum)."[53] To be an essent means to belong in its particular specific position in the hierarchy of the created and, as so brought about, to correspond to the cause of creation (*analogia entis*).[54] Truth itself is understood as *homoiosis* and *convenientia*, the correspondence or adequation of things with their preconceived idea in the divine mind. To know the truth about what is, the only reliable way left for man is to devote himself to the revealed teaching, the *doctrina* of the Church doctors. In its essence truth now appears in the character of 'doctrine' and its knowledge consists in the '*Summa*', the systematic collection of the whole heritage of the various doctrinal views in so far as they are consonant with the teaching of the Church.

Scholars adopting this approach to the essent as a whole are called 'theologians' but, Heidegger remarks in an interesting passage,[55] their 'philosophy' is philosophy in name only. "A 'Christian philosophy' is even more of an absurdity than the idea of a square circle. Square and circle have at least this in common that they are both spatial constructs, whereas Christian faith and philosophy are divided by an abyss. Both, it might be said, teach the truth, to which the answer is that truth here is conceived by each in wholly disparate ways. That the Medieval theologians studied Plato and Aristotle, re-interpreting them in their own way, is much the same as Karl Marx using the metaphysics of Hegel for his political doctrine. Properly and strictly speaking, the *doctrina Christiana* does not mean to impart knowledge about the essent, about what is; its truth is entirely concerned with salvation, with insuring the salvation of the individual immortal soul."

III THE MODERN AGE

The modern age begins with the liberation of man from the authority of the revealed truth of Christianity and Church doctrine such that, standing on his own, man himself becomes his

53. *Ibid.*, p. 132.
54. *Holzwege*, p. 83.
55. *Ibid.*, p. 132.

own lawgiver.[56] This liberation, however, is itself conditioned by its bond with revealed truth, through which man was assured of the salvation of his soul and made secure in that certainty. As Heidegger points out, "The liberation *from* the revelation-based certainty of salvation had, therefore, to be a liberation *into* a certainty in which man secures truth as what is known to him through his own activity of knowing. This was possible only when man himself, seeking to liberate himself, guaranteed the certainty of what is knowable, which in turn he could do only by determining, from within himself and for himself, what is to count as knowable to him and what is to be understood by knowledge and by the assurance of the known, i.e., by certainty." What is of decisive importance here, Heidegger says, is not that man throws off his shackles but that with this freedom, his own essence is transmuted and he becomes a subject. For Aristotle and the Greeks, the subject (*subjectum, hypokeimenon*) was what a statement was about, that which lies before, that which underlies as its basis, the permanently present. But for Descartes, the permanently present, the given, is found in the *ego cogito*, which thus becomes the ultimate subject, the subjectness of the ego as subject lying in the certainty of self-consciousness. Man becomes an essent in whom all that is is grounded as to the mode of its Being and its truth. Correspondingly, the nature of the essent in its totality also undergoes a change. The world turns into an image, a picture in man's grasp and at his disposal, and "the essent as a whole is set out as something which man may prepare himself to meet and which he accordingly seeks to bring in front of himself, to have and keep it, in a positive sense, before himself (*vorstellen*, taken literally)." The world is conceived as a picture and the essent as something which *is* only in so far as it is set up by the representing, producing activity of man. The Being of essents is sought and found in the representedness (*Vorgestelltheit*) of essents; the presence of the present appears, since

---

56. For this account of Descartes and the rise of modern philosophy see "Die Zeit des Weltbildes" in *Holzwege;* also *Nietzsche II*, pp. 131–192.

Descartes, in the mode of objectivity. This is indeed a far cry from the early Greek conception of Being as the presence of the present, of what lies in front (the *hypokeimenon* or subject in the Greek sense), in the unhiddenness or truth of which man shares through apprehension and so *is* man. "Representation (*Vorstellen*) has no longer the character of an apprehension of what is present, in the unhiddenness of which this apprehension itself belongs, with its own mode of presence. In representation there is nothing more of the opening oneself for . . . , but only a grabbing and grasping of. . . . Here it is not what is presented that has its sway; it is the attitude of attacking that prevails." The nature of truth itself undergoes transformation, so that truth is conceived from now on, not as unhiddenness, but as the *certainty* of adequation and correctness.

Liberated from the authority of revealed truth, man has to find certitude within himself and to find a metaphysical foundation for this certitude. Such a *fundamentum absolutum inconcussum veritatis,* absolutely unshakable in its character as a foundation, Descartes provides in the *ego cogito,* in the 'I' conceived as the thinking, representing principle determining what 'being' is to mean. The *cogito ergo sum* of Descartes formulates, Heidegger points out,[57] an intrinsic connection between *cogito,* representing, and *sum* or being, such that it is not merely *I* who am as representing but that the being of every essent consists in its being represented. Further, *cogito* is always *cogito me cogitare;* every 'I think (represent)' is at the same time a representing of oneself as representing. It is of the nature of representation as such to incorporate within it the reference to the representing 'I' for which it is a representation and which itself *is* as represented in what it represents. The ego *is* as representing (*sum cogitans*) and as itself a representation of such representing. As Heidegger remarks,[58] "*sum res cogitans* does not mean that I am a thing

57. *Nietzsche II,* p. 162.
58. *Ibid.,* p. 164.

endowed with the property of thinking; it means that I am an essent whose mode of *being* consists in representing, such that this re-presenting (*Vorstellen,* putting in front of oneself) puts, at the same time, the representing 'I' itself in the position of being represented." Man, in quest of the certitude of what he knows and of himself as knowing, thus becomes the subject, the underlying basis and ground of everything that is, in terms of whose representing activity the Being of everything is determined and for whom everything is an object, including himself. This thorough subjectivity is at the same time extreme objectivity. The essent is objectivized by virtue of a re-presenting which aims at holding any thing that is before oneself so that calculating man can, in his concern for certitude, secure and be certain of the essent. This conception of the Being of essents as objectivity of representation and of truth as certitude was for the first time developed in the metaphysics of Descartes, Heidegger says, and modern metaphysics in its entirety, not excluding Nietzsche, moves and keeps within the perspective opened up by Descartes in his interpretation of the essent and of truth. Descartes marks "the beginning of the consummation of Western metaphysics", a beginning of which the far-reaching metaphysical significance emerges with growing clarity and force in the views of succeeding philosophers.

The subjectivistic trend in modern metaphysics is deepened still further in Leibniz's conception of the subject as *ens percipiens et appetens.* The Being of what is (i.e. the presence of the present) manifests itself not only as representation but as will, which henceforth is an essential aspect of the way Being is understood in modern times right up to Nietzsche, by whom it is explicitly recognized as the only reality. Leibniz's conception of representation, the true *subiectum,* which is at the same time force (*vis primitiva activa*) and is characterized by the synthetic function of bringing into a unity all that is (Being as unifying ground, *Logos*), prepares the way not only for Kant but is destined to constitute "the historical foundation of the modern period."[59] The Principle of Sufficient Reason, after its long period of incubation, at last emerges into clear and explicit formulation by Leibniz and philosophy, conceiving truth as certainty, forthwith becomes a quest for the "conditions of the possibility of"; thinking comes into its own in the shape of Reason.[60] The name of Leibniz stands, Heidegger says, not for a past system of philosophy but "designates the contemporaneity of a thinking of which the full impact has yet to be endured. . . . Only when we blance back at what Leibniz thinks can we realize how very much the present era, called the Atomic age, is under the domination of the *principium reddendae rationis sufficientis*."[61] In Leibniz, Being reveals itself as Ground and as Reason, as the very principle of the calculability of essents and their subjugation by man.

Plato interpreted Being (presence) as *idea,* consisting of the 'what' of anything, and the Idea as *agathon,* enabling it to be what it is; with Descartes, the *idea* becomes the *perceptum* of a *perceptio,* a representation. The *agathon* character of the *idea,* i.e., Being as enabling and rendering possible, as ground, having been brought once again to light by Leibniz, manifests itself in all its power in the Kantian metaphysics. The innermost core of the history of modern philosophy, Heidegger says,[62] consists of the process by which Being acquires its indisputable character of being essentially the condition of the possibility of essents, i.e., in the modern sense, of what is represented, i.e., of what stands opposite, i.e., of objects. The decisive step in this process is taken by the metaphysics of Kant, the peak or *centre* to which the subjectivism of the modern period, initiated by Descartes, leads

---

59. *Ibid.,* p. 442.
60. Cf. *Der Satz Vom Grund,* passim; the whole of this book is devoted, by way of a continuous discussion of the Principle of Sufficient Reason, to the philosophy of Leibniz and is important also for the elucidation of Heidegger's conception of the destiny of Being (*Seinsgeschick*) and of the history of Being (*Seinsgeschichte*) in relation to the history of thought.
61. *Ibid.,* p. 65.
62. *Nietzsche II,* pp. 230 f.

up and which points beyond to the speculative-dialectical interpretation of Being as the absolute concept by Hegel.[63] The basic
metaphysical position of Kant finds expression in the fundamental principle, the "supreme principle" upon which the whole
of the Transcendental Philosophy rests (as H. J. Paton describes
it and as Kant himself explicitly recognizes). In its final formulation the principle runs: "The conditions of the *possibility of experience* in general are likewise conditions of the *possibility of
the objects of experience.*"[64] In the *Critique of Pure Reason,*

63. Cf. *Nietzsche II*, p. 231; also *Kants These über das Sein*, p. 36. The
central place (*die Mitte*) that Heidegger assigns to Kant in the history of
modern thought is reflected in his unceasing preoccupation with Kant in his
own thinking. Apart from the major work *Kant und das Problem der
Metaphysik*, written during the *Being and Time* phase, scattered discussions
of Kant's views can be found in most of his later writings. Heidegger's latest
published work (1962), *Kants These über das Sein*, an essay, and *Die Frage
nach dem Ding*, a full-sized book, is devoted entirely to Kant. See also the
report of the discussion with Ernst Cassirer at the Davos Conference in:
Ergänzungen zu einer Heidegger-Bibliographie by Guido Schneeberger.
H. J. Pos gives an interesting account of the encounter between the two
philosophers at Davos in his "Recollections of Ernst Cassirer" (*The Philosophy of Ernst Cassirer,* ed. by Schilpp). A less biased and more detailed
account has been recently provided by Carl Hamburg ("A Cassirer-Heidegger Seminar" in *Philosophy and Phenomenological Research,* XXV, 2.) who
also gives a full translation of the discussion-report in Schneeberger. *Die
Frage nach dem Ding* is subtitled, *Zu Kants Lehre von den Transzendentalen Grundsätzen* (on Kant's doctrine of Transcendental Principles) and
is in the main a study of Chap. II (System of all Principles of Pure
Understanding) of Book II (Analytic of Principles) of the Transcendental
Analytic in the *Critique of Pure Reason,* thus making good what was lacking
in *Kant und das Problem der Metaphysik,* as Heidegger says. In the perspective of the inquiry into the thingness of a thing, i.e., of the *a priori* determination of the most general characteristics of the Being of an essent, Heidegger considers this as the very heart and core of the whole work, in accordance with Kant's own innermost intentions. Heidegger's procedure in
this book is one of straightforward exegesis; the implicit and the unsaid in
Kant's view of Being is brought out in the recent essay mentioned above.
The exegesis is, nevertheless, one which seeks to go beyond the one-sided-
ness and bias of the Idealistic and the Neo-Kantian interpretations.

64. *Critique of Pure Reason,* A 158, B 197. About this sentence, Heidegger writes (*Die Frage nach dem Ding,* p. 143), "He who grasps this
sentence, grasps Kant's *Critique of Pure Reason.* He who grasps the latter,
knows not just a book in the literature of philosophy but has a grasp of the
basic attitude characterizing our historical existence, which we can neither
circumvent, nor leap over nor disavow in any other way. We must, on the
contrary, by appropriating and transforming it, bring it to a decision in the
future."

Kant's aim is to discover how ontological or tra. knowledge (the *a priori* synthesis) is possible. Such kno. concerned, not with the essent as such but, transcendi. ...., with the possibility of a prior comprehension of its Being, with the ontological constitution of the essent, i.e., with the structure of transcendence. "The supreme principle of all synthetic judgments", quoted above, sums up this structure as the unity of the two elements it mentions, experience and the objects of experience. In order that an object should be given, there must occur a prior "turning oneself toward" it, in the form of the ontological synthesis, of which the core, according to Heidegger, is constituted by the transcendental synthesis of the imagination. This turning-oneself-toward is the condition of the possibility of experiencing an object. In the second place, the object itself must be rendered possible by a pre-given horizon in which it may appear. This horizon is the condition of the possibility of the object in respect of its objectivity (that it can stand opposite us, confront us). As Heidegger puts it,[65] "The turning oneself-toward and letting (the object) stand-opposite as such fashions the horizon of objectivity in general. . . . The transcendence is in itself ekstatic-horizonal." The transcendental object, with which ontological knowledge is concerned, is not an essent hidden behind the phenomenon but is the correlate of the unity of apperception, the X as Kant calls it; it is no thing at all but sheer horizon. The X is "object in general", i.e. the horizon of objectivity, the transcendence in and through which the Being of essents manifests itself *a priori*.

It is, Heidegger holds, the transcendental imagination which primarily renders possible such ontological knowledge by building, prior to all experience of objects, the pure schema or view of a horizon of objectivity as such, the horizon of 'constant presence' in which an object may manifest itself as present. Heidegger further suggests that it is the faculty of the imagination that constitutes the 'hidden' common root of the Sensibility and

65. *Kant und das Problem der Metaphysik,* p. 111 (E.T., p. 123).

Understanding; he identifies the transcendental imagination, as Kant himself failed explicitly to do, with primordial Time, which constitutes and generates time in the modalities of past, present and future through the operation of the three-fold synthesis. Without being himself explicitly aware of it, Kant has brought together Time and the 'I think' and identified them; the pure self, i.e., the finite human subjectivity, is essentially of the nature of time. Kant was bound to light upon time as the root determination of finite transcendence because the understanding of Being in Dasein, by itself as it were, projects Being in terms of time. And he was bound at the same time, Heidegger adds, to be carried back from the vulgar concept of time to the transcendental understanding of time as pure self-affection, which in its essence is one with pure apperception and in this unity renders possible the pure sensuous Reason in its wholeness. Unknown explicitly to the author, "time in its essential unity with the transcendental imagination acquires a central metaphysical function in the *Critique of Pure Reason*."[66] Had Kant realized the implications of this, the dominating position of reason and understanding, the age-old pre-eminence of 'Logic' in metaphysics including his own concept of a 'transcendental logic' taken as something absolute, would have been thoroughly shaken and become questionable. But in the second edition of the *Critique of Pure Reason*, Kant gives back to the Understanding its dominating place, with the consequence that metaphysics becomes, with Hegel, more radically 'Logic' than ever before.[67] If only Kant

66. *Ibid.*, p. 219 (E.T., p. 252).
67. From another direction this is also the conclusion of Heidegger's second book on Kant. Kant determines the nature of human knowledge so that thought becomes subservient to intuition, thus losing its old supremacy. This radically transforms the nature of thinking and hence of logic. But as Heidegger remarks, it was not within the power of Kant to realize this fully and work it out, for that would have meant nothing short of jumping over his own shadow. "This no one can do. But the uttermost exertion in making this forbidden attempt—this is the decisive and basic movement of the act of thinking. In Plato, in, in Leibniz, above all in Kant, finally in Schelling and Nietzsche, we can observe in different ways this basic movement. Hegel

had seen that the horizon of transcendence is constituted by the pure schemata regarded as transcendental time determinations, he would have concluded, as Heidegger does in *Being and Time,* that the ontological structure of essents, i.e., their Being, is essentially rooted in Time. The possibility of ontological knowledge is shown, in Kant, to be grounded in the structure of transcendence, i.e., of the finite subjectivity of the human subject. Kant, "who was alive, in his philosophizing, to the problem of the possibility of metaphysics as no one before him or since," shrank back, Heidegger says, from explicitly recognizing the transcendental imagination (Time) as the ground of ontological knowledge because to have done so would have meant abandoning the firm ground of pure reason on which he himself stood and because it would have forced him to go beyond metaphysics itself to its true ground in the truth of Being as such.

"Kant is the first," says Heidegger,[68] "to raise once again, since the philosophy of the Greeks, the question of the Being of essents as a question to be unfolded." In accordance with the dominant tendency of the age, his thinking moves in the dimension of Reason, the faculty of representing something as something. It is the dimension of subjectivity, in which what is *is* only as an object for a subject. The certifying ground, the ultimate *a priori* condition of the possibility of objects is the objectivity, the objectness, of objects. The conception of objectivity as constituting the Being of all essents which can be experienced, of objectivity for rational subjectivity, is the view of Being implicit in Kant's thinking, for, according to him, it is only in the light of a prior glimpse of Being as objectivity that anything can appear at all *as* an object. Being, i.e., the presence of the present, reveals itself in the

---

alone has apparently succeeded in jumping over this shadow—but only by eliminating the shadow, i.e., the finitude of man, and leaping into the Sun itself. Hegel has passed over the shadow which does not mean that he has leapt over it. And yet every philosopher *must* want to do this. In this 'must' lies his vocation. The longer the shadow, the more far-reaching is the spring." (*Die Frage nach dem Ding,* pp. 117 f.; E.T., pp. 150 f.).

68. *Der Satz vom Grund,* p. 131.

Kantian philosophy in the character of objectivity (standing opposite) as against the way the Greeks encountered the essent as facing them in its own character as constant presence. The original and basic conception of Being as presence is presupposed and implied in the Kantian determination of the essent as an object of experience; objectivity is the form in which the presence of the present appears in the age of subjectivity. The supreme principle of Kant's metaphysics, quoted earlier, says, according to Heidegger, "that the conditions of the possibility of representing (vor-stellen) what is represented are at the same time, i.e., none other than, the conditions of the possibility of what is represented. They constitute the representedness which is the essence of objectivity, i.e., of the Being of essents. The supreme principle says: Being is representedness. Representedness, further, is a kind of being handed over or delivered, such that the representing self can be secure of what is thus presented and brought to stand. Security is found in certitude, which is how the nature of truth is determined."[69] The connection between Being (eon, understood as presence) and Unity (hen) or the logos as gathering together and disclosing, left unexplained by the Greeks, appears in Kant in the form of the supreme principle of the Synthetic Unity of Apperception, which renders possible both the objectivity of the object as well as the object as such. The unity is conceived, however, as one of synthesis (sym = together; thesis = positing). The logos is here shifted and transferred to the 'I' as subject and yet, as apperception, it remains in contact with affection through the senses. The subjectivity of man is, with Kant, not yet absolute but still remains a subjectivity of finitude.[70]

The transcendental method is the inquiry not into objects but into the nature of their objectivity (i.e., their Being) and hence into the subjectivity of Reason, for which it is objectivity and in which it is rooted. And it is further an inquiry which is itself, as

69. *Nietzsche II*, p. 231.
70. *Kants These über das Sein*, p. 18.

Heidegger notices in his later phase, part of objectivity, a manifestation of the way Being reveals itself as the objectivity of the object of experience. The transcendental method is itself a mode of representation springing from the subjectivity of Reason in which Being itself, in revealing itself as objectivity, conceals itself *as* Being to the utmost degree.[71] The self-certitude of knowledge through representing the essent in its Being as objectivity, characteristic of modern subjectivism, finds expression in Kant's doctrine of Reason as assuring itself both of itself in its self-legislative supremacy as well as of its object by prescribing its nature to it. But in his doctrine of the transcendental imagination Kant has also for the first time seen and realized in his thinking the inventive or creative nature of Reason, as Heidegger points out,[72] thus preparing the way for the conception of Absolute Reason in the metaphysics of the German Idealists. "The categories of reason are horizons of imaginative creation (*Ausdichtung*) through which what is encountered is provided with a free and open area, placed within which, and from out of which, it becomes capable of appearing as something stable, as that which stands opposite (*Gegenstand*)." Schematization is the essential creative core of Reason, of thinking as it appears in the form of reckoning and calculation to guarantee certitude in the realm of what is by positing it as object. Kant himself speaks of Being as what is posited in transcendental reflexion, in the representation of representation, thus conceiving Being in terms of an act of the human subjectivity. In this respect, Kant only follows to its logical end the central tendency of the whole history of philosophy, i.e., the determination of Being regarded as presence in terms of thinking as a representation of what is.[73] But the Being of what is, not being itself an essent, cannot be grasped by representational

71. *Der Satz vom Grund*, p. 137.
72. *Nietzsche I*, p. 584.
73. Cf. *Kants These über das Sein*, in which Heidegger discusses Kant's statement that Being is not a real predicate but the pure positing of a thing (*Critique of Pure Reason*, A 598, B 626).

thinking, nor itself be adequately characterized in terms of constant presence, of simple givenness, of the 'is'. Hence the need to reopen the question of Being again and to explore the possibility of giving utterance to it, not in terms of thinking, nor of an essent of any kind but in terms of its own self, i.e., of the temporality that has been lying concealed within the view of Being as constant presence.

With all his subjectivism, Kant never lost sight of the finitude of Reason and of man's knowledge, a finitude which is not due merely, or primarily, to the fact that human knowledge is subject to fickleness, inaccuracy and error. Finitude, Heidegger points out,[74] is inherent in the very essence of knowledge, for man's knowledge is not, like divine knowledge, *intuitus originarius* (creative knowledge) but is necessarily receptive and dependent upon something given to it and, *therefore,* also in need of the activity of thinking. "Thinking as such is hence the seal of finitude." The attack against the thing-in-itself, which Reason cannot assimilate into itself and upon which it is dependent, launched by the German Idealists, is based on a growing forgetfulness of Kant's basic insight into the finitude of man's knowledge. This forgetfulness, in turn, results in the transformation of metaphysics, which is an expression of man's need for ontological knowledge, i.e., of his finitude, into Logic as Hegel conceives it in the form of Absolute Knowledge: "Logic is accordingly to be conceived as the system of pure reason, as the realm of pure thought. This is the realm of Truth as it is in and for itself, without any veil. Its content, one may therefore say, is the representation of God as He is in His eternal essence before the creation of nature and of a finite spirit."[75] The quest for the real as the other to thought culminates here in the undisputed sovereignty of thought as the only reality, with nothing to limit it and completely transparent to itself and so in full possession of truth, indeed as Truth itself.

74. *Kant und das Problem der Metaphysik,* p. 31 (E.T., p. 30).
75. *Wissenschaft der Logik I,* p. 31.

Philosophy, Hegel said, comes to port, the secure haven of self-consciousness, with Descartes.[76] But, as Heidegger remarks[77], it comes into full possession of the land, where it has since made itself at home, only with Hegel, who conceives the unshakable certitude of thought as the Absolute itself. Philosophy, according to Hegel, is the actual knowledge of what truly is, actual being understood in the sense of the Aristotelian interpretation of presence as *energeia,* subsequently transformed into *actualitas* and objectivity and the latter understood as spirit and self-consciousness. Real or actual knowledge is absolute knowledge of the Absolute in its absoluteness, i.e., the certitude of the spirit in its unconditioned self-awareness. The Absolute is not something external to knowledge, regarded as a means—instrument or medium—for grasping it. The Absolute is already present with us and our attempt to know it is already illuminated by its *parousia.* For Hegel, philosophy is science or ascertained knowledge (*Wissenschaft*), the unconditioned certitude of knowledge in self-consciousness. The subjectivity of the subject lies in its representational relation to the object and so to itself. Representation presents the object by representing it to the subject, a representation in which the subject as such presents itself. The absolute self-certitude of such presence (in presentation) is the absoluteness of the Absolute, the absolute certainty of Spirit as self-consciousness, which is realized in philosophy as absolute knowledge or science. Truth, understood previously as correspondence and so as an attribute of representation, becomes with Hegel certitude and identical with representing itself. Knowledge, with its certitude immanent in itself, severs itself from its relation to objects; representation liberates and absolves itself completely, as Heidegger puts it, from its objective reference and in this independence of self-representation attains to total absoluteness.

76. The following account is based on Heidegger's essay, "Hegels Begriff der Erfahrung" in *Holzwege,* a commentary on the sixteen paragraphs of Hegel's "Introduction" to his *Phenomenology of Mind.*
77. *Holzwege,* p. 118 (E.T., p. 27).

The *Phenomenology of Mind*, which gives an exposition of knowledge as a phenomenon (appearing in the original sense of *phainesthai*), does not describe so much the passage of the mind from the natural consciousness to absolute knowledge and is not so much, Heidegger says, an *itinerarium mentis in Deum* as itself a manifestation of ascertained knowledge, as the emergence of Science itself. Hegel's distinction between the natural consciousness and real knowledge does not imply, according to Heidegger, that the former is 'mere' appearance; it is the consciousness which is untrue, not in the sense of being false or illusory, but as the not yet perfectly true, being driven forward towards its own truth by the power of the will of the Absolute. The natural consciousness is itself a mode of knowledge (*Bewusstsein*, being in the state of having known) and as consciousness, it is presence (Being) in the mode of a gathering together of representations, i.e. as subjectivity. It is not real knowledge in the sense that it represents only the essent, paying no heed to the essent in its Being. But the natural consciousness is able to represent the essent only because, without explicitly knowing it, it has already represented to itself the Being of essents in a general and indeterminate way. As opposed to actual knowledge, which has the Being of essents as its object, it is only, as Hegel says, a notion of knowledge, not real knowledge assured of the actuality of the actual. The natural consciousness, Heidegger asserts, is not necessarily coincident with the sensuous consciousness; it is a confinement, not to the perceptual, but to *any* kind of immediate object it may represent, be it the nonsensible entities of logic and reason, be it the supersensible entities of the spirit. Representation as such is the hallmark of the natural consciousness. Consciousness itself is neither the natural consciousness taken by itself nor real knowledge taken by itself but the original unity of both, in and for itself. Consciousness itself is the unrest of its own self-differentiation into natural and real knowing and thus contains in itself, itself *is*, the principle of its movement beyond the natural.

The object of consciousness, as immediately present in representation and without any reference to the act or agent of the representation is called by Hegel Being, which for him means the essent. Being in this sense is for him what is not yet, really and in truth. Being has for him always this narrow sense of 'mere Being' because what truly is, is the *ens actu,* the actual, of which the actuality consists in the knowledge of the certitude fully aware of itself; the latter alone 'is' the true and the whole Reality. Being, supposed to have been left behind in absolute knowledge thus comes back again, though, as Heidegger comments, Hegelian 'Science' takes no notice of this fact. In contradistinction to Hegel's usage, Heidegger uses the word 'Being' for what Hegel, with Kant, calls objectivity, as well as for what he conceives to be the truly actual and what he calls the actuality of the spirit. As he remarks,[78] "We interpret the *einai,* Being, of the Greeks not like Hegel in terms of its view as the objectivity of the immediate representation of a subjectivity that has not yet found itself, i.e., not in terms of subjectivity, but in terms of the Greek *aletheia,* as presence in and through unhiddenness," a presence (*ousia, Anwesen*) which has its basis in an as yet unthought character of time of which the true nature has yet to reveal itself. As Heidegger remarks, according to his own usage Hegel should not, strictly speaking, apply the word Being, as he is inevitably led to do, to the reality of the real, to the spirit which, for him, is self-consciousness (*Selbst-bewusst-sein, being*-self-conscious). Being, in Heidegger's sense, discloses itself in Hegel, at the same time concealing its own truth, as the absoluteness of the Absolute.

Hegel realizes that the distinctions between knowing and its object, between the object and its objectivity, between knowing and the knowledge of this knowing, all fall within consciousness itself. But, Heidegger points out, because Hegel's thinking moves within the sphere of metaphysical representation, he is unable to grasp the real significance of these distinctions, ultimately trace-

78. *Ibid.,* p. 142 (E.T., p. 69).

able to the unnoticed ambiguity of the *on* (which means both the essent and its Being) on which metaphysics itself is based. In terms of his own distinction between the ontic and the onto-logical, Heidegger designates the natural consciousness as the ontic consciousness, primarily concerned with representing the essent, its immediate object. "But," he says,[79] "representing the ob-ject is at the same time representing it, though without explicit awareness, *as* object. This consciousness has gathered together the object in its objectivity and is therefore ontological. But, while representing the object it does not direct itself to objec-tivity as such; the natural consciousness is ontological and yet not quite such. We may, therefore, describe the ontic consciousness as pre-ontological. As such, the natural consciousness *is* the implicit distinction between the ontically true and ontological truth." Consciousness *is* itself as this distinction and hence, as natural, not cut off from the ontological but resting on it, and yet confined mostly to the ontic, not going behind to the truth of its true object, the essent. This truth, underlying its true immediate object, is indeed not something hidden behind or under the ob-ject, as Heidegger puts it, but is rather the prior, fore-given horizon of light within which objects can at all show themselves and be known as such. What Hegel calls the self-examination of consciousness is the process of continuous comparison between the ontic and the pre-ontological by which consciousness comes to its own real Being as fully manifest ontological consciousness. This is the dialectical movement which consciousness executes on itself—on its knowledge as well as on its object—in the sense that out of it the new and true object arises, which Hegel calls ex-perience.[80] This is Hegel's term for the Being of what is, the full presence, appearance or epiphany of consciousness, of the sub-jectivity of the subject. The basic feature of consciousness is to be already what, at the same time, it is not yet, to hold itself in the not-yet of the already, to be on its way to that. As Heidegger puts

79. *Ibid.*, p. 163 (E.T., p. 108).
80. See *The Phenomenology of Mind,* trans. by Baillie, p. 142.

it, "The Being (presence) of consciousness consists in its self-moving character. The Being which Hegel conceives as experience is fundamentally characterized by movement."[81] This movement is dialectical in the sense of a continuing dialogue between the natural and the real, between the ontic and the ontological knowledge, through and as which consciousness gathers itself together and realizes itself in its complete truth, the absolute notion. The movement culminates in experience, the self-manifestation of consciousness as self-representation, "the presentation of the absolute subject as representation, and thus as absolving itself fully." Experience, Heidegger continues, "is the subjectivity of the absolute subject. Experience is the presentation of absolute representation and as such the *parousia* (complete presence) of the Absolute. Experience is the absoluteness of the Absolute," the way consciousness *is* as presence and appearance. Experiencing is the mode in which consciousness sets forth on its ascent to its own notion—as what it truly is—reaching out for and attaining to its truth, in which consummation its own nature as appearance shines forth. "Experiencing is a mode of presence, i.e., of Being. Through experience, emergent consciousness comes into its own presence, abiding in itself as thus emerging forth. Experience gathers consciousness together into the collectedness of its own essence . . . the truth of what is true, the Being of what is, the shining forth of what emerges."[82] In experience thus conceived, there is a reversal (*Umkehrung*, turning round) of consciousness from the habitual representation of what appears to its appearance, from the essent to its Being, a reversal or conversion which is due to our own agency (*unsere Zutat*) in the sense that, setting aside our private opinions and predilections, we *let* that which appears (consciousness) shine forth by itself and appear as it is in its own Being, impelled by the Absolute which, as Will, realizes itself in experience. The exposition of the experience of consciousness in the *Phenomenol-*

81. *Holzwege*, p. 167 (E.T., p. 116).
82. *Ibid.*, p. 170 (E.T., p. 120).

ogy of Mind is itself the fulfilment of the Absolute's will, a manifestation of the way man is related in his essence to the Absolute,
as fulfilling its will, part of the Absolute's *parousia.*

According to Heidegger, the exposition of the emergence of
absolute knowledge in the *Phenomenology* represents Hegel's
ontology of the actual consciousness in its actuality, of the subject as subject, i.e., of the true essent as Hegel conceives it in its
wholeness. The Science or absolute knowledge of which this is
only a part leads on to its proper completion in his *Science of
Logic,* which exhibits, Heidegger says, not the self-manifestation
of the Absolute, but how the Absolute is present to itself in its
absoluteness, the self-comprehension of the Absolute in absolute
notion. This is the theology (or theiology, as Heidegger prefers to
call it) of the Absolute. The Science of the Absolute, Heidegger
says,[83] is for Hegel, about the time when the *Phenomenology of
Mind* was first published, "the onto-theological knowledge of the
true essent as essent. In its entirety, it unfolds itself in its two
aspects in the *Science of the Phenomenology of Mind* and in the
Science of Logic. Hegel's *Science of Logic* is at this time conceived as the Theology of the Absolute and not as Ontology. The
form taken by the latter is the *Science of the Experience of Consciousness* (the title under which the *Phenomenology* was first
published in 1807). The *Phenomenology* is the 'first Science', the
Logic the Science proper, within the first philosophy, constituting
the truth of essents as such. This Truth is of the essence of
metaphysics." Hegel dropped the first title of the *Phenomenology,* Heidegger suggests, perhaps because he shrank back from
acknowledging the original force of the word 'experience', with
its suggestion of reaching out and arriving, a mode of presence,
of *einai,* of Being." The term 'phenomenology', which was substituted for it, carries, nevertheless, the same meaning: the
phainesthai, the self-emergence or appearance of the absolute
subject, the spirit. The Phenomenology of the Mind is the ap-

83. *Ibid.,* p. 184 (E.T., pp. 142 f.).

pearance of the Spirit, as gathered together in the dialogue between the ontic and the ontological consciousness, in its *parousia.*

Both the *Phenomenology* and the *Logic* are, Heidegger points
out, theologies of the Absolute, the first, of the Absolute in its
parousia (i.e., its presence with us) and the second, of the Absolute in its absoluteness. And both are ontologies, worldly, inasmuch as they represent the worldliness of the world, the essent
(conceived as subjectivity) in its totality. But, as Heidegger remarks, "the science of absolute knowledge is not the worldly
theology of the world because it secularizes the Christian
Church theology but because it is itself implied in the very
essence of ontology." Hegel's metaphysics demonstrates the metaphysical character of theology itself and provides confirmation of
the essentially onto-theological character of metaphysics, as it has
developed since the age of the Greeks. True to the metaphysical
tradition, Hegel's thinking is concerned, as Heidegger points out
elsewhere,[84] with the essent as such and as a whole, with the
movement of Being from its emptiness and abstraction to its
concrete fullness. Like all metaphysics, it thinks the essent as
such, i.e., in general, and the Being of the essent as the unity of
the most general, conceived as the most universal basis to which
one can penetrate; and it thinks the essent in its totality and its
Being as the unity of this whole, conceived as the foundation on
which all that is can be grounded, i.e., as the highest Being. It is
ontology and theology in one—the *logos* of the most universal
Being and of the highest (*theion*). For Hegel, the true Science or
metaphysics is 'Logic', not because it has thought for its theme,
but because for him, too, the main concern of thinking is with
Being, as presence, in the form of the ancient *Logos,* the ground
which provides the foundation, with Being conceived as ground.

Hegel declares that the goal of philosophy, in its dialectical
progress from the abstract universal, Being, to the full concrete-
ness of Absolute spirit, is truth, finally reached in his own

84. See *Identität und Differenz,* pp. 53–55 (E.T., pp. 56–58).

Science.[85] Taking truth in the sense of the absolute certitude of the self-knowledge of the absolute subject, Hegel does not realize that just this certitude itself is dependent upon truth in a more fundamental sense, upon truth understood as disclosure or unhiddenness, *aletheia*. Whether in the initial emergence and manifestation of Spirit as pure Being or in the final self-manifestation of Spirit as Absolute Idea, truth as prior disclosure or unhiddenness must already be presupposed. And this leads, Heidegger says, to "the further question whether the unhiddenness has its seat in spirit, conceived as absolute subject, or whether, on the contrary, unhiddenness is itself the locus and a pointer to the location in which alone such a thing as a representing subject can 'be' what it is."[86] Thinking of historical reality in terms of Being conceived as absolute subjectivity and approaching it in the speculative, dialectical manner, Hegel, despite his taking 'the kingdom of pure truth' as the goal of philosophy, is debarred from the awareness that truth in the primordial sense of unhiddenness (*aletheia*) still remains the Unthought of philosophy, the mystery that it has always been. "Hegel takes Being, when he conceives it as indeterminate immediacy, as what is posited by the determining, conceiving subject. Accordingly, he cannot allow Being, in the Greek sense of *einai,* to be detached from its connection with the subject and set it free in its own essence. The latter, however, is presence, i.e., a coming out of concealment into unhiddenness, into presence."[87] *Aletheia,* which has its sway even before philosophy proper begins, still remains a mystery. Being can reveal itself as presence only with the prior occurrence of unhiddenness. But the latter, *aletheia,* still remains unthought in its essence.[88]

85. See for this paragraph, *Hegel und die Griechen* in the *Gadamer-Festschrift.*
86. *Ibid.,* p. 53.
87. *Ibid.,* p. 54.
88. As with all the other philosophers considered in this chapter, only an outline of the way Heidegger interprets Hegel is given here. The wider question of his relation to Hegel, to Plato and Aristotle, to Medieval thought and Christianity, to Kant and Nietzsche cannot be dealt with here. How

Hegel's metaphysics of absolute knowledge as Spirit, according to Heidegger, marks the beginning of the last stage in the development of metaphysical thought but not yet its final consummation. Although unconditioned certitude has come into its own in Hegel as absolute actuality, the will, implicit in the conception of Reality since Leibniz and implied in Kant's as well as Hegel's concept of Reason, is yet to emerge explicitly and be acknowledged expressly as the Being of what is.[89] The consummation of metaphysics, the ultimate stage of its development, occurs in the thinking of Nietzsche, with whom the possibilities latent in metaphysics since its Platonic inception are fully explored and exhausted. The full implications of the awareness, present in Leibniz, Kant, Fichte, Schelling, Hegel and Schopenhauer, that the Will constitutes the Being of all that is, are drawn out and carried to their logical conclusion by Nietzsche, who saw, and thought through, as no thinker before him, the dark shadow cast over the present and the coming world-history by the Nihilism inherent in the metaphysical (i.e., the Platonic-Christian) tradition of the West. He conceived his own work as a reaction against and an overcoming of metaphysics, a fight against Platonism. But, like all counter movement, like everything 'anti-', as Heidegger puts it, it remains itself necessarily stuck up in what it attacks. "Nietzsche's countermove against metaphysics is, as its mere inversion, itself ensnared in metaphysics, inextricably and without a way out left; it has cut itself off from its own essence and, as itself metaphysical, become incapable of recognizing its own essential nature."[90] Nietzsche's philosophy is

much of the thought of the past, and in what form, is alive in Heidegger's own philosophy is also a question for the future. For Heidegger's relation to Hegel in particular, see Jan van der Meulen, *Heidegger und Hegel* (2nd ed., 1954).

89. Cf. *Vorträge und Aufsätze*, pp. 76, 114.

90. *Holzwege*, p. 200; cf. *Platons Lehre von der Wahrheit*, p. 37: "The concept of value, emerging in the 19th century as the inner consequence of the modern conception of truth, is the latest as well as the weakest offspring of the *agathon*. . . . In so far as Nietzsche's thought is dominated by the idea of value . . . without awareness of its metaphysical origin, Nietzsche is also the most unbridled Platonist in the history of Western metaphysics."

itself a manifestation of the last epoch of metaphysics, the entire history of which is itself one long drawn out epoch in the history of Being and of the way Being has revealed and dispensed itself to man through its own withdrawal.

Seeking to take Nietzsche seriously as a thinker, not just as one who philosophized existenzielly (which, Heidegger says, he never did), Heidegger finds that his thinking is no less pointed, detached and stringent than the thinking of Aristotle. "The customary, but none the less questionable, juxtaposition of Nietzsche with Kierkegaard," Heidegger remarks,[91] "fails to recognize, due to a failure to appreciate the true nature of thinking, that as a metaphysical thinker Nietzsche has his place secure near Aristotle," which cannot be said about Kierkegaard, although the latter refers to Aristotle more frequently. It is widely held that Nietzsche is not a strict thinker but a poet-philosopher; that he cannot be counted among the philosophers, who excogitate only abstractions, shadowy and remote from life; that if he is at all to be called a philosopher he must be regarded as a 'philosopher of life' (*Lebensphilosoph*) who has at last done away with abstract thinking. This estimate of Nietzsche, Heidegger holds, is utterly mistaken. It was Nietzsche who said, "Abstract thinking is for many hard and a torture,—for me, on favourable days, it is a feast and an intoxication." Nietzsche's philosophy, despite its aphoristic style and unsystematic form, is metaphysics and has its place on "the long course of the age-old leading question of philosophy: What is the essent?"[92] The diverse themes which recur in his thought are linked together by an inner unity and, Heidegger believes, constitute a meaningful pattern which in essence is metaphysical. This, of course, can be seen only if we look at Nietzsche's thought from the perspective of the history of Being, a perspective which was not available to Nietzsche and which, in fact, is accessible only to a thinking that has taken the

91. *Holzwege,* p. 230.
92. *Nietzsche I,* pp. 12 and 14.

leap out of metaphysical thinking and so can see in Nietzsche the final culmination of such thinking.

Heidegger sums up the central concepts of Nietzsche's philosophy in five basic key-terms in his thinking.[93] These are: the Will to Power; Nihilism; the Eternal Recurrence of the Same; the Superman; Justice. Metaphysics is the truth of essents as such in their totality. This truth is the unhiddenness of the 'what' of the essent (the *essentia* or *Seiendheit,* being-ness) as well as of its 'that' (the *existentia,* that and how the essent as a whole is). Further, the truth of essents appears in varying forms, depending on the way the essent is conceived from time to time, being thus historical in its very nature. Finally, according to the way truth appears in any period of its history, it requires a type of humanity which corresponds to it, establishes it, makes it known and preserves it. In Nietzsche's metaphysics, Heidegger says, "The Will to Power names the Being of essents as such, the *essentia* of essents. 'Nihilism' is the name for the history of the truth of essents as thus determined. The 'Eternal Recurrence of the Same' is the way the essent as a whole is, the *existentia* of essents. The 'Superman' refers to the type of man demanded by this whole (as conformable and adequate to it). 'Justice' is the essential character of the truth of essents as Will to Power."[94] Each of these concepts involves the others and must be understood with reference to them. They constitute, in their unity, Nietzsche's metaphysics, his vision of the truth of essents as such in their totality.

The Will to Power, Nietzsche says, is "the innermost essence of Being."[95] Will here must be understood, hence, not in the psychological sense of a mental faculty, but metaphysically, as the basic character, the Being, of the essent as such, in terms of

93. The following account is based on the essay entitled "Nietzsches Metaphysik" in *Nietzsche II.*
94. *Nietzsche II,* p. 260.
95. See Chapters I (*Der Wille zur Macht als Kunst*) and III (*Der Wille zur Macht als Erkenntnis*) of *Nietzsche I* for detailed treatment of the Will to Power.

which Nietzsche comprehends all essents, physical or mental. The will is not any sort of wishing or striving but, fundamentally and in essence, commanding. It is again not something separate and external to power, and the latter is not a goal which the will seeks to attain as something outside it. Both together constitute an indivisible unity, the will to power being the essential character of power itself, which is never a final possession but ceaselessly tends to exceed itself, which *is* as such constant self-enhancement. Power is always, therefore, for more power, power over power, and the will essentially the Will to will. Concerned with its own preservation and increase, the will to power prescribes for itself the conditions which render this possible. The process of Becoming, the movement towards more power in herent in the will to power, secures itself by setting up 'points of view', outlooks, which can be counted upon, and must be reckoned with—the will to power is, as Nietzsche calls it, intrinsically 'perspectivistic'. These points of view are measures and quantities, i.e., values; the 'seeing' characteristic of the will to power is by its very nature a reckoning with values. Value is essentially the point of view employed by "the commanding-calculating seeing of the will to power." Such points of view condition the complex fabric of science (knowledge), art, politics and religion, shapes taken by the will to power, which may, in turn, be themselves called value-structures. "The Will to Power is, in accordance with its innermost nature, a perspectivistic reckoning with the conditions of its possibility, which are as such set up by itself. The Will to Power is in itself value-positing."[96] It is a will that wills values and is itself the valuational principle, and hence the thinking which takes the truth of things as will to power is necessarily a thinking in terms of values. "The metaphysics of the Will to Power—and only that—is properly and necessarily a thinking in terms of values. . . . In such value-thinking consists the self-consciousness of the Will to Power. . . . Value-thinking

96. *Nietzsche II*, p. 272.

is implied in the way the Will to Power is itself, the *subiectum.*
. . . The Will to Power reveals itself as the subjectivity of which
the distinctive mark is evaluative thinking."[97]

Plato, with whom metaphysics begins, conceived the Being of
the essent as idea, the principle of the unity of what is diverse,
and at the same time the good, the enabling or the condition of
the possibility of what is.[98] The ideas, which alone truly are,
belong to the super-sensible realm and viewed from Nietzsche's
metaphysical position they are values. The essent as such in its
totality is comprehended in terms of the super-sensible—whether
understood as the God of Christianity, as the moral law, as Reason, as progress or as the happiness of the many—, the Ideal or,
from Nietzsche's point of view, the highest values. All metaphysics is Platonism, and Christianity, including its modern secularized forms, is 'Platonism for the people'. Taking the concept of
value as the clue to his historical reflection on metaphysics, the
basis of Western history, Nietzsche interprets and examines
metaphysics in terms of the Will to Power as the sole principle of
valuation. He regards all metaphysics as a system of values, but
without explicit recognition of the Will to Power as the supreme
principle. Hence he conceives his own metaphysics of the Will to
Power as providing the "principle of a new scheme of values,"
involving a "revaluation of past values." Such revaluation constitutes the ultimate character of Nihilism. According to Nietzsche,
Nihilism means the devaluing of the highest values. In Heidegger's words, "Nihilism is the process of the devaluation of the
highest values prevailing hitherto. The annulment of these values
is the collapse of what has hitherto been taken as the truth about
the essent as such in its totality . . . the fundamental happening
in the history of the West, a history of which metaphysics has
been the foundation and guiding principle. In so far as meta-

____

97. *Ibid.,* p. 272.
98. On Nihilism, see *Nietzsche II,* Chapters V ("Der Europäische Nihilismus") and VII ("Die Seinsgeschichtliche Bestimmung des Nihilismus");
also the essay, "Nietzsches Wort 'Gott ist Tot'" (in *Holzwege*) and *Zur
Seinsfrage.*

physics has received its peculiar theological mould through Christianity, this devaluation must also be expressed theologically, in the words, 'God is dead'."[99] 'God' means here, Heidegger adds, the supersensible realm in general, the true, eternal world, beyond this earthly one, as the real and only goal, both as conceived by Christian faith and in its secularized form (Conscience, Reason, Progress, the Social Instinct). But though the devaluation of the highest values, the vanishing of all value from the world, is part of the Nihilistic process and the fundamental happening in the history of the West, it does not yet exhaust the full essence of Nihilism. The collapse of the highest values prevailing hitherto demands the setting up of new ones, a revaluation of all values. Hence, Nihilism does not stop short at mere nullity but has a liberating, affirmative character. As a historical process, "Nihilism is a devaluation of the hitherto highest values, aiming at the thorough revaluation of all values"; it implies the total rejection of past values and a grounding of the essent as a whole on entirely different conditions. But, Heidegger points out, "even with this recognition of the affirmative character of European Nihilism we do not come to its innermost core; for Nihilism is neither just *one* historical occurrence nor even the *central* feature of Western history, but is itself the law of this history, its 'logic'."[100] As such, Nihilism manifests itself in a series of stages, beginning with Pessimism, the preliminary form of Nihilism, with its two sub-forms, the pessimism of the weak and the pessimism of the strong. 'Incomplete Nihilism' denies indeed the values hitherto taken as the highest, but only puts new ideals in the place of the old (Communism in place of primitive Christianity; Wagner's music in place of dogmatic Christianity), without abandoning that 'place', the self-subsisting super-sensible dimension, itself. For 'extreme' or complete Nihilism there are no self-

99. *Nietzsche II*, pp. 275 f. Cf. Karl-Heinz Volkmann-Schluck: "Zur Gottesfrage bei Nietzsche" in *Anteile—Martin Heidegger zum 60. Geburtstag.*
100. *Ibid.*, pp. 277 f.

subsistent eternal truths whatever. Extreme Nihilism, in so far as it remains content with such negation, remains 'passive', whereas 'active' Nihilism, rejecting both this world as well as the ideal, super-sensible world, goes on to affirm a new principle of valuation and, as truly liberating man from the bondage of the old, is characterized by Nietzsche as 'ecstatic Nihilism.' "Despite the appearance of being merely negative, it affirms, neither anything given nor an ideal, but rather the 'principle of valuation' itself, the Will to Power,"[101] thus becoming full-fledged and complete, 'classical' Nihilism, as which Nietzsche understands his own metaphysics. Revaluation for Nietzsche does not mean, Heidegger remarks, "that in the old and the same place of the hitherto prevailing values new ones are set up; the term means, in the first place and always, *that the place itself is determined anew*."[102] It is through the "revaluation" that, for the first time, values are conceived *as* values, i.e. as the conditions of the Will to Power. The revaluation is, strictly speaking, a re-thinking of the essent as such in its totality in terms of 'values'.

According to Nietzsche's doctrine, the total worth of the world cannot be evaluated, for it makes no sense to speak of the total value of the essent as a whole which, as Will to Power, sets up values as the condition of its own maintenance and increase.[103] In itself it is worthless, having no intrinsic meaning, aim or purpose. This, however, must be understood not in a merely negative sense but as asserting something positive about *how* the essent as a whole is: the Eternal Recurrence of the Same. This "most difficult of all thoughts", as Nietzsche calls it, must be grasped in its inseparable connection with the Will to Power, as characterizing, together with the latter, the essent as a whole. As Heidegger expresses it, "The essent, which *as such* has the funda-

101. *Ibid.*, p. 281.
102. *Ibid.*, p. 282.
103. On the Eternal Recurrence, see the detailed treatment in Chapter II ("Die Ewige Wiederkehr des Gleichen") and in Chapter IV ("Die Wiederkunft des Gleichen und der Wille zur Macht") of *Nietzsche* (in Vols. 1 and 2 respectively).

mental nature of the Will to Power, can be, *as a whole*, only the Eternal Recurrence of the Same. And conversely, the essent, which *as a whole* is the Eternal Recurrence of the Same, must *as essent as a whole*, i.e., to the process of Becoming, its unique state The values or ends set up by the Will to Power are not something "in themselves", outside this Will, with the attainment of which it can come to rest; these ends, points of resistance or hindrance essential for the operation of power, are set up by the will and are immanent in it. The Will to power as power beyond power is intrinsically a perpetual return into itself, giving thus to the essent as a whole, i.e. to the process of Becoming, its unique state of movement, not directed towards any ultimate goal extraneous to itself, and yet ceaselessly moving towards self-imposed ends and so ever returning to itself. Further, the essent as a whole, conceived in its Being as Will to Power, must be a fixed quantity because power, with ceaseless increment inherent in it, cannot increase infinitely in the absence of any surplus, as Heidegger puts it, beyond itself, from which it can feed itself. The world, as power, must not be conceived, Nietzsche says, as unlimited, for it *cannot* be so conceived, the concept of infinite power being self-contradictory. The world is incapable of eternal novelty. Since the essent as such is conceived as Will to Power and hence as eternal becoming which advances towards no pre-determined goal beyond it, and since this eternal becoming is limited as to the possible forms and power-structures in which, as Will, it can manifest itself, therefore, the essent regarded as the Will to Power must be, as a whole, a perpetual return of the same. This circular movement, "the primordial law of the essents as a whole", is the mode of presence (Being) of what is as such ever varying or becoming, but in a way that guarantees the utmost constancy and invariability as a whole. As Heidegger remarks, the Eternal Return is the most unvarying perpetuation of what is ceaselessly varying. In Nietzsche's doctrine, the conception of

104. *Nietzsche II,* p. 284.

Being as constant presence, as old as metaphysics, appears in the guise of the Eternal Recurrence of the Same. "To set the stamp of Being on Becoming—in this lies the highest Will to Power," as Nietzsche says, adding, "that everything returns is the utmost approximation of a world of Becoming to one of Being." The conception of the Eternal Recurrence of the Same, the summit of Nietzsche's metaphysical vision, is, as the truth about the essent in its totality, neither a merely personal experience of this thinker, with its validity confined within the limits of a personal view, nor is it amenable to scientific, empirical demonstration. The Will to Power itself, the basic character of the essent as such, and not a 'Mr. Nietzsche', as Heidegger puts it, sets up and determines the thought of the Eternal Recurrence of the Same.[105]

Neitzsche's conception of the Superman or Overman (as Walter Kaufmann translates *Übermensch* in his *Nietzsche,* finding the English 'superman' misleading) has nothing to do with a supersensible ideal of humanity, nor does it announce the impending emergence somewhere of a 'suprahuman' personality.[106] It is not, Heidegger says, the product of the arrogance of a 'Mr. Nietzsche' and it does not mean the crudely magnified capriciousness of the deeds of violence in the manner common to humanity so far. As against a mere inflating and carrying beyond all bounds of man in his existing character, the Overman marks a reversal of the hitherto prevailing nature of man. The Overman, in Heidegger's words, is man nihilistically

105. For a more detailed account of this central concept of Nietzsche's philosophy, see the brilliant Chapter II of *Nietzsche I.* As Heidegger remarks there (pp. 257–258), "Nietzsche's doctrine of the Eternal Recurrence of the Same is not just one theory about what is among others. It has developed as a result of the most bitter argument with the Platonic-Christian mode of thinking and with the way the latter has worked itself out and developed in the modern age. This mode of thinking is at the same time judged by Nietzsche as the distinctive feature of Western thought and of its history in general." For a criticism of Heidegger's views on this doctrine, see Karl Löwith: *Nietzsches Philosophie der Ewigen Wiederkehr des Gleichen,* pp. 222–225.

106. On the Superman, see also "Wer ist Nietzsches Zarathustra?" in *Vorträge and Aufsätze.*

reversed. He is the type of man who corresponds metaphysically to Nietzsche's vision of the essent, which is as such the Will to Power and in its totality the Eternal Return of the Same. The Overman is the complete negation of the man of the past, of man as shaped by the Platonic world-view and Christian morality, but it is a negation that springs from the affirmation of the Will to Power. In the epoch of 'metaphysics', man is conceived as, and is, in consequence of the way he is related to Being, the rational animal. The Overman represents a denial of this nature of man, but it is a nihilistic denial of this nature in the sense that it merely reverses the relative positions of rationality and animality, making Reason a mere tool in the service of the latter. The metaphysical emergence, in Hegel, of Reason as absolute subjectivity, i.e. as the Being of what is, prepares the ground for the total, nihilistic inversion of the role of Reason in Neitzsche. "The nihilistic denial of the metaphysical primacy, determining what is to count as being, of unconditional Reason—not its complete rejection—is the affirmation of the unconditioned role of the body as the warrant and point of reference for all interpretation of the world."[107] The will, inherent previously in Reason as representing it and in its service, now emerges as dominant, with Reason subservient to it as calculative thought and evaluation. It is transformed into the Will to Power, its own sole lawgiver and the Being of all that is. The subjectivity of the Absolute spirit, though unconditioned, was yet incomplete, but the inversion of rational subjectivity into the subjectivity of the Will is its final consummation. The reversal of the subjectivity of unconditioned representation into the subjectivity of the Will to Power is the overthrow of the primacy of Reason as the guiding principle and arbiter for the conception of what is, a phenomenon described by Nietzsche as the death of the God of Christian morality. The Overman is the necessary consequence of this ultimate, completed subjectivity. With the collapse of the super-sensible realm

107. *Nietzsche II,* p. 300.

in general, there remains, in the midst of essents as such and as a whole, only man who, as the ultimate subject and sole embodiment of representing, value-positing Will, must offer himself to the Will to Power as the abode of its pure presence. The Overman, going beyond the man of the past, is the subject in whom the pure essence of the Will to Power finds its dwelling; in willing itself, the Will to Power must will its own highest condition, the Overman. Man as he was up till now was characterized by Reason as his distinctive mark and was therefore 'the animal not yet fixed in his nature', but as the Overman, with his animality as itself the very essence of the Will to Power, he is at last defined and established in his true nature, the prototype of a humanity in accord with the essent conceived as the unconditioned, completed subjectivity of the Will to Power, fit for absolute mastery over the earth. The Overman is the guardian and the repository of the truth of the essent as such and in its totality, as this truth is determined by the Will to Power and the Eternal Recurrence of the Same.

In Nietzsche's subjectivistic thinking, Truth retains its character of certitude and permanence but in conformity with his nihilistic revaluation, it ceases to be a super-sensible light and becomes, as a condition of the Will to Power, a value.[108] Truth, for him, is a value necessary for the Will to Power and, as producing the illusion of permanence in what is ever a becoming, it is a kind of error. As the condition of the maintenance of the Will to Power, truth is necessary but not sufficient, for the Will to Power is primarily the will, not merely to the retention of power but to its incessant enhancement. For the latter, art alone suffices and hence, for Nietzsche, "art is of greater value than Truth." As 'error', truth also continues to be understood in his thinking as a kind of correspondence. But the original character of truth as *aletheia*, unrecognized but still implicitly present in all modern

---

108. See also *Nietzsche I*, pp. 612–616, for Nietzsche's conception of Truth, where righteousness is also discussed in the section entitled, *Die Wahrheit als Gerechtigkeit.*

thought in a changed, perverted and disguised form, also shines through in Nietzsche's conception of art. The modern liberation of man from truth as certitude of salvation, leading man to seek assurance in himself, shows its real full nature in the metaphysics of the Will to Power. We see here the final overthrow of creative Reason bearing the stamp of the *Logos*—the divine creative power—of Christian theology. Man's new freedom now finds assurance and justification in a new kind of righteousness or justness, a manifestation of the Will to Power itself as setting up conditions of its own preservation and enhancement. In Nietzsche, as Heidegger puts it, Righteousness (*Gerechtigkeit*), "because it is the highest mode of the Will to Power, is the real basis for the determination of the nature of truth. In the metaphysics of the unconditioned and complete subjectivity of the Will to Power, truth exhibits itself as 'righteousness'."[109] In Nietzsche's sense of this term, however, all its associations deriving from Christian, humanistic morality must be excluded. Keeping in view the fact that in the metaphysics of the Will to Power the right can only be what the Will sets up for its own perpetuation, we must understand righteousness as a pure function of Power. "Looking out beyond the petty and narrow perspectives of good and bad", prevailing thus far, righteousness opens out the wholly new point of view from which man is seen as pushing on to absolute mastery over the earth. Nietzsche himself, Heidegger points out, never explicitly realized that and how righteousness is the aspect in which he conceives truth, i.e., the unhiddenness by virtue of which the essent manifests itself as such and in its totality as the Will to Power and the Eternal Recurrence of the Same. "The metaphysics of unconditioned and complete subjectivity, without explicitly saying it, thinks its own nature, i.e., the nature of truth, as righteousness. The truth of essents as such as a whole is accordingly truth about the essent but such that its own nature is determined by the basic character of the essent, i.e.,

109. *Nietzsche II*, p. 325.

by the Will to Power as its highest form."[110] Nietzsche's meta-physics is, as all metaphysics necessarily is, the truth of essents as such and as a whole in a double sense: truth about the essent because truth itself derives from the Being of essents. Such truth is essentially historical in character, each of its historical mani-festations depending upon the way Being reveals itself to thinkers in different ages.

With Nietzsche's philosophy, in which the tradition of Western thinking comes, in an important sense, to a focus and fulfills itself, we come to the end of the metaphysical epoch in the history of that tradition. "The decisive question," Heidegger says, "for him who still can, indeed must, raise a philosophical ques-tion at all at the end of Western philosophy, is not the question about the basic character of the essent, how the Being of essents is to be characterized; the question rather is: What is this Being itself? It is the question about 'the sense of Being', not merely about the Being of essents; and 'sense', moreover, is defined pre-cisely as that in terms of which and by virtue of which Being can at all reveal itself as such and become manifest in its truth."[111] It is to what Heidegger has to say on this question that we, there-fore, turn now.

110. *Ibid.*, p. 332.
111. *Nietzsche I*, p. 26.

chapter four

THE QUESTION OF BEING

"In the treatise *Being and Time,* the question about the sense of Being is posed and developed, *as a question,* for the first time in the history of philosophy."[1] Negatively, it has been shown there that to 'be' is not merely to be simply given or to be the object for a knowing subject, these being themselves derivative modes of Being presupposing a more fundamental sense of the term. Positively, it has been suggested that not merely the being of man but Being as such is inseparably bound up with time. How far and in what sense the notions of truth, of nothingness, of transcendence, of ground and of language are interlinked with that of Being is discussed in subsequent works and answered with some finality. In the writings of the second phase, there is a determined, self-conscious attempt to shed the vestiges of the metaphysical way of conceiving Being, i.e., in terms of and from the point of view of the essent. *An Introduction to Metaphysics* attacks the question of Being directly and may be taken, as Heidegger suggests in the 'Foreword' to the Eighth Edition (1957) of *Being and Time,* as complementary to that work, approaching as it does the question mainly from its historical aspect. Like *Being and Time,* it is introductory, leading on to the problem only, and incomplete, in the sense that it confines itself to showing, in its historical part, how the prevailing conception of Being as "constancy of presence", coming down from the Greeks,

1. *Einführung in die Metaphysik,* p. 64 (E.T., p. 70).

is inadequate. Traditional metaphysics, taking the generality and emptiness of the concept of Being for granted, occupies itself with the essent as such, with the essent in its Being (the *Seiendheit* or being-ness of a being) rather than with Being as such, seeking to fill up the emptiness of Being with notions derived from the side of the essent. Heidegger seeks to demonstrate in this work that 'Being' is not just a universal, the most general concept, and therefore empty of all content but, as the light in which all that is discloses itself to us, is inexhaustible in the richness of its meaning, strangely complex in its structure and a power determinative of man's historical existence. He does this, first, by showing that even the word 'Being', in its grammar and etymology, is not so empty as it sounds and, secondly, by a detailed examination of the Greek conception of Being, and exhibiting how highly determinate it is in its contrast with the notions of Seeming, Becoming and the Ought.

The main reason for the fact that the word 'Being' (Ger. *Sein;* Gr. *einai;* Lat. *esse*) sounds empty and nebulous in its meaning lies, Heidegger explains[2], in the character of its grammar and etymology. The German *das Sein* (Being) is a verbal substantive based on the infinitive *sein* (to be). The infinitive is a word-form that, as it were, cuts off what is meant in it from all determinate relationships of signification, that abstracts from all particular relations. It is an abstract verbal concept, designating only the most general, indeterminate meaning of a verb. And when the abstract infinitive, in the present case *sein* (to be), is transformed into a substantive (*das Sein,* Being), this indefiniteness is further aggravated and the emptiness lying within the infinitive is as it were still more firmly established and stabilized. In addition, the substantive form carries the ineradicable suggestion that what is called 'Being' itself *is,* though obviously only the essent is and not, over and above that, Being also. Thus the term becomes a name for something utterly indeterminate. A consideration of the etymology of the term, however, is more reward-

2. *An Introduction to Metaphysics,* Chapter 2.

ing. Etymologically, the various inflections of the verb *sein* (as also of the English 'be') are derived, Heidegger says, from three different roots: 1. *es* (Sans. *asu*, be, live, that which stands and moves and rests in itself, the living, self-standing. Cf. Sans. *asti;* Gr. *estin;* Lat. *esse;* Ger. *ist;* Eng. *is*); 2. *bhu* (Sans., arise, emerge, come to stand by itself. Cf. Gr. *phuo, phuin,* shine forth, appear; Lat. *fuo;* Ger. *bin;* Eng. *be*); 3. *vas* (Sans., dwell. Cf. Sans. *vasami;* Gr. Lat. *vesta;* Ger. *wesan, gewesen, wesen;* Eng. *was*). Three concrete meanings have thus entered originally into 'Being': to live, to emerge, to dwell; but today these have become extinct and only the abstract sense of 'to be' remains. The three meanings have got mixed up, effacing one another, so that no determinate sense stands out explicitly. These, however, are mere facts of linguistic science and however suggestive, as such they contribute little to the question about Being itself; the question of Being is not a matter of etymology and grammar.

From the point of view of linguistic usage, however, two important facts about 'Being' and 'is' stand out as philosophically relevant. Firstly, when we say that something 'is'—really meaning it, and as determined by a particular situation, aim and mood, and not merely as just a propositional specimen—the 'is' may be variously meant. In the 'is' Being discloses itself in a variety of ways—*to on legetai pollachos,* as Aristotle said, but in a deeper sense.[3] But this diversity of meanings, far from being arbitrary, shows a single determinate trait running through them all, holding our understanding of 'Being' within a definite horizon of sense, that of constant presence (*ständige Anwesenheit*), as which the Greeks initially experienced Being. This is further indicated by the fact that the verbal substantive *Sein* (Being) is understood by us in terms of the infinitive, which in turn we comprehend, "involuntarily and almost as if there were no alternative," in terms of 'is', with all its diversity of use. "The specific verb form 'is', the third person singular of the present indicative, has here a pre-eminent status." The sense in which we under-

3. For examples, see *Ibid.,* p. 75; also *Nietzsche II,* p. 246.

stand 'Being' today is thus historically determined, suggesting that the inquiry into the sense of Being cannot dispense with the historical dimension. It is true, in the second place, that we are concerned neither with the word as such nor with its 'meaning' but with what they are about, the thing itself, i.e., with Being. The latter, however, is no entity. No thing corresponds to the word 'Being' and its meaning, from which it by no means follows that Being consists only of the word and its meaning. This points, Heidegger concludes, to the peculiar fact about 'Being' that here the word and its meaning are more profoundly dependent on what is meant (i.e., the thing itself) than in the case of other words. And, conversely, Being also is itself dependent on the word in a quite different and deeper sense than any essent. "In each of its inflections the word 'Being' bears an essentially different relation to Being itself from that of all other nouns and verbs of the language to the essent which they denote." Hence, the inquiry into Being is inextricably bound up with a reflection on language, the shrine of Being. As explained earlier, the Greek conception of Being, determining ours, is inadequate and so is the way the Greeks looked upon language, its logic and its grammar, which were themselves moulded by that conception of Being and have in turn given their stamp to the way *we* talk now. And once this is realized, it becomes imperative to make a fresh start and seek, by means of more appropriate language, to come closer to the true nature of Being. The path to this, however, lies through a consideration of the various ways in which metaphysics, by its very character as essent-centred, represents, not Being itself, but the Being of essents and the way it conceives the relation between what is and its Being.

I BEING AND METAPHYSICAL THOUGHT

Metaphysics determines the nature of man in terms of his relationship to essents.[4] But since metaphysics is concerned with the essent in view of its Being, man's relationship to essents itself requires that he should be conceived in terms of the more basic relationship with Being. Metaphysical thinking, however, unaware of its own foundation, can hardly recognize the latter relationship as such, except in terms of the former. And yet, in all our dealings with the essent we necessarily and inevitably stand in some kind of relationship with Being. As Heidegger puts it, "We have dealings with essents and at the same time hold ourselves in the relationship to Being. Only so do we have a footing in the essent as a whole and our sojourn in it." We always stand, in other words, in the midst of the distinction between beings and Being, the distinction on which, in fact, our relationship both to Being and to essents is dependent. "We cannot evade the distinction between Being and beings, not even when we presumably cease thinking metaphysically. Everywhere and always, we stand and move on the narrow path of this distinction which carries us from essents to Being and from Being to essents in all our relationship with essents, of whatever kind or rank, of whatever degree of certainty or accessibility it may be. . . . Perhaps the distinction is the real core of that natural disposition of the human mind for metaphysics (of which Kant speaks)." What man is and what his relationship to Being is are grounded, Heidegger holds, on this distinction. This distinction, far from being a mere invention and a mental construct, is the very ground on which metaphysics itself can originate, for it alone renders possible any thinking about the essent as such, i.e., in its Being. It is the unrecognized and unacknowledged but nonetheless constantly employed foundation of all metaphysics. This distinction, further, is not 'made' by anybody, is not the result of an 'act' of a distinguishing 'subject' and yet it *is*. Heidegger therefore prefers to designate this distinction by the more impersonal phrase "Ontological Difference" or just "Difference", meant to suggest that essents and Being are somehow held apart, separated and yet kept together in their relationship with each other, in and by themselves and not merely as a distinction of the intellect. (In conformity with this dynamic conception of Being, the Difference

also is not just a static 'relation' but is to be conceived dynami-
cally, as differentiation, as an 'issue' for settlement [*Austrag*]
between the two 'terms' of the relation.) Though based as to its
own possibility upon the Difference, metaphysics cannot recognize it *as such* and so remains shut out from the possibility of
thinking about Being *as* Being.[5]

The perennial question of metaphysics, as Aristotle explicitly
laid down, is: "What is the essent? (*ti to on*)." The answer that
the Aristotelian First Philosophy gives to this question is that "a
being is spoken of in many ways" or, in Heidegger's translation,
that the essent, in respect of its being, becomes manifest in many
ways. But Aristotle does not inquire why and how and to what
extent the Being of Beings unfolds itself in the four modes which
he merely asserts without seeking to determine their common
origin. What is the common meaning of Being as expressed in
these four ways of regarding Being: Being as property, Being as
possibility and actuality, Being as truth, Being as schema of the
categories? "What is the sense of Being expressing itself in these
four headings? How can they be brought into a comprehensible
harmony?" We cannot become aware of this unified sense, Heidegger asserts, without first raising and clearing up the question:
From where does Being as such (not merely the essent as such)
get its determination?[6] But this question metaphysics is not in a
position even to raise. As concerned with the essent as such and
in entirety (i.e., in its Being), metaphysics presupposes, and

5. According to Max Müller (op. cit., p. 73) during the preliminary
drafting of Division III of *Being and Time* (which was to bear the title,
"Time and Being"), Heidegger sought to distinguish three kinds of Difference: the 'transcendental' or Ontological Difference in the narrower sense—
the difference between the essent and its beingness (*Seiendheit*); the 'trans-
cendence-having' or Ontological Difference in the wider sense—the difference between the essent and its beingness on the one hand and Being itself
on the other; the 'transcendent', or Theological Difference in the strict
sense—the difference of God from the essent, from its beingness and from
Being. This attempt was, however, given up as a merely speculative construction, not based on the experience of thought.

6. Cf. Richardson's *Heidegger*, p. x. Pöggeler illustrates the multiple
speakability of being with reference to the 'transcendentals' of scholastic
philosophy: *res, unum, aliquid, bonum* and *verum*.

bases itself upon, the Ontological Difference. It seeks to conceive Being, but it does so not as Being, not in its difference from beings, but always in terms of the essent and as subserving its concern with the essent. Metaphysics is the movement of thought away from and beyond the essent as a whole toward its Being but it is at the same time a movement that comes back to the essent as its ultimate destination. In the direction *away* from the essent, it conceives Being as the most general determination of the essent and in the direction *towards* the essent, its ground and generative principle (*arche*, as, e.g., in the Christian conception of the creation of everything that is by a First Cause or in the Enlightenment idea of governance by cosmic reason). All the time, it is the essent that is in the forefront, as requiring explanation, as the measure and the goal, as the realization and fulfilment of Being; even while the latter is conceived as an 'Ideal', and thus higher in rank than the essent, it is still in a way in the service of the essent. For metaphysics, the essent as a whole thus has the pre-eminence, a position of supremacy over Being. Going beyond the essent to its Being, here, is itself oriented to the eventual movement back from Being to the essent. The awareness or light of Being itself is never absent in our dealings with essents but to metaphysical thinking it always appears as *their* Being and determined by its relationship to *them*. As a form of presence (the presence of what is present), Being reveals itself as *chreon*, as *moira*, as *logos*, as *idea*, as *energeia*, the latter afterwards progressively deformed into *actualitas*, reality (or actuality) and objectivity, culminating, in its extreme subjectivistic form, in the Will to Power.[7] Concerned with Being from the

---

7. Also as substance. Sections 19–21 of *Being and Time* are devoted to a discussion of the Cartesian determination of the Being of beings as substance. In a recent article entitled, "Aus der letzten Marburger Vorlesung" (in *Zeit und Geschichte, Dankesgabe an Rudolph Bultmann*, 1964), Heidegger offers a revised extract from a lecture-course on Leibniz given at Marburg in 1928. He discusses here Leibniz's conception of the substantiality of substance as monad and of *vis activa* (with its character as *perceptio* and *appetitus*) as its unifying essence.

point of view of the essent and conceiving it under the limited temporal horizon of the present, metaphysics characterizes Being in a variety of ways. Some of the principal ways in which metaphysics thus conceives Being (as presence) may here be reviewed briefly.

The question, "What is the essent as such?" is a question about the Being of essents. The nature of this is determined in terms of its "what" and its "that", which together make up the essent in its Being. The "what" is determined by Plato as *idea* and when later this is termed "essence (*wesen*)", this only means that the Being of beings is conceived in terms of its 'whatness', to the neglect of its 'that'. The Being of beings is here approached from the side of essents and conceived in its relation to essents as the genus and the universal from which they derive their character as essents. The *essentia* is the quiddity, the *genos* in the double sense of origin and genus, the one (*hen*) in the many (*polla*), the universal (*koinon*). It is the 'what' of anything, irrespective of whether that thing exists, and is thus pure possibility. As against this, the 'that' is the *existentia,* the existence or actuality of what is. *That* the essent is, is its *existentia* which, according to Plato, is to be found in what truly answers to the 'what', the real Being, the Idea as the *ontos on,* as opposed to the essent which, properly speaking, 'is' not, for Plato. Being is differentiated into what anything is and that it is. With this differentiation (Aristotle) and the preparation for it (Plato), Heidegger says, begins the history of Being as metaphysics. Since Aristotle, who first explicitly formulated the distinction between the *ti estin* (the 'what') and the *oti estin* (the 'that'), however, it is in the actuality of the actual, in existence, that the real and proper Being of anything is thought to lie, *existentia* being, as Heidegger puts it, the commonest metaphysical name for Being. For Aristotle, what is present (i.e., the essent) is what which, having come forth into unhiddenness, stands there as the invariant 'this', the particular (*tode ti*). The movement of coming forth or of production comes to a rest in this and hence the presence or Being of the present is characterized by motion and its consummated mode, rest, which is the fulfilment and gathering together, the *telos* or end of motion. As such consummation of motion, the essent, tarrying there in the steadiness of the 'look' or aspect (*eidos*) it presents, is conceived by Aristotle as *ergon*, as a work. The presence (Being or *ousia*) of a particular 'this' has for him, therefore, the character of *energeia* or, as he also calls it, *entelecheia*. On the basis of this general conception of *ousia* as *energeia*, there arises then the distinction between *ousia* in the primary sense of the particular 'this' and in the secondary sense of the look presented by it, its 'what', which is common to all the particular instances of its manifestation.

This distinction between existence and essence, Heidegger points out, is not coincident with the distinction between Being and essents but falls within Being itself. Plato takes one term of the pair (essence) as identical with Being, whereas Aristotle emphasizes the other (existence). Aristotle's conception of Being as *energeia*, embodied in the particular 'this', is, according to Heidegger, more comprehensive and nearer the original Greek spirit, the view of Being as *physis*, in the sense that though the *eidos* (the 'look' of the 'this') can be conceived in terms of *energeia* as a mode of presence, the *tode ti*, the particular essent, remains, as *me on*, inconceivable in terms of the Platonic idea. The two modes of *ousia*, *idea* and *energeia*, constitute, in the interplay of their distinction, the basic framework of all metaphysics as it unfolds itself in the course of its history. Sometimes one of them comes to the forefront as the basic character of Being and sometimes the other, each undergoing radical modification with the development of metaphysical thought. The history of metaphysics is the history of the modification of *idea* into idea and representation, of *energeia* into *actualitas*, existence, actuality and objectivity, but it is a history in which the primal nature of Being as the unity underlying these two remains hidden. Since the transformation of the Aristotelian *energeia* into *actualitas*—later, *existentia*—this remains the dominant conception of Being and hence, as Heidegger puts it, the history of Being reveals itself primarily in the history of *energeia*. The essent is conceived henceforth as what is actual (as against the merely potential or possible), that which possesses causal efficacy, its actuality (Being) lying not merely in its being the ground (*arche*) of what is but primarily in its character as cause (*aition*). From this the theological conception of Being as the highest essent or God, itself present in complete actuality as *actus purus* and supreme cause, follows inevitably.

As its very name suggests, metaphysics goes beyond the essent to its Being. The latter is for it 'sheer transcendence', as Heidegger expressed it in *Being and Time*. Metaphysics rises above the essent to its what-ness, its *essentia*. This ascent to the *essentia* is transcendence in the transcendental sense of Kant. At the same time, transcendence means the transcendent in the sense of the *existentia*. Ontology, Heidegger says, represents transcendence as the transcendental; theology represents it as the transcendent. This two-fold ascent of metaphysics, however, is only for the sake of representing the essent itself, i.e., of an eventual return to it. In its upward movement metaphysics does not stop to contemplate Being itself but passes it by, as Heidegger puts it, "for it has already conceived Being in its own way, namely, as the essent in so far as it, the essent, is" (i.e., as the is-ness of what is). All transcendence, ontological or theological, according to him, is conceived relatively to the subject-object relation, in terms of which man understands himself and his world in the era of subjectivity.

The Platonic conception of Being as *ousia*, i.e., the Being of essents regarded merely as their being-ness or is-ness (*Seiendheit*), also leads to its being taken as the abstract universal. Being in this view, is the most general (*to koinaton*), the highest universal arrived at by a process of abstraction from the particular essents. It is, therefore, utterly empty, carrying no other meaning except that of subsuming all that is under itself. In later philosophy, indeed, this is established as logically obvious. But, as

Heidegger points out, this characterization of Being as the most general concept says nothing about the nature of Being, a nature which every metaphysical doctrine understands in a specific, concrete sense of its own. At the most, it describes how we arrive at the concept through the process of generalization. "Through the interpretation of Being as the most general nothing whatever is said about Being itself; it only says how metaphysics thinks about the *concept* of Being." Evidently, this is only a way of refusing, on the part of metaphysics, to notice the difference between Being and beings while yet making use of it all the time.[8]

Being in the sense of the is-ness of what is, in the next place, is not regarded merely as the highest universal but also as what comes before, the Apriori or the '*Prius*'. Plato and, following him, Aristotle, have determined the *ousia* of the essent as the *proteron*. Plato has demonstrated that to see two things as having the same colour, for example, we must already know sameness. The two coloured things, of course, come first in our experience—they are first in relation to us (*pros hemas*) and the sameness comes later. But in respect of its own Being (*te physei*), sameness comes first and the particular essents later. Sameness, as enduring presence

---

8. See also *Identität und Differenz*, pp. 63–64 (E.T., pp. 65–68). (In speaking of it as a universal), we conceive Being in a manner in which It, Being, is never given. It is utterly impossible to conceive 'Being' (infinitely more so, Heidegger says, than the reality of a universal, as illustrated in Hegel's story of the man who found that only fruits were to be bought but never fruit) as the universal corresponding to particular essents, Being ever appears in this or that historical form (i.e., as it dispenses itself from epoch to epoch), as *Physis, Logos, Hen, Idea, Energeia*, Substantiality, Objectivity, Subjectivity, Will to Power, Will to Will. But what comes as such historical destiny is not to be found laid out neatly like apples, pears and peaches, on the counter of the historian's representation. The description (below) of Being in terms of the Difference and of the latter in terms of an issue for resolution (*Austrag*), Heidegger says, perhaps brings into view something common and pervasive which runs through the entire destiny (dispensation) of Being from beginning to end. But it still remains difficult, Heidegger admits, to say how this universality is to be thought, if it is neither a universal valid for all particulars nor a law secure from the necessity characteristic of a dialectical process.

(the Being of what is the same) must have already come in our view (as *idea*) before two things can show themselves as having the same colour; as the Being of these it is also prior to them. The knowledge of what is thus *a priori* is therefore, from the point of view of essents, metaphysics. Since Plato, this conception of Being as the *a priori* is dominant throughout the whole history of Western philosophy, which may thus be rightly described as the history of Platonism. Actually, Heidegger remarks, the *a priori* is not just a property of Being but Being itself in its unhiddenness, though with the interpretation of truth (*aletheia*) in terms of apprehension (*noein*), it afterwards came to be regarded as a property of knowing. In conceiving Being as the *a priori*, as coming before essents, metaphysics conceives it exclusively from the point of view of the essent and as referring back to that, irrespective of whether the *a priori* is taken to mean what is prior in itself or in the order of knowing or as determining the possibility of objects. "So long as the Being of essents is conceived as the *a priori*, this way of determining Being itself prevents a consideration of Being as Being, a consideration which could perhaps enable us to realize how far Being as Being enters into this *a priori* relationship with essents and whether this relationship is merely incidental to Being, only following in its wake, or whether Being itself is this relation."[9]

Another consequence of the Platonic doctrine of Ideas is the conception of Being as a condition of the possibility of what is. Plato conceived Being, in the sense of the is-ness (*Seiendheit*) of what is, as *idea* and the essential nature of all Ideas, the Idea of Ideas, as the *agathon*, the good in the sense of the enabling and the empowering. The *idea tou agathou* is *epikeina tes ousias*, beyond even the is-ness of what is, in the sense that the enabling character of the Idea is what really constitutes the is-ness or Being of all that is. Since Plato, Being has thus been understood not only as *a priori* but also as that which enables essents to be,

9. *Nietzsche II,* p. 347.

renders them possible. Being means the condition of the possibility of whatever is. In modern philosophy, with the transformation of the Platonic *idea* into re-presentation, the enabling character of Being comes under the sway of subjectivity. Being is conceived as the representedness of what is represented, the former being regarded as the condition of the possibility of the latter. In Kant, the is-ness of the essent, conceived as object, is its objectivity and the latter is the *a priori* condition of the possibility of objects in general. As Heidegger remarks, "through Kant's interpretation of Being, the is-ness (*Seiendheit*) of what is is for the first time expressly conceived in the sense of the condition of the possibility, which then leaves the way open for its unfoldment into the conception of value in the metaphysics of Nietzsche."[10] This way of conceiving Being, like those mentioned before, is primarily concerned with the essent in its character as essent, with the essent in its Being and not with Being as such, and therefore remains confined within the metaphysical sphere of the truth of essents, without access to the truth of Being itself.

It lies in the very nature of metaphysics as representational thinking to represent the Being of essents as their ground. In representing anything to ourselves, we represent it *as* this or that. With this "as this or that", we accommodate the thing represented somewhere, deposit it there, as it were, provide it with a ground.[11] Only what is brought to a stand in a representation for which adequate ground has been provided, i.e. is an "object" in the modern sense, counts as an essent, as something that is. The enormous power of the demand made on us by the *principium reddendae rationis* (the Principle of Sufficient Reason), incubating so long, has, in the modern phase of the history of Being, emerged with Leibniz to the surface and the man of today is completely in its grip, as Heidegger shows in *Der Satz vom Grund*. Metaphysics seeks to ground essents in Being but, in

10. *Ibid.*, p. 232.
11. *Der Satz vom Grund*, p. 39.

doing so, it turns Being itself into an essent, be it the highest essent in the sense of a first cause, be it the pre-eminent essent in the sense of the subject (of subjectivity regarded as the condition of the possibility of all objectivity) or, as a combination of the two, the highest essent as the Absolute in the sense of unconditioned subjectivity. The question of Leibniz, later taken up by Schelling, "Why are there essents at all and not rather nothing?" is a question that asks for a first cause and for the highest ground, itself essent, of all that is. It is the question, as old as Plato and Aristotle, about the *theion,* the Divine, which for metaphysics is necessarily the essent ground of essents. Metaphysics is not only ontology, the inquiry into the essent as such in respect of its *essentia* but also theology, the inquiry into the highest essent. The metaphysical concept of Being as ground converts Being into a being and, because of its concern with essents, thinks of it in terms of these. How far is it possible to think of Being as Being and yet as Ground, how far and in what sense Being itself can be thought as Ground and not merely from the point of view of essents, how far the Being-centred conception of Ground can itself be understood in terms of play is, Heidegger suggests, still a task for the future. These are questions, however, of which the beginnings of an answer are suggested by Heidegger in his conception of *Ereignis.*

The above mentioned ways of characterizing Being are metaphysical in the sense that they approach Being from the perspective of beings, seeking to grasp *their* truth and not letting Being itself shine forth in its truth. For metaphysics, Being is always the essent in its Being, never Being in its own truth. In thinking about the essent as such it has a fleeting glimpse of Being, in passing and on its way to the essent. It thinks indeed of the essent as such but it does not ponder the "as such" itself, as Heidegger puts it. This "as such" is the unhiddenness of the essent, which metaphysics ignores, Being itself is the unhiddenness in which the essent has its presence. But this unhiddenness itself remains hidden to metaphysics. This is so, not because of a failure of thought on the part of metaphysics but because Being itself stays away. The illumination which lights up the essent itself remains inaccessible to metaphysics in its own nature as such illumination. Metaphysics thus does not think of Being *as* Being, does not let it 'be' itself, but always understands it from the point of view of its own concern with the essent and so in terms of the latter. For it, Being as such is a nullity and for this reason, as Heidegger asserts,[12] "metaphysics, as metaphysics, is the real Nihilism. . . . The metaphysics of Plato is no less nihilistic than the metaphysics of Nietzsche. In the former, the Nihilistic essence is still hidden, in the latter it comes fully into view."

Being itself is none of the things metaphysics conceives it as being. As Heidegger puts it,[13] "It is itself. To realize and to say this is what the thinking of the future must learn. 'Being'—that is not God and not a World-ground. Being is farther away than all that is, whether it be a rock, an animal, a work of art, a machine, an angel or God. Being is the nearest. And yet the nearest is what remains remotest from man." As mentioned before, metaphysics by its very nature is not only ontology but also theology, for it is concerned not only with the essent as such but also with the essent as a whole. Its wholeness constitutes the unity of essents, unifying by virtue of being the generative ground. In the essay on "The Ontotheological Structure of Metaphysics" (in *Identität und Differenz*), Heidegger has gone more deeply into this question than in his earlier discussion in the 'Introduction' to *What is Metaphysics?*, seeking to delve into the unitary essence of metaphysics and discover the single source in which this triple character of metaphysics has its origin.[14] Having had experience of theology, both that of religious faith as well as of philosophy, in his own origin and development, he "prefers now to be silent

12. *Nietzsche II,* p. 343.
13. *Brief über den 'Humanismus',* p. 76.
14. For the following, see "Die onto-theo-logische Verfassung der Metaphysik" in *Identität und Differenz.*

about God in the sphere of thinking."[15] The onto-theological character of metaphysics, he says, has become questionable for thought, not because of any sort of atheism but because of a realization that ontotheology is itself rooted in an as yet unthought unity of the essence of metaphysics. The question how God comes into philosophy must, therefore, be explicitly raised. And to do this is to ask, taking the 'step back', what the source of the onto-theological structure of metaphysics is.

Metaphysics is 'Logic', in the first place, not because its theme is thinking, but because it its concerned with the Being of essents as originally revealed in the shape of *Logos* (gathering together and laying down as a unity, the *hen panta*), the self-fathoming and self-substantiating Ground, and which therefore takes into its service thinking as proving and grounding. Metaphysics is Ontology because, concerned with the essent as such, it thinks of Being as the unity of the utmost generality, as the unity to be found at the bottom of things. And it is Theology in the sense that it thinks of Being as the unity of the essent as a whole, i.e. as the highest above all, as the unity which provides the ground and establishes. In each case, the Being of essents is taken as Ground and metaphysics may, therefore, be described as being concerned, basically and radically, with the grounding of essents, "giving an account of the Ground, accounting for it and in the end calling it to account." The Being of essents as such manifests

15. For Heidegger's "experience" of theology, see Chapter I pp. 7–9 above.

In his article, "Martin Heidegger und die Marburger Theologie," (*Zeit und Geschichte. Dankesgabe an Rudolph Bultmann*), H–G. Gadamer gives a fascinating picture of the theological climate at Marburg during the twenties, of the young Heidegger in theological debate, of "the breath-taking radicalism of Heidegger's questioning, which drew even theology under its sway." This article vividly brings out the significance of Heidegger's preoccupation with Aristotle at this time, the theological relevance of many of his ideas in *Being and Time* and his influence on Bultmann's theology and beyond it on the hermeneutic philosophy of Gadamer himself. From the very beginning, Gadamer says, the questions that clamoured within him were theological ones. "The *Urform* of *Being and Time* was an address at a gathering of Marburg theologians in 1924."

itself as having the character of a ground and this is such in a complete sense only when conceived as the first Ground, *prote arche*. For metaphysics, the primary concern of thought is thus with Being conceived as Ground in the sense of a self-caused First Cause (*causa prima, ultima ratio*) or *causa sui*. This is the God of metaphysics, irrespective of whether its character as Ground appears in the form of *logos* or *hypokeimenon,* substance or subject, in the course of its historical unfoldment. The Onto-logical Difference, on the basis of which Being and essents get differentiated, is the ultimate source of the onto-theological struc-ture of metaphysics. In the course of this dynamic 'Differentia-tion,' Being appears as Ground (*Logos*) and the essent as the grounded, the two being held apart in an intimacy of relationship such that "not only does Being as Ground provide a foundation for the essent but the latter (in its wholeness), on its part and in its own way, grounds and generates Being." In the light of Being as Ground, the grounding itself appears as something that is, an essent, and therefore itself in need of being accounted for in terms of a highest essent conceived as the first cause. "Because Being reveals itself as Ground, the essent is the grounded and, as the highest essent, itself the grounding first cause. As meta-physics thinks the essent in respect of its Ground as that which is common to every essent as such, it is 'Logic' in the shape of Onto-logic. As metaphysics thinks the essent as such in its totality, i.e., in regard to the highest, all-grounding essent, it is 'Logic' in the form of Theologic." The happening of Differentiation, through which Being reveals itself as Ground or *Logos,* is itself generative of metaphysics and the ultimate 'explanation', if it may be called such, for the fact that the essent appears both as grounded and, representing to itself (as 'Logic') its own ground as something that is (i.e., itself as its own utmost generality and totality), the self-caused First Cause. This is how God comes into, and is the form in which He is known to, philosophy. But, as Heidegger remarks, "To this God man can neither pray nor make offerings and sacrifices. Man can neither kneel down in awe before the *causa sui* nor can he sing and dance before this God. Accordingly, the godless thinking which is compelled to give up the God of philosophy, God conceived as *causa sui*, is perhaps closer to the (really) godly God, freer for Him, than (metaphysics as) onto-theo-logic would like to admit."[16]

II TRUTH OF BEING—*EREIGNIS* AND *GEVIERT*

The step back out of metaphysics into the source which generates the whole sphere in which metaphysical thinking can function leads to that which makes the central question of metaphysics—What is the essent in its Being?—itself possible. This is the 'Difference', so termed "provisionally and unavoidably in the language of tradition",[17] between Being and beings, the two-foldness (*Zwie-falt*) of essents and Being. The participation (*methexis*) of the essent in Being (as idea), of which Plato speaks and into which, following him, the entire history of philosophy inquires, already *presupposes*, Heidegger says, such two-foldness of Being and beings. To speak of Being is to speak of the Being of essents and to speak of the essent is to speak of the essent in its Being. The one is implied in the other. "We speak", as Heidegger says,[18] "always on the basis of the two-fold-

16. See on this whole problem, W. Schulz, *Der Gott der Neuzeitlichen Metaphysik*. As Pöggeler has remarked, the question of God has been there on Heidegger's path of thought from the very beginning and so also his wrestling with the claims and credentials of theology. In the pre-*Sein und Zeit* years he gave lecture-courses, none of which have been published, on the philosophical foundations of medieval mysticism (1911–20), on the phenomenology of religion (1920–21) and on Augustine and Neo-Platonism (1921), held a colloquium, with Ebbinghaus, on the theological foundations of Kant's *Religion Within the Limits of Pure Reason* (1923) and gave a lecture on phenomenology and theology (1927). His views, expressed in conversation, have been reported by H. H. Schrey (in *Martin Heideggers Einfluss auf die Wissenschaften*) and by H. Noack (*Anstösse*, I, (1954). In 1959, Heidegger conducted a day-long seminar (unpublished) on "Christian Faith and Thinking" at a meeting of the "Old Marburgers", of which the impact on theologians is recorded in *The Later Heidegger and Theology*, ed. by Robinson and Cobb. Heidegger's Address on "Time and Being" was also given at a meeting of the "Old Marburgers" in 1962.

17. *Identität und Differenz*, p. 46 (E.T., p. 50).

18. *Was heisst Denken?*, p. 174 (E.T., p. 227).

ness. It is always already given, for Parmenides as much as for Plato, for Kant as much as for Nietzsche. The two-foldness has already laid open the sphere within which it becomes possible to represent the relation between essents and Being", either as the Platonic *chorismos* or as transcendence—both of these presuppose the distinction or two-foldness and therefore cannot themselves generate it. Accordingly, Heidegger argues[19], Being should be thought in its difference from the essent and the latter in its difference from Being. For, "Being as well as the essent, in their different ways, emerge from and through the Difference." When we thus think of Being in terms of Difference, of Being as Difference, Being shows itself in the character of going over to the essent, as coming down to it and revealing it and the essent appears as that which, through such descent of Being, comes into unhiddenness and appears as if it were by itself unhidden. As against the traditional conception of transcendence as the movement from Dasein to Being (in terms of which he mentioned the Ontological Difference earlier), Heidegger thinks of the Difference now as the interplay and resolution (*Austrag*) of Being's descent into beings and the latter's emergence into unconcealedness. Being is the revealing descent (*enthergende Überkommnis*) and the essent is the coming into and enduring in the haven of unhiddenness, the arrival (*sich bergende Ankunft*) which hides its own self in this unconcealedness. Both emerge, as thus differentiated, from the Difference, their identical source. The Difference between Being and essents is not just a static and formal 'relation' between two terms but the interplay, the working out or the process of resolution (*Austrag*) of the two opposed movements of revealing (descent) and concealing (arrival). This conception of *Austrag* carries Heidegger into a dimension more basic than the differentiation of Being and the essent on which metaphysical thought rests, "beyond Being" (the Platonic *epikeina,* but in a more fundamental sense!), a dimension into which entry

19. See "Die Onto-theo-logische Verfassung der Metaphysik" in *Identität und Differenz* for the whole of this paragraph.

is rendered almost insuperably difficult by the inherently 'metaphysical' character of the Western languages themselves. As Heidegger remarks[20], "What is called here *Austrag*, leads our thinking into a realm, to speak about which the principal terms of metaphysics, Being and essent, Ground and the grounded, do not any longer suffice. For what these words name, what the mode of thinking governed by them conceives, originates, as the Different (i.e., the Being of what is in general and as the highest), from the Difference, of which the genesis is beyond the purview of metaphysics and cannot be thought in its language."

Just as a consideration of the Difference leads Heidegger beyond the 'Being' of metaphysics, so also does reflection on the Identity between the essence of man (as a thinking being) and Being itself.[21] The unity of a thing with itself, its identity (which is never a bare, abstract unity but is always self-mediated and complex)[22] constitutes, according to the whole tradition of Eu-

20. *Identität und Differenz*, pp. 69 f. (E.T., p. 71).

21. For the following, see Heidegger's Jubilee Lecture, *Der Satz der Identität in Identität und Differenz*. This lecture, Heidegger points out in his Foreword, glances both forward and backward: ahead into the sphere with which the lecture on "The Thing" is concerned and back into the sphere of the Difference from which metaphysics derives its essential character.

22. The Principle of Identity does not, Heidegger claims, merely say that every A is itself the same but rather that every A is with itself the same (*idem, to auto, das Selbe, Identity* as distinguished from sameness). In self-sameness there lies the relation of 'with', hence a mediation, a union, a synthesis, unification into a unity. This is the reason why throughout the history of Western thought, Identity appears in the character of Unity. But this Unity is by no means the monotonous vacuity of what, in itself without relation, persists un-wearyingly in its indifferent oneness. But Western thought needs more than two thousand years until the relation of the same with itself, lying within Identity and already glimmering in the beginning, comes to light definitely and in its characteristic form. Only the philosophy of Speculative Idealism, prepared by Leibniz and Kant, gives accommodation, through Fichte, Schelling and Hegel, to the intrinsically synthetic nature of Identity. After the epoch of Speculative Idealism it is no longer permissible for thought to conceive the unity of Identity as mere sameness and to ignore the mediation inherent in unity. Where this happens, Identity is conceived only abstractly.

According to Heidegger, it may be added, the Principle of Identity, like the Principle of Sufficient Reason, refers primarily to the Being of what is

ropean thought, a principal feature of the Being of all that is. But, as Heidegger points out, the earliest Greek utterance in which this Being is expressly mentioned, viz. the saying of Parmenides that Being and apprehension (thought) are the same (*to gar auto noein estin te kai einai*), expresses something entirely different. As against the traditional doctrine of metaphysics, according to which Identity belongs to Being, Parmenides suggests that Being inheres in an Identity, that thinking and Being belong in the Self-same, that they belong together through this Self-same. The sameness of *to auto,* the Self-same, lies, according to Heidegger, in a belonging-together, though a belonging-together which must be interpreted otherwise than in terms of the later metaphysical conception of Identity as a feature of Being, for here Being itself is regarded as a feature of this Identity. Without taking the Parmenidean conception of belonging-together as the last word on the identity of thought and Being, Heidegger proceeds to consider what belonging-together in the sense of mediated Identity means.

Belonging-together in the customary sense is a belonging-*together* in which the sense of belonging is determined by the 'together', i.e., in terms of its unity. Here, to 'belong' means, Heidegger says, to be co-ordinated and incorporated into the order of a 'together', given its place in the unity of a manifold, put together into the unity of a system mediated through the unifying centre of an effective synthesis. "Philosophy conceives such belonging-together as *nexus* and *connexio,* as the necessary connection between one thing and another." On the other hand, belonging-together may also be understood as *belonging*-together, such that the 'together' is determined in terms of belonging. "Belonging-together" can yield a sense in which it is not the unity of togetherness that determines the sense of 'belonging' but in which togetherness itself is understood in the light of belong-

and only consequentially to thought. "The Principle holds as a law of thought only in so far as it is a Law of Being." See *Identität und Differenz,* pp. 15 f. (E.T., pp. 25 f.).

ing. It is in this sense that thought and Being belong together in
the Self-same. Man (with thinking as his distinctive character)
and Being *belong* together; they are held together in a unity, but
not in the sense of being coupled together, as the traditional
concepts of man and Being represent. May it not be, Heidegger
asks, that this togetherness or unity is rather one of mutuality, of
belonging *to* each other? In fact, as he points out, even in the
traditional concepts of man and Being there is an inkling of this
mutuality of the two. As himself an essent, man is included
within the order of Being. But his distinction lies in the fact that,
as a thinking being who is open to Being, he faces Being, remains
related to it and thus corresponds (is responsive) to it. Properly
speaking, man *is* only this relationship of correspondence or
responsiveness. "In man there prevails a belongingness to Being,
a belongingness which is receptive to Being because it is delivered up and entrusted (*übereignet*) to the latter."[23] Similarly,
Heidegger asserts, Being in the sense of presence *is* and endures
only as, through its claim, it solicits man and is of concern to him;
man, open to Being, alone lets it come as presence. Such occurrence of presence wants the open area of a clearing (*Lichtung*)
and because of this need remains delivered up to the nature of
man. Man and Being are, as Heidegger puts it, entrusted to each
other and belong to each other. It is on the basis of this conception, not further examined, of the belonging-together of man and
Being that the nature of each was later given its metaphysical
determination. But so long as we represent everything, as metaphysics does, in terms of system and mediation, with or without
dialectic, this relationship can only be conceived as one of connection and inter-linking, brought about either from the side of
man or of Being. Access to this *belonging*-together, a deeper
insight into it, is possible, Heidegger asserts, only when we break
loose from the attitude of representational thinking, when we
take the spring away both from the current conception of man as

23. *Identität und Differenz*, p. 22 (E.T., p. 31).

animal rationale, a subject for his objects, as well as from Being conceived as the Ground of all essents as such. The *belonging-together* of man and Being can properly be realized only by such a leap. "This leap has the abruptness of an unbridged entry into the belongingness which alone bestows the interrelation of man and Being and hence the 'constellation' of the two. The leap is the sudden entrance into that realm which has enabled man and Being to have ever already reached each other in their essence, by virtue of both being enrtusted to each other out of a mutual sufficiency."[24]

The present-day constellation of man and Being, the way they concern each other, is that of technology, regarded not as merely a production of man but as manifesting in its essence the way in which Being addresses itself to us and claims us. The claim or demand under which today not only man but all essents, including nature and history, stand in respect of their Being is that of planning and calculation. In our very depths we are today challenged to apply ourselves in every sphere to planning and calculation: the essent as such addresses itself to us in respect of its calculability. Being is itself subject to the challenge of letting the essent manifest itself under the aspect of calculability and, in the same measure, man is challenged to treat the essent as an object of his planning and reckoning. The gathered complex of this challenge, which delivers man and Being to each other so that they challenge each other in this fashion is called by Heidegger the *Ge-Stell* (con-figuration, mutual 'placing'; coined analogously to *Ge-setz,* what is laid down, the Law). The constellation in which our age stands is determined by this mutual challenging of Being and man, claiming us in the mode of the *Ge-Stell.* The *Ge-Stell* is not something that can be encountered within the horizon of representational thinking, through which we think of the Being of essents as presence, and it is not itself something ultimate but only a secret hint of that which has the real sway over the con-

24. *Ibid.,* pp. 24 f. (E.T., p. 33).

stellation of Being and man. "The *belonging*-together of man and Being in the manner of reciprocal challenging brings dismayingly home to us that and how man is taken up into the ownership (*vereignet*) of Being and, on the other hand, how Being is dedicated (*zugeeignet*) to the nature of man and is taken up into that.[25] In the *Ge-Stell* there prevails a singular owning and being owned (dedication). It is important to realize, in a simple, straightforward manner, this relationship (of mutual fittingness and owning, *eignen*) in which man and Being belong (*ge-eignet*) to each other (and are so in harmony with each other), i.e., to meditate on what we call the *Ereignis*."[26] The configuration of man and Being in the modern world of technology, the *Ge-Stell*, is itself one manifestation of a deeper mutuality of man and Being, a prelude, as Heidegger calls it, to the primordial *Er-eignis*. This conception hence opens out a possibility of the *Ge-Stell* being overcome and transformed into a deeper 'owning' through the *Er-eignis,* thus retrieving the technological world from its position of domination and taking it back into that of servitude within the realm which enables man to reach up truly into the *Er-eignis*.[27]

25. Kurt F. Leidecker's translation of *Vereignen* by "alienation" (in the English translation of *Identität und Differenz* entitled *Essays in Metaphysics: Identity and Difference*) is not the only incredible rendering in this translation. The *Ereigins* as the source of the relationship between Being and man has a doubly positive character—viewed from the side of man, it is *Vereignen* and from the side of Being, it is *Zueignen*. My own understanding here is based on the (oral) explanations of Dr. Walter Biemel and has the sanction of Dr. Otto Pöggeler's account in his article, "Sein als Ereignis."

26. *Ereignis* simply means "event". Heidegger uses it then in the special *etymological* sense *Er-eignis*, the occurrence of owning. The original meaning of the word, Heidegger points out, is: eyeing, seeing, beckoning with the glance, appropriating (*aneignen,* taking into possession). He intends the term to be taken as "a leading-word in the service of thought . . . as little amenable to translation as the Greek *Logos* and the Chinese *Tao*."

27. See the remarkable lecture, *Die Frage nach der Technik* (in *Vorträge und Aufsätze*) for a discussion of the Greek concept of *techne* as a mode of 'knowing' or, more precisely, of disclosure and unhiddenness and, in terms of that,' for an elucidation of the *Ge-Stell*. The latter is the mode in which truth—the aspect in which everything discloses itself to us—prevails in the present age, which is not of our making but within which we move and have

What the term *Er-eignis* aims at disclosing is the nearest, the most intimate, of all that is close to us and in which we are already held; for, as Heidegger puts it, "Could anything be closer to us than what brings us nearer that to which we belong and within which we *are* as the 'belonged', the *Er-eignis?*" The *Er-eignis* is that domain, suspended in itself, which enables man and Being to reach one another in their essence and, by shedding those determinations which metaphysics has given to them, to attain to their real nature. The Self-same (*to auto*) from which Being and Thought derive their mutual belongingness and in which they themselves belong is the real Identity which metaphysics conceives as an attribute of Being. Heidegger, on the contrary, seeks to show how "Being belongs, along with thought, in an Identity of which the nature has its source in that letting belong-together which we call the *Er-eignis.*" The essence of Identity, he asserts, is a property of the *Er-eignis*. The Principle of Identity, which presupposes Identity as a trait of Being, is thus no longer a principle in the ultimate sense but, interpreted in terms of the *Er-eignis,* is transformed into a leap, "a spring which breaks away from Being as the ground of essents and so becomes a leap in the abyss.[28] This abyss, however, is neither an empty

---

our being. As Heidegger says here, both the Greek *poiesis* and the present-day *Ge-Stell* are "modes of disclosure, or *aletheia*. The *Ge-Stell* manifests the occurrence of unhiddenness, such that modern technology in its functioning discloses the real in the character of an enduring quantity at our disposal (*Bostand,* used technically here). It is therefore neither a merely human doing nor indeed a mere means for such doing. The purely instrumental and anthropological determination of technology falls to the ground; it cannot be rendered viable by being propped up with the help of metaphysical and religious interpretations." In "Hölderlins Erde und Himmel" (op. cit., pp. 17 and 35–37), Heidegger remarks that the *Ge-Stell* is the disguise in which the *Ereignis* itself manifests itself in the present age, holding within it, thus, a promise of the advent, of a possible coming, of the primordial, true belongingness in the future.

28. For a similar interpretation of the Principle of Sufficient Reason, passing from the principle regarded as a *Satz* in the sense of statement (about the essent) to the principle considered as a *Satz* in the sense of a leap (into the nature of Being as Ground), see *Der Satz vom Grund,* p. 96.

Nothingness nor dark chaos but— the *Er-eignis*." A consideration of what Being in its difference from beings means has thus led to the Difference as fundamental to both and the nature of Difference has been determined in terms of the *Austrag*. The latter leads into the sphere "beyond Being",[29] the sphere of the *Er-eignis,* the primordial Identity (not to be thought as a static state of affairs but as event, or rather, as eventuation) from which man and Being both derive not only the intimacy of their mutual relationship but also their own respective natures. The *Austrag* (referring to the dynamic character of the relation between Being and beings, with its inter-play of revelation (of beings) and concealment (of Being) is itself consequent upon the coming together of man and Being, which does not exclude their drawing apart, withdrawal itself being a mode of being-with through the *Er-eignis*. Heidegger's quest for the "sense", or essence, of Being thus terminates in the conception of *Er-eignis* as the ultimate, in terms of which Being itself can be understood.[30] The essent in its Being, the essence of Being itself and

29. This Platonic phrase, it should be noted, is never used by Heidegger himself.

30. This is not quite equivalent to saying, as Otto Pöggeler does in "Sein als Ereignis", that "with the determination of Being as *Ereignis,* Heidegger reaches the goal he set before himself in *Being and Time.* . . . The occurrence of such mutuality of relationship in history *is* Being." Heidegger remarks in the course of a recent discussion of *Ereignis* in its relation to language (*Unterwegs zur Sprache,* p. 260, note, ". . . It may appear unbelievable to many that the author has been using in his manuscripts the word *Ereignis* . . . for more than twenty-five years. What it refers to, though in itself something simple, continues for the time being difficult to think. For thought must first disaccustom itself from slipping back into the idea that here it is "Being" that is conceived as *Ereignis.* The *Ereignis* is intrinsically different in its richness from any conceivable metaphysical determination of Being. Being, on the other hand, can be thought, as regards the derivation of its essence, in terms of *Ereignis.*"

In his book on Heidegger, Pöggeler quotes frequently from an unpublished work of Heidegger entitled, *Beiträge zur Philosophie* (written during 1936–38), which deals at length with *Ereignis.* Other unpublished works from which also he quotes are: *Die Überwindung der Metaphysik* (1938–39), *Das Ereignis* (1941), *Hölderlins Hymnen* (lectures-course, 1942) and *Einblick in das, was ist* (four addresses given at Bremen in 1949 entitled, *Das Ding, Das Gestell, Die Gefahr* and *Die Kehre*). For these references, see

the nature of man must indeed be so understood, if we are not to remain imprisoned within the representational thinking of metaphysics, if we are to enter once again, surrendering our self-will, into the simplicity and the translucent depth of what is and to prepare thus a shrine into which the light of the Holy may descend, so rendering possible the manifestation of the Divine.

Being thus derives its sense or nature from something more fundamental, the *Ereignis,* and from the point of view of its essence, therefore it can no longer be called "Being". As Heidegger expresses it,[31] when Being is thought in its truth it undergoes a transformation and in consequence loses its name; in the *Er-eignis* Being itself is "got over".[32] This possibility, it may be pointed out, already lay inherent in the original asking of the question about the *sense* of Being in *Being and Time.* The very asking of the question was to move away from metaphysics, exposing oneself to the possibility that what metaphysics conceives as "Being", and through such conceiving itself develops *as* metaphysics, is in its essence something different and profounder. As Heidegger remarks,[33] "Metaphysics does not acknowledge Being *as* Being. 'Acknowledging' this, however, means to let Being, in regard to the origin of its essence, have free play in all its dubiousness. It means to endure the question of Being, to persist in asking it. And this implies meditating on the origin of presence and perpetuity and so leave open for thought the possibility that 'Being' may, on the way to 'as Being', give up its own character in favour of a more fundamental determination. The talk of 'Being itself' always bears a question mark." It drives, he says elsewhere,[34] the attempt to represent it from one predicament to

---

also Orlando Pugliese: *Vermittlung und Kehre* (1965). The whole question of the relation between man and Being in Heidegger has been discussed critically by R. Pflaumer in his article, "Sein und Mensch im Denken Heideggers" (*Philosophische Rundschau,* XII, 1966).

31. *Nietzsche II,* p. 336.
32. *Vorträge und Aufsätze,* p. 71.
33. *Nietzsche II,* p. 338.
34. See *Zur Seinsfrage,* passim, for the following.

another, while the source of this perplexity remains hidden. Nothingness goes with Being as a possible manifestation of that; in essence it is nothing other than Being. Nihilism is itself rooted in the metaphysical revelation of Being as the truth of things, in the metaphysical conception of Being itself and for this reason, to go beyond "Being", and only that, is to go beyond Nothingness. The overcoming of Nihilism depends upon the surmounting or surpassing (*Verwindung*) of metaphysics.[35]

Being is turned towards man, gives itself to him, but this does not mean that "Being" is something by itself and then occasionally also turns towards man. "Perhaps this 'turning towards' itself is, in a way that is still obscure, that which we call, awkwardly enough and vaguely, 'Being'"—of which the turning away or withdrawal, in the age of Nihilism, is itself a mode of turning toward. The turning towards and the turning away of Being are not to be thought as if man came upon them only now and then and for the moment. The nature of man rather rests on this that at all times he abides, in this fashion or that, in this turning toward and turning away. "We say of 'Being itself' ever *too little* when, in saying 'Being', we leave out the presence *to* (as entering into) the nature of man and so fail to recognise that this nature (*Wesen*) itself is a constituent of 'Being'. We also say of man ever *too little* when, in saying 'Being' (not being human), we set man apart and only subsequently bring what is thus set up into relation with 'Being'. And we say *too much* if, on the other hand, we think of Being as the all-encompassing, thereby representing man as only a special kind of being among others (plants, animals) and then putting the two into a relation. This is so because in the essence of man himself lies the relation to Being, which is determined as such by virtue of the relationship of resorting to in the sense of needing (*Brauchen*), and which is thus drawn out of

35. Curiously enough, Kluback and Wilde (in their English translation of this essay, entitled *The Question of Being*) translate *Verwindung* as 'restoration' which completely distorts the sense of the text and contravenes Heidegger's express rejection of the notion of a *Restauration* (i.e., restoration), a few lines below, in this context.

its alleged 'in and for itself'." The talk of a "turning-toward (or bestowal) of Being" remains, Heidegger says, a make-shift and thoroughly questionable, because Being depends on this turning-towards, which therefore can never be just added on to "Being". To be present ("Being") is as such to be present for a human being always, a call that addresses man in his essence. And man's nature is in itself receptive to this call, for it belongs in the call of this behest, in this coming to be (*An-wesen*). The ultimate, in each case, is the Self-same, the belonging-together of call and hearing. Can this still be called "Being"? It is, Heidegger says, no longer "Being" at all in the sense in which it has revealed itself traditionally, viz., as presence. This isolating, disconnecting word "Being" has to be abandoned as also the name "Man". Once the belonging-together is seen to be the more basic truth, the whole question about the relation between the two reveals itself as inadequate, for it is incapable of entering the realm of that which it aims at inquiring into. As Heidegger remarks, we cannot, in fact, even say that "Being" and "man" "are" the same in the sense that they belong together; for when we speak in *this* manner, we turn each of them into independently existing entities.

If the turning-toward is intrinsic to "Being", so that the latter rests on the former, then "Being" is dissolved into the turning-toward, as Heidegger puts it. This now becomes the main thing to be inquired into; Being henceforth is considered as that questionable something "which has reverted and been absorbed into its own essence." Accordingly, a preliminary attempt to explore this realm of the "turning-toward" of what has been called *Ereignis* above and which constitutes the "sense", the "truth" or "essence" of Being[36] ("Being itself") can refer to "Being", Heidegger says, only by writing it as crossed out.[37] The striking out of the word by means of a cross is intended, in the first place, to

36. In his latest writing Heidegger prefers to speak of the "essence" or nature (*Wesen*) of Being, whereas in the *Being and Time* phase he speaks of the "sense", and later, of the "truth" of Being.

37. Earlier, Heidegger also tried for a time the device of spelling "*Sein*" in the old fashion, as *Seyn*.

have the defensive function of keeping off the almost ineradicable habit of representing "Being" as something that stands
over against man, existing by itself and only at times reaching up
to man. According to this way of conceiving, man has the appearance of being excepted or excluded from "Being". Actually,
Heidegger remarks, he is not only not left out, i.e., he is not only
included in "Being", but "Being", needing man in his essence, is
obliged to give up the appearance of being a separate, independent reality (*Für-sich*). And for this reason it is also something
having quite a different nature than the conception of a totality
comprehending the subject-object relation would like to admit.[38]
Being present ("be-ing", *An-wesen,* as Heidegger now writes the
word for "being present", *Anwesen,* to mark the departure from
the traditional concept, at the same time avoiding the word
"being") as such turns towards man's essence in which (or
where) through man's mindfulness of it, the turning-toward is
consummated. Man in his very essence is the remembrance of
Being in the Sense of 'Being' crossed out and intrinsically part of
it. Be-ing (*An-wesen*) is grounded in the turning-toward, which
as such uses the being of man so that the latter may expend
himself for that.

Obviously, the cross-mark over Being cannot, as Heidegger
points out, be merely a negative sign of cancellation; it, in fact,
hints at the positive content of the conception of a Being beyond
Being, the *Ereignis.* "It points rather," Heidegger says, "into the
four regions of the Square (*Geviert*) and their gathering at the
place of intersection."[39] The four regions of the Four-fold are
Earth, the Heavens, Gods and Mortals. The Earth is that which

38. Cf. Karl Jaspers' conception of the Encompassing (*das Umgreifende*).
39. Cf. Heidegger's account of these, all too brief, in "Bauen Wohnen
Denken" and "Das Ding" in *Vorträge und Aufsätze;* also "Hölderlins Erde
und Himmel." In English, Vycinas (*Earth and Gods*) and Richardson (*Heidegger*) give good expositions; more perceptive and lucid in James M.
Demske's "Heidegger's Quadrate and Revelation of Being" in *Philosophy
Today,* 1964, selected and translated from his book, *Sein, Mensch und Tod,*
(1963), a finely written study of the concepts of death and mortality in
Heidegger's earlier as well as later thought.

serves and supports, out of which everything emerges. As Hei-degger says elsewhere,[40] "This coming forth and emerging itself, as a whole, was called in ancient times *physis* by the Greeks. We call it the Earth. . . . The Earth is that into which the emer-gence of all that comes forth is as such referred back," in which it remains embedded as its sustaining principle. It is the hidden-ness involved in all unhiddenness, the closure out of which all disclosure arises and in which it is rooted and preserved; it is that which manifests itself as the hidden in all unhiddenness, recal-citrant to all disclosure, intrinsically shut up in itself. The celes-tial region of Heaven is the pure principle of light, in which everything that emerges into unhiddenness shines forth as what it is. It is the wide horizon of openness—the sun in its course, the changing faces of the moon, the round of the seasons, of day and night—overarching the Earth as its necessary correlate. The Im-mortals are "the beckoning messengers of Divinity"; they bring with them the area of holiness in which God may appear, even though as His own absence. This is the dimension of the Holy, invoked by the great poets, which once made it possible for the world to be filled with the gods and with God; the forsakenness of the world, the absence of the gods, is itself something positive both as reminder and as promise[41]. The Mortals are men; they

40. "Der Ursprung des Kunstwerkes" in *Holzwege*.
41. Apart from the incidental remarks in the Hölderlin essays, there is very little in Heidegger's published writings which can throw further light on his conception of the Holy and of "God and the gods". W. Schulz has pointed out (loc. cit) that in these essays the Holy has been determined as the Unmediated and the poet as the mediator. But the poet himself needs the mediation of the gods to give utterance to the Holy. The gods are the intermediaries, upon whom the poet depends and who in turn depend upon the poets. See also W. Schulz, *Der Gott der Neuzeitlichen Metaphysik* (pp. 54–58). Vincent Vycinas, in his *Earth and Gods* discusses Heidegger's view with reference to the Greek conception of divinity. As Demske points out, however, it would be misguided to interpret Heidegger's talk of the 'Im-mortals', inspired by Hölderlin's usage and by his spiritual quest, as an attempted revival of paganism: "The use of the category 'the Immortals' here, far from constituting a decision for Greek paganism as opposed to Christianity, seems to fit smoothly into a Judaeo-Christian framework which includes the legitimate 'pagan' insight of the presence of the Divine, how-

are called so not because their life on earth is terminable but because they alone are capable of dying (*sterben*), of taking, in the midst of life, death upon themselves *as* death. Accepting death as 'the shrine of Nothingness' and as part of life, they embody, as mortals, the relationship to Being as Being (for Nothingness is, as the "veil of Being", Being itself experienced as the sheer other to what is, from the point of view of the latter). Each of these four is involved in the other and together they constitute an indissoluble unity. Each, in itself at one with the other, belongs to the other and together they are united in the simple unity of the Four-fold. Each of the four reflects in its way the nature of the other and each is in its way mirrored back into

---

ever hazy and ill-defined this idea may be, in the things of human "experience." See, in this connexion, the criticism offered by Hans Jonas in his article on Heidegger and theology in the *Review of Metaphysics*, XVIII, 1965.

Keeping clear of the way of faith as also of the metaphysical conceptualizations of speculative theology, and seeking to think of the Divine in terms of the truth of Being, not of the truth of beings as Western religious thought has done so far, Heidegger finds in Hölderlin a poet who directs the thinker to the future which is open for a non-metaphysical experience of Divinity and its arrival. The metaphysical-moralistic God, as Nietzsche saw, is dead but not so Divinity, which lives on and abides as a task for future thought. The absence of God, like all absence, is not nothing; "it is just the presence, which still remains to be appropriated, of the hidden fullness of that which has been and which therefore is ever a gathered together abiding of the Divine in the Greek, in prophetic Judaism, in the Sermon of Jesus. This no-longer is itself a not-yet of the veiled arrival of its inexhaustible essence." (*Vorträge und Aufsätze*, p. 183). Hölderlin's poetry was for Heidegger a pointer in the direction of a rethinking about God in terms of the Holy and of Truth, of the arrival of the Divine as an event to be awaited and prepared for by a deeper insight into the meaning of Truth and Being. The Godlessness of the present is due neither to a mere failure of belief among men nor to a moral incapacity but is part of the history of Being itself. We can begin to overcome this when we realize, with Hölderlin, that primordial Truth (*aletheia*), is the Holy, itself above gods and mortals. The Holy is the necessary element or medium for the manifestation of Divinity. The Holy, in itself pure immediacy, finds expression in the poetic word and is revealed through the mediation of a god, a being in whom the light of the Holy is gathered as in a single ray which claims and addresses mortals. Cf. Pöggeler (op. cit., pp. 193-95, 215-35 and 260-67) for the relevance of Hölderlin in this regard and Richardson's *Heidegger* for full summaries of the Hölderlin essays.

its very own within the artless unity of the four. The Four-fold represents the happening of a mutual owning and acknowledging of each by each and of each into the unity of the *Geviert,* such that each is at the same time expropriated into the freedom of its own nature. This owning-expropriating four-foldness in its unity is called by Heidegger the mirror-game (*Spiegel-Spiel*) of the Four-fold, its play of reflection, play, because not explicable by anything outside itself. In "Hölderlins Erde und Himmel," Heidegger speaks of the inter-relationship of earth and heaven, God and man as "the in-finite relation", following Hölderlin's usage. The relation which holds these together is called infinite because standing within it, each of the four is freed of its onesidedness and finitude. The mediating centre or core of this relation, its intimacy (*Innigkeit*), is itself neither earth nor Heaven, neither God nor man. It is the *Ereignis,* or what Heidegger here calls *Geschick,* which holds the four together in their intimacy and thus constitutes the heart of "the in-finite relation".[42]

This play of earth and heaven, gods and mortals is called, in its unity, the World by Heidegger. Earlier, in *Der Ursprung des Kunstwerkes,* Heidegger had conceived world, the area of openness for the play of man's historical existence, as the polar opposite of the earth, the impenetrable and the closed, in order to show how truth comes to pass through the warring of these antagonistic principles as they are embodied in a work of art and to emphasize, further, how truth comprehends in itself hiddenness as well as unhiddenness, resulting in what Heidegger calls "the strange opponency of presence" in everything that is. The world is not caused and has no ground; it happens or opens out as its own "world-ing". This means that, as he puts it, it can neither be explained in terms of something else nor does it have a foundation outside itself. Concepts like those of cause and ground are inappropriate in the context of the "world-ing" of the world. 'World', Heidegger points out, has no longer a meta-

42. *Hölderlin-Jahrbuch,* 1958–1960, pp. 25, 31.

physical sense here and means neither the secularized conception of a *universum* of Nature and History nor the theological conception of creation (*mundus*), nor does it mean simply the totality of all that is (*kosmos*).[43] The mirror-game of the world, the play of the Four-fold in its unity, is the round dance of the occurrence of owning (*Ereignen*).[44] The being-in-the-world which was described in *Being and Time* as constitutive of Dasein is now characterized simply as 'dwelling', which is the way mortals have their sojourn on earth. Man is man in so far as he has his home on the earth, under the heavens, in front of the gods, with his fellowmen. Mortals *are* in the Four-fold in the sense that they truly dwell in the world, that they take care of, cherish and tend the Four-fold by saving the earth and leaving it free in its essence as earth, by receiving the heaven as heaven, by awaiting the arrival of the gods, by shepherding themselves, in their own essence, towards death. But for mortals, the sole way of dwelling in this four-fold manner in the *Geviert* is through their sojourn with things (*Dinge*). Only in such sojourn with things is it possible for men to enter into relation with Being and the world. "We are", as Heidegger puts it, "in the strict sense of the term, the be-thinged (*die Be-Dingten,* i.e., conditioned by our relationship with things). We have left behind the arrogance of being in any way unconditioned."[45] Dwelling in the Four-fold and with things, man tends the former by drawing its essence into the things. And the Four-fold is preserved in the things only when they are allowed to unfold their own nature as things through the

43. Commenting on Heidegger's preoccupation with "World", W. Marx says, "We can see here Heidegger's attempt to help in building a new cosmos to take the place of the traditional one that Cartesianism had destroyed. It is not a cosmos of immutable Essences, teleologically ordered as conceived by the Greeks, nor is it the meaningful order and hierarchy of divine Essences of medieval times. It is rather a cosmos, a world, of an ever active manifestation of the ways that Being *west.*" ("Heidegger's New Conception of Philosophy", *Social Research,* XXII, 1955).

44. For further explanation of *Gering, Ring, reigen* etc., see, besides "Das Ding", "Hölderlins Erde und Himmel."

45. "Das Ding", in *Vorträge und Aufsätze,* p. 179.

cultivating-building care of man. Man dwells in so far as he builds and the essence of building is to permit true dwelling— with things.

A thing, e.g., a bridge or a jug, gathers together in itself earth and heaven, gods and mortals. It is not merely a symbol for such gathering but, as a thing, it is itself the gathering together of the quadrate (*Geviert*) of the four in its unity. The thing 'in itself', the reality of the thing, is such gathering together (as the old High German word 'thing' literally means). A thing is such because it 'things', gathers together, bringing to pass the Four-fold and making it abide for a while in this or that thing. An essent is a thing neither in the Roman sense of *res*, nor in the sense of the medieval *ens*, nor at all in the modern sense of an object. It is a thing, as Heidegger puts it, in so far as it 'things'. The presence of a present thing, e.g., a jug (i.e., the Being of this essent) in fact, comes to pass and is determined out of (in terms of) the 'thing- ing' (gathering) of a thing. In bringing the quadrate of earth, heaven, gods and mortals to bide together in its simple unity for a while in itself, the thing, any and every thing, 'things' the world, gathering it together into itself. The four regions of the quadrate, constituting the world, are gathered together at the point of intersection of the cross over 'Being', the point which thus represents the thing. All that a thing is, is granted to it by world. Only when we let the thing *be* as the gathering together of the world in its 'worlding', do we think, Heidegger says, of the thing as thing, the thing as it is in itself. In their turn, things unfold, by virtue of their gathering character, the world in which they are as this or that thing for a while.[46] Things bear, bring forth, world, conjuring it into existence, as it were. Manifesting themselves through and out of the world, they bring this world to man and so provide him with his world.[47] World and things are

46. *Unterwegs zur Sprache*, p. 22.
47. See the account, in "Der Ursprung des Kunstwerkes", of how a work of art, a temple, for example, represents the occurrence of truth or unhid- denness and as such opens out and sets up a world, from which then all things derive their character and which determines man's attitudes and decisions.

not two separate entities but are held apart in a relationship of intimacy through the Difference (which Heidegger now writes as *Unter-Schied,* corresponding to the change from the language of 'Being' and 'essent' to that of 'world' and 'thing'). The Difference, from which world and thing derive their respective natures, lets things rest in the favour of world, in what it grants to them and it lets the world acquiesce in the way in which and the extent to which the thing gathers it together. And as with the difference between Being and beings, the difference between world and thing, the 'between' itself, is the self-mediation of an Identity in which things and world (which include men or 'mortals') both belong. This is the *Er-eignis,* the togetherness of man's owning and being owned within the *Geviert,* the Four-fold of the world, for which Being has always remained a 'provisional name'.[48]

III LANGUAGE, TRUTH, TIME AND THOUGHT

The inter-play of world and thing in their difference and mutuality as well as the happening of Identity (*Ereignis*) are bound up with language in the most intimate fashion. "Language is the softest and also the most vulnerable vibration, holding everything in place, in the swaying edifice of the *Ereignis*. In so far as our nature is owned in language, we dwell in *Ereignis*. . . . The *Er-eignis* is vibrant with the essence of that which speaks as language, once called the house of Being."[49] Language, Heidegger says, is something more than an activity of man, more than expression or a means to it, more than a representation of the actual or the imaginary. Primarily, it is language

48. *Vorträge und Aufsätze,* p. 229.
49. *Identität und Differenz,* pp. 30, 32 (E.T., pp. 38, 39). In *Being and Time,* language is touched upon within the limits of the existenzial analytic and described in terms of the ontological constitution of Dasein. In *Erläuterungen zu Hölderlins Dichtung* the mode of being of language is then more explicitly hinted at as the house in which man dwells together in the neighbourhood of Being. *Unterwegs zur Sprache,* finally, thinks of language in terms of the *Geviert* and the *Ereignis,* completing, as it were, the "step back" from the representational thinking of metaphysics to the meditative, reminiscent thinking which alone is appropriate in this "realm of all realms", the *Ereignis.*

itself which 'speaks', not man; *his* speaking is only an echo of and response to that, depending upon how he hears what language itself says. The essence of language lies in stillness—the rest in which all motion is gathered together—the stillness which the Differentiation, the 'between', brings to the thing as a thing in the world, enabling it to be itself, and to world in its world-ing intimacy with thing. Language is the chime of stillness (*Geläut der Stille*), itself nothing human in its essence. Man's essence, on the other hand, lies in speech and he realizes his own nature in so far as, needed by the still essence of language, he gives himself over to that. "Men are capable, in *their* way, of uttered speech only in so far as they belong in the chime of stillness."[50] The speech of mortals is a call and an invitation to things and to world, invoking them by giving them names, to emerge from the pristine simplicity of the 'between' of their togetherness; it is out of this originally poetic character of speech that man's everyday language develops through a process of degeneration. Man speaks only in so far as he hears, in so far as he listens to the silent call of the 'between', i.e., to what language itself speaks. "Man speaks, in so far as he co-responds to language. To co-respond is to hear. And to co-respond is to hear because it is to be owned by the call of the silent."[51]

It is the word that gives its Being to everything. "No thing is, where the word fails", as Stefan George's poem has it. Everything that is, that and how it is, depends upon the word. The relationship between word and thing is not an external relation between two independent entities; the word itself is the relationship which sustains in itself the thing so that it 'is' a thing, which holds everything in Being and preserves it so. Everything, as the essent that it is, owes its 'is' to the word which, hence, does not merely stand in relation to the thing but is itself the relationship. But the word itself is not a thing, nothing that is; in the sense in which it

50. *Unterwegs zur Sprache*, p. 30.
51. *Ibid.*, p. 33.

is itself a thing, it cannot either constitute or generate the 'is' or things. The word has no Being and the 'is', likewise, is no essent. Neither the word nor Being 'are', nor, in consequence, the relationship between them. And yet, 'it gives' (*es gibt*) both, the word even in a profounder sense than Being, which makes every essent 'be'. The word, which 'it gives', itself gives Being and so is itself never something given but is ever itself the giver, pure and simple. The essence of language—of which thinking and composing (*Dichten*) are the two modes, most near to each other and yet distinct, lies in what Heidegger terms Saying (*Sage*, from *sagan*).[52] Saying in this primary sense is showing something, letting it appear, be heard and seen, emancipating it into its own, in a manner both revealing and concealing, the dispensing of that which has been called world above (i.e., 'Being' in Heidegger's earlier usage).

According to the classical view of language as laid down for posterity by Aristotle (in his *peri hermeneias* or *de interpretatione*) language is made up of written words, which indicate vocal sounds, themselves the indications of the happenings of the soul and these in turn indicate things. Language here is conceived, Heidegger remarks, in terms of vocal utterance, i.e., in physical terms. But the physical (metaphysically conceived as belonging to the realm of the 'sensible') is itself rooted in what has been called Earth above. It is therefore more appropriate to speak of language, with Hölderlin, as the flower of the mouth. "In language the Earth opens out to the blossoming of Heaven."[53] The word thus points to the region, is itself the region, in which Earth and Heaven, the flow of the deep and majestic height, meet together. The manifestation of language as vocal sound, the earthy in language, cannot be explained in physiological or physical terms or in terms of phonetics but derives from the silent

---

52. Cf. "Sprache und Heimat" (in *Dauer im Wandel*, p. 186); also the essay "Moira" in *Vorträge und Aufsätze* for the derivation of 'Saying' (*die Sage*) from the *phacis* of Parmenides and the *logos* of Heraclitus.
53. *Unterwegs zur Sprache*, p. 206.

chime, from the evocative call of the Saying that gathers together world and lets it manifest itself in things. The four regions of the Four-fold—Earth, Heaven, God and Man—are brought and held together in their mutuality by what Heidegger calls the Nearness (*Nähe*, the source of all nearing), the still centre from which all movement flows, the temporalization of time, the spatialization of space, the inter-play of the four world-regions—the World-Play. The Nearness, the unmoving but dynamic core of this inter-play, is the chime of stillness and is identical with that Saying which dispenses and makes manifest the world (i.e., the 'Being' of metaphysics). Language as the Saying of the world-quadrate is not something to which man bears some relationship; it is itself rather "the relationship of all relationships," the very principle of relationship, within which man is held and which sustains him. "It (language) holds together, sustains, gives to each and enriches, the mutuality of the world-regions, keeps and tends it, and it does so by keeping itself to itself."[54] Just as Being, in revealing essents, conceals its own self, so also the *Sage*, in revealing world, keeps its own essence hidden. Not the spoken word—itself a thing—but the Saying (*die Sage*), as the chime of stillness of which the spoken word is but an echo, bestows world and hence also "that which we call by the little word 'is'." Word and thing, Saying and Being, are bound together in a unity. The ancient *logos*—meaning both the saying which discloses the essent in its 'is' as well as Being, the presence of the present—bears testimony to this hidden unity.[55]

The attempts to penetrate the mystery of language, beginning with Greek antiquity, and seeking to grasp it in terms of speech and so as a mode of human activity, converge to their pinnacle, according to Heidegger, in Wilhelm von Humboldt's reflexions on language, as finally expressed in the great "Introduction" to his work on the Kawi language of Java, separately published (1836) under the title, *Über die Verschiedenheit des menschlichen*

---

54. *Ibid.*, p. 215.
55. See also the essay, "Logos" in *Vorträge und Aufsätze*.

Sprachbaues und ihren Einfluss auf die geistige Entwicklung des Menschengeschlechts. This work has decisively influenced, directly or indirectly, the whole of linguistic science and philosophy of language that have developed since its publication. Language as the embodiment of speech is, according to Humboldt, not merely a means of communication but "a true *world*, which the *spirit* has to set up between itself and *objects*, through the inner labour of its energy." Despite his profound insight into the deeper nature of language, in particular its dynamic character, Humboldt's views do not reach into its essence. Language for him is *one* type and form (among others, though the most significant) of the world-views built up by human subjectivity. And his thoughts on it are formulated, moreover, in the language of the metaphysics of his age, that of Leibniz in particular. Humboldt is concerned with language, Heidegger says, not *as* language, not with language as it is in itself, but with language as a manifestation of the spiritual (intellectual) development of the human race. Such attempts to comprehend language in terms of something other than itself—energy, activity, power of the spirit, world-view, expression—do indeed say something true *about* language, but, seeking to have a grasp on it through something else, they fail to touch its essence.

Saying something (as distinguished from speaking, for much may be spoken but nothing said and, contrariwise, nothing be spoken and yet a great deal said) is showing or exhibiting it. And such showing is not primarily or exclusively a human activity. "Showing or letting something manifest itself characterizes, as appearing, the presence or absence of every kind and level of essents. Even where the showing is done by our saying, this showing, as a pointing-to, is preceded by a letting-itself-be-shown."[56] Speaking, further, is at the same time, hearing, primarily so, in fact. Hearing does not merely accompany and envelop speaking, as in the case of a conversation. Speaking, Heidegger says, is

56. *Unterwegs zur Sprache,* p. 254.

in itself intrinsically a hearing; it is listening to the language that we speak. We speak only in so far as we listen to what language itself says, i.e., shows, and we can hear what language says only in so far as we are in our very essence taken up into the essence of language, belong to it. There is no such thing as *the* language, but only particular languages, into which particular peoples and races are born, in which they are nurtured and have their dwelling. Language is essentially mother-tongue, dialect, the language of home and, so regarded, itself a home for man. In this sense, language is, in what it says, creative and revelatory in its very essence. Language opens up to man his world, determining the way in which he is integrated and taken up into the unity of the Four-fold, whether and how he dwells in the world as in a home.[57] Saying (*Sage*), i.e., language in its essence, is the still stream that unites, while itself generating them, its two banks: what is says and our speech echoing that. Saying does not constitute merely the subsequent expression of what is already manifest; all shining forth and its cessation depend rather upon Saying as a showing. Saying governs and directs the free area of that clearing (*Lichtung*) in which appearing and disappearing occur. What is it that stirs and quickens, that gives its motion, to Saying, that makes it open out a path to speech and thus renders anything manifest? This unknown and yet intimate moving principle is insusceptible of being 'placed' by means of a topological discussion (logical topography, *Erörterung*), for it is the place, the locality, of all locations and of the play of time and space. It can barely be named as a kind of fittingness, a kind of owning (*Eignen*, which carries both meanings, appropriation as well as appropriateness). This is what has been described above as the happening of Identity, of mutual owning, adequacy and unity—the *Ereignis*, which bestows the free area of a clearing in which anything can manifest itself as present or absent. The *Ereignis* grants to mortals, as Heidegger

57. Cf. "Sprache und Heimat," op. cit.

puts it, the sojourn in their own essence, so that they become capable of speaking. Because the manner in which Saying shows is an appropriating (in the double sense indicated above), the ability to listen, and so belong, to Saying also rests upon the *Ereignis*. The owning of man, as one who can hear, in Saying, emancipates man into his own, solely in order that, as one who can speak, he may respond to Saying out of his very own, thus bringing the soundless Saying into the utterance of language. The *Ereignis* enables Saying to emerge into speech; it is the *Ereignis* that, forging paths from Saying to speech, moves the former towards the latter. Itself resting in the *Ereignis*, Saying, as showing or bringing into view, is the most specific and proper mode of appropriating (*Ereignen*). The *Ereignis* is inherently self-saying, language-generating. In its essence, language can therefore be described, with Heidegger, as the melody of the *Ereignis*. In consequence, the way language itself speaks at any particular time, the relationship in which we stand to language and the way we respond to it, depends upon the way and the extent to which the *Ereignis* reveals or withdraws itself from epoch to epoch. Language was described by Heidegger in the writings of his middle phase as "the house of Being" because all being-present (i.e. Being) is in its guardianship. But the shining forth of the latter is itself "consigned to the care of the appropriating showing of saying. Language is the house of Being because, as Saying, it is the song of the *Ereignis*."[58]

The *Ereignis*, not resulting from anything else, is itself the source of all giving, the giving of which the ampleness even grants anything like an 'it gives (*es gibt*)', of which even 'Being' has need in order to come into its own as presence. It is the ultimate, irreducible to anything more basic, inexplicable in terms of anything reaching further back. "The *Ereignis* is the most inconspicuous of all that is inconspicuous, the simplest of all that is simple, the nearest of all that is near and the farthest of all

58. *Unterwegs zur Sprache*, p. 267.

that is far; it is that within which we mortals reside for life. . . . If law means that which lets everything abide in its very own nature, which lets everything belong in what is fit and proper to it, then the *Ereignis* is the simplest and gentlest of all laws, indeed, *the* Law, in that it gathers mortals into the adequateness to their own essence and into being owned by it and keeps them within that."[59] In this "realm of all realms", this swaying edifice of the *Ereignis,* suspended in itself, also lies hidden the mystery of *aletheia* is the happening of the *Ereignis* itself. Being as presence ment and disclosure necessarily implied in it. Truth in the primordial sense is not a property of statements, neither does it reside in things or even in the "Being" of what is. Truth as *alethia* is the happening of the *Ereignis* itself. Being as presence itself depends upon the prior occurrence of unhiddenness, of a clearing (*Lichtung*), an open, lit up area in which anything can manifest itself and *be.* This lit up area is what has been called World above.[60] Man's relationship to the clearing is nothing other than this clearing itself; as part of the world quadrate, man is owned in it, needed by it and in turn himself tends it. The happening of disclosure (*Entbergung*), through which anything comes into manifestness and is, occurs, as explained above, through Saying. Such disclosure or entry into the clearing (*Lichtung*) does not merely illuminate or bring to light something that already is but rather grants it its presence and gathers and contains it in it. But the showing or disclosure brought about by Saying, the chime of stillness, does not itself generate the *Lichtung* but rather presupposes such occurrence of overtness in and through the *Ereignis* itself. Both *aletheia,* Truth, and Saying, the light and the vibration, have their source in the *Ereignis,* the coming together, the mutual owning of man and Being, the supreme identity. As Inherently self-saying the *Ereignis* is also the illuminating; it is the former because it is the latter, for, as Heidegger says, "the whole essence of language rests on dis-

59. *Ibid.,* p. 259.
60. Cf. *Vorträge und Aufsätze,* p. 276.

closure, on the sway of *aletheia*."[61] The "realm of all realms", the *Ereignis,* is also the realm of Truth as the primordial happening of openness—*aletheia* itself. Being itself rests in its truth (i.e., in the *Ereignis* as described above) and "the truth of Being *is* as the Being of truth."[62] In this happening of Truth, man, belonging together with Being in the *Ereignis,* has an ineliminable share, for it is through his responsive gesture that Truth is embodied and "descends" (thereby truly "ascending" into its own), "trues" itself and is "trued", into a "work" (art, poetic utterance, thought). The primary form of this is the human word, thinking in the basic sense. As a thinking being, man is owned, claimed, used and called upon to fulfil and realize the Truth, watch over it and so let the Truth prevail.

Contrary to the traditional conception (mainly religious) which regards Truth as sheer transparency and pure light, Heidegger insists that the unhiddenness characterizing truth as *aletheia* is inseparably bound up with hiddenness—the two together constitute the full nature of Truth, which is hence called "the Mystery" by Heidegger. The essent or thing, as earth, is at bottom itself opaque and inscrutable, never surrendering its full secret. In disclosing the essent (or thing), Being, as the two-foldness of the Differentiation (or World), itself remains hidden; in revealing World and Thing in their togetherness, the Saying (the chime of silence) itself remains hidden; in generating the last, the *Ereignis* itself remains hidden. All disclosure and overtness, in bringing about unhiddenness, itself remains hidden.[63] But the concealment (*Verbergung*) that attends upon disclosure

61. "Hegel und die Griechen," in *Gadamer-Festschrift,* p. 56.

62. *Was ist Metaphysik?,* p. 40 (E.T., p. 382).

63. Cf. "Der Ursprung des Kunstwerkes" (*Holzwege,* p. 42), where Heidegger speaks of the hiddenness pervading all that is (i.e., is unhidden), while itself remaining hidden, as having a two-fold character, denial (*Versagen*) and dissembling (*Verstellen*). The essent, Heidegger says, denies itself to us (i.e., does not manifest itself to us in all the richness of the "thing" that it truly is) up to the very limit where we can barely say that it is; and it dissembles by showing itself as other than what it is and so deludes us.

(*Entbergung*) and constitutes its matrix is, as Heraclitus divined, not sheer antagonism to the latter but remains ever "turned towards" it; concealment and disclosure "love" each other (*physis kryptesthai philei*), are inclined towards and friendly to each other, together constituting a unity. Concealing itself is not mere closing itself up but, as Heidegger says,[64] a sheltering and guarding, in which the possibility of emerging into light is essentially preserved, in which such emergence belongs. "Self-concealment guarantees to self-disclosure its essence." Truth, as such inter-play of covertness and overtness, is not something eternally abiding in its fulness in some remote Empyrean but a happening, and one in which we are most intimately involved. It is in the main a happening of the withdrawal of Being, its self-concealment from man, and of the revelation of beings—the destiny of Nihilism as reflected in the rise and development of the Western metaphysical tradition. Historically, the light of truth has taken possession of the Western mind in various forms from one epoch to another—as *a-letheia*, as *homoiosis*, as *doctrina*, as certitude, as the Eternal Recurrence of the Same, as *Ge-Stell*. Truth is therefore not only history but destiny (*Geschick*), in the sense that, from epoch to epoch, man finds himself thrown into and in the grip of the particular form in which truth prevails in a particular epoch, so that all his thinking and doing, the way things show themselves to him, the way he comports himself towards them and what and how he thinks about them, the way he *is* in the world, is determined by the particular epochal light of truth in which he happens to live. But this dependence of man is not a onesided determination of man by the concealing-revealing light of Truth. Truth, as determinative of man's existence, needs being tended and cherished by man in order to prevail *as* truth. As Heidegger remarks,[65] "Some day we shall learn to think our worn-out word truth (*Wahrheit*) in terms of guarding and watching over (*die Wahr, wahren*) and realize that truth is the

64. *Vorträge und Aufsätze*, p. 271.
65. *Holzwege*, p. 321.

tendance of Being and that Being as presence belongs in it." The
step back from metaphysical thinking into the remembrance of
the truth of Being and so of the true nature of Truth itself is, in
Heidegger's eyes, a preparation for a future which will permit
this pristine truth to prevail in all its liberating power.

The basic trait of that which revealed itself to Western thought
as Being is manifested in presence and representation. "From the
early days of the Greeks up to the late period of our century
"Being" means being present. Every sort of presence and presentation has its origin in the happening of presence" (i.e., the
revelation of Being as presence).[66] Western thought in its entire
course does not even say clearly and fully what presence itself
means, far from bringing into view that on which the presence of
what is present depends. "It would, therefore," Heidegger says,
"be falling into an error to suppose that the Being of what is must
mean, solely and for all times, the presence of the present."[67]
Once the conception of time as made up of a succession of 'nows'
is seen to be derivative and its true nature is realized, presence
also reveals itself in its real character, being itself understood
now in terms of the integral essence of Time, as the arrival
(*Ankunft*), the coming, of the "has been" in the form of the yet
to be—as the Moment. The conception of Being as presence and
that of time as a series of 'nows' go together, one implying the
other. And both together involve the conception of thinking as
representation and a kind of grasping (*Be-greifen*).

Of all Western thinkers, Nietzsche, and he alone, had a
glimpse into this profound truth about the way presence, 'now'-
time and representation are linked together.[68] In *Thus Spake Zarathustra* (Part II), he characterizes the thinking of man hitherto
as inspired by the spirit of vengeance. Vengeance, as such, is
vengeance against Time, Nietzsche says; "this, and this alone, is
revenge itself: the Will's revolt against time and its 'it was'."

66. *Zur Seinsfrage,* p. 21 (E.T., p. 63).
67. *Was heisst Denken?,* p. 143 (E.T., p. 235).
68. For the following, see *What is Called Thinking?* passim and *Vorträge
und Aufsätze,* pp. 101–128; also *Nietzsche I,* Chapter 2.

What Nietzsche himself sought and longed for was a way out that might bring to man deliverance from this spirit and from the way of thinking inspired by that. "That man might be redeemed from vengeance, this is for me the bridge to the ultimate hope and a rainbow after prolonged foul weather." In his dealings with essents, man represents the essent in respect of the fact that it is, what and how it is, i.e., in respect of its Being. Such re-presention is the nature of metaphysical thinking and of man's relationship to what is. In accordance with the manifestation of Being as Will (explicitly so in the modern age), man also appears to himself as essentially willing. His relationship to Being, i.e. thinking, is also thus willing in the form of re-presenting essents. All representing is willing, a kind of pursuing, chasing, ambushing, a defiance and derogation of what is. Such representing finds in Time its greatest stumbling-block, for time in its essence (as 'now'-time) is a passing away. As Heidegger puts it, "Time passes. And it passes so that it passes away. The passage of time is, of course, also a coming but it is a coming that is inevitably a going away into the past. The coming of time (i.e., the future) never comes to stay but only to go."[69] Hence, transitoriness or vanishing into the past is the very essence of time. Time *is* what Nietzsche calls the "it was" of time. "Representation, with the willing intrinsic to it, tosses and knocks in vain against this irrevocable 'it was', unable to prevail against it, and 'it was' stiff and frozen in its finality, in which the passing of time itself passes away into the deadness of the past. The redemption from this need to say "no" to time, this great misery of the Will's own revolt, cannot lie for Nietzsche in a liberation from all willing (as in Schopenhauer and Buddhism[70]), for this will mean a lapse into utter nothingness (since Being-Will) and it cannot be a liberation from time as such, for it is the 'now', the present in which alone anything 'is' (since Being-presence). For him the redemption from the refractory and the contrary in time, its in-

69. *Was heisst Denken?*, p. 39 (E.T., p. 96).
70. *Vorträge und Aufsätze*, p. 117.

eluctable pastness, can only be through a perpetuation of what "goes" into a "coming" again, so that the passing away sheds its deadness and comes ever anew—the Eternal Recurrence of the Same. If the Being of all that is is willing,[71] if time it taken in the Aristotelian sense of being a flow of 'nows', if the 'now', i.e., the presence of the present, is what to "be" means and if, in consequence, thinking consists in representing and conceiving, then the doctrine of the Eternal Recurrence is the only way out for the Will, the only way in which the Will can heal itself, through such representation, of the wound that Time inflicts upon it. And so long as Time is understood in the Aristotelian sense and Eternity as the 'now' brought to a stand (*nunc stans*), Being, as *presence,* can never be liberated from its thraldom to time nor can the Eternity of which Schelling speaks, non-dependence upon time, ever belong to Being.

In *Being and Time,* Heidegger developed a way of thinking about time which enables us to regard its three ecstasies, past, present and future, as manifestations of a deeper temporality of which these are 'temporalizations'. Time in this sense was described there as the transcendental horizon of the comprehension of Being, as that in which Dasein's transcendence itself is rooted. As against the traditional conception, according to which time, consisting of a flow of 'nows' i.e., as basically the present, is itself something that is present in the present, i.e., as essent, it was suggested that time in the primordial sense is that in terms of which Being itself may be understood, in terms, that is, not of

71. Heidegger quotes (*Ibid.,* p. 112) the following sentences from Schelling's treatise on Human Freedom (*Philosophischen Untersuchungen über das Wesen der Freiheit und die damit zusammenhängenden Gegenstände,*) as the classical formulation of this conception, (followed by Schopenhauer's *Die Welt als Wille und Vorstellung,* 1818) in which the conception of representation finds a similar classical utterance:

"In the last and ultimate instance there is no other Being whatsoever except Will. Will is primal Being and to it alone (i.e., Will) are applicable all the predicates of that (i.e., primal Being): Unfathomability (having no ground outside itself), Eternity, independence from time, self-affirmation. The whole of philosophy is only an effort aiming at giving expression to this sovereign Being."

presence only but of the integral unity of future, past and present. As against the traditional conception, moveover, emphasis was placed on the 'futuristic', the future-oriented, character of time rather than on the past, with the 'going' of the latter incorporated into the 'coming' of the future. In *Kant und das Problem der Metaphysik,* still approaching time from the point of view of Dasein's transcendence, Heidegger identified primordial time with the transcendental imagination (the faculty of synthesis in the general, as he interprets it), in which pure sensibility and pure understanding are themselves rooted and united and which generates, through pure intuition,[72] time as a series of 'nows'. Time in this sense thus constitutes, as self-affection, the basis of the specific finitude of the human subject—rationality dependent upon sensibility—and so man's finite self-hood itself. Transcendental time and the "I think", the I, neither of them 'in time' themselves, are the same and constitute the ultimate horizon in which anything can appear as present. Time is the being of Dasein and, as the ultimate horizon for the manifestation of anything as essent, identical with Being itself. Being in its truth is for Heidegger pure happening; it is, as he says, nothing other than its own happening, the happening of primordial disclosure as the *Ereignis,* in which, while lighting up or opening out world, Being in its essence withholds its own self. The 'history of Being' (i.e., Being in the sense of Ereignis) begins with its *epoche,* its keeping itself to itself, and the epochs of this history are the epochs of man's progressive oblivion and falling out of his relationship to Being. This falling out is itself, however, something positive and a manifestation of his relatedness to Being, a relatedness which even in the extremity of man's alienation remains big with the promise of a revelation of Being in its truth, of a transmutation or absorption of Being in its own true essence, the *Ereignis.* This is what Heidegger once called the eschatology of

---

72. See also *Die Frage nach dem Ding,* pp. 115, 154–157 (E.T. pp. 147, 197–201), for a discussion of Space and Time as pure intuitions.

Being.[73] As *Ereignis,* the truth of Being is itself the happening of
the·belonging-together of man and Being (the ʹisʼ), the happening of truth as concealing-revealing illumination. To what extent
this belonging-together reveals itself to man, in which light of
truth man stands in a particular epoch, how Being (presence)
discloses itself to him in its difference from beings, is the dispensation (*Geschick*), varying from age to age, of the truth of
Being, i.e., of the *Ereignis* itself. The history of Being is not a
series of events ʹin timeʹ but "Being itself" and the ʹit givesʼ of
Time with its still source in that togetherness out of which man
and Being (presence) both emerge.

True Time, Heidegger says, is not a mere flow of duration but
"the arrival" of what has been. This is not something that has
vanished into the past but is the gathering together of what
continues to be; it is prior to all arrival because, as such gathering, it withholds itself preserved in its own beginning."[74] What is
early, in other words, in generating the later, does not as it were
pour itself out fully into that and itself vanish into the nothingness of a dead and petrified past but remains quick with its rich
essence, a treasure hidden and held in trust, as the hiddenness
sustaining and nourishing the unhiddenness of all that comes into
the present as presence.[75] The hidden treasure lying thus suspended in what has been releases itself, so to speak, in what is
yet to come, approaching the present from the direction of the
future, as the future. Space and Time, Heidegger remarks further,[76] are not what they appear to be for calculating, representational thought, mere parameters for measuring off nearness and
remoteness conceived as intervals of distance. In this age of the
peculiar constellation of man and Being characterized as the *Ge-
Stell* above, they appear so but their true nature is revealed when
we think nearness and remoteness, temporal or spatial, in terms

73. See "Der Spruch des Anaximander" in *Holzwege.*
74. *Unterwegs zur Sprache,* p. 58.
75. *Vorträge und Aufsätze,* p. 143.
76. *Unterwegs zur Sprache,* pp. 208–214.

of the Self-same, the togetherness of man and Being as itself the principle of all near-ing. The nearness which is true neighbourliness can never depend upon space and time in their character as parameters. Facing and being turned towards each other, mutuality (*Gegen-einanderüber*), characteristic of neighbourliness, is the way earth and heaven, God and man are united together into true nearness in the world-quadrate. Here, each, open in its self-concealment, opens out to the other, the one extending and yielding itself to the other and so each remaining itself; each guards and tends the other and at the same time covers it over. Nearness in this sense is closed to time (as also space) as a parameter because its 'nows' never open out to each other; they cannot even be said to shut each other out, for such closure itself is a mode of mutuality and presupposes it. The parametrical, only possible in a world dominated by technology, is the devastation of all mutuality and a standing denial of true nearness.

"We can say of Time that it temporalizes (*zeitigt*), of space that it spatializes," keeping in mind that the meaning of Identity is letting-belong-together, mutual owning.[77] Time temporalizes, in the sense of ripening, bringing on and bringing forth. It brings on, in unified fashion and contemporaneously, what it has 'matured' equally, the has been, presence and what we await, the future. Thus temporalizing, it transports us all at once into its three-fold ecstasy, at the same time bringing back to us, through the opening up of each, the concordant unity of has been, presence and awaiting. Carrying away and bringing to, in this fashion, time gives its motion to the triple ecstasy. Time itself in the entirety of its essence does not move but rests in stillness. Both the carrying away and bringing back of Time and (in a similar way) the rooming-in, letting in and out of Space, belong together in the Self-same, the play of Stillness, which Heidegger admits, is for the present recalcitrant to further thought. The Self-same, holding time and space gathered together in their essence,

77. *Unterwegs zur Sprache,* p. 213.

gives motion and direction to the mutuality of the four world-regions, thus bringing to pass the Play of the World.

The step back from metaphysics into its origins leads to a transmutation of 'Being' into something more fundamental. This contains within itself the unity of Being with the essence of man and is such that its meaning is not confined to the unhiddenness of a mere "constancy of presence" but includes within it the 'not' of hiddenness as well as the 'has been' and the 'waiting' of past and future in their indivisible unity with the present. Such Being is not Will, implicitly or explicitly, for it is neither Ground nor Creator when thought about in terms of itself rather than from the point of view of essents. The *Ereignis* is rather a 'letting be' (*Lassen*), the Play of a belongingness that unites together earth and heaven, gods and men within the Four-fold of World, uniting world and things into each other's favour, uniting Word and Being through a permissive letting be. Since Being or Truth in the primordial sense of the *Ereignis* is not something that can ever 'present' itself or be given as an object to thought, it cannot be grasped within a concept, cannot be represented, whether as subject, object or substance. Thinking in the traditional sense of conceiving and representing, in all its various historical forms, is no longer adequate to it. The step back has led, further, to a conception of man in which man is not an independent entity 'having' a relationship to Being but 'is' in his essence this relationship itself. Man also in this sense cannot be brought within the grip of a concept. In consequence, the relationship between man and Being, i.e., thinking, cannot itself be a concept or representation. Time itself, as it emerges into view when we step out of representational thinking, is no longer a succession of presented 'nows', mere sempiternity, but a gathering together of what has been and the coming, an 'arrival' charged with the inexhaustible yet to be, lying within the has been. As one with Being, time, like the former, is never itself presented in the present of a bare now but is the integral unity of the has been and the coming that arrives in a concrete present no longer shorn of its riches but equally incapable of conceptual representation.[78]

Throughout the entire history of Western Philosophy, Being has been approached from the point of view of and interpreted in terms of its relationship to thinking; and thinking, as an activity of the human subject, is understood as serving the double purpose of providing the horizon, the setting, for the interpretation of Being and also the organon or tool for it.[79] But, as we have seen, the original Greek revelation of Being as presence itself constitutes the basis on which thinking in the form of representation can manifest itself. In consequence, not only can thinking in this sense not provide the prior horizon for the interpretation of Being but it can also not be regarded as a neutral instrument, self-validating and self-evident in its universality, for such interpretation. "Logic" as the theory of thinking cannot, hence, be taken as the measure and starting-point, whether as horizon or as organon, for the interpretation of Being. Being (*einai*) and thinking (*noein*) belong together in an Identity (*to auto*) prior to both; it is the happening (*Ereignis*) of primordial Truth (*Lichtung*) which determines both the form in which Being (presence) reveals itself as well as the mode of thinking corresponding to it. Neither "Being" nor "Thinking" are entities with a permanently fixed character and the historicity of forms in which the former manifests itself is reflected in a corresponding transformation in the way "thinking" itself is understood. Throughout the history of Western philosophy, not only has the conception of Being as presence (with its various historical forms) remained an unexamined presupposition but also, along with that, the concep-

---

78. It must be pointed out, expressly and emphatically, that the above account of Difference and Identity (*Ereignis*), World and Thing, Language, Truth and Time, i.e., the account of Heidegger's thinking about the truth of Being, belongs to the sphere of "what is to be thought" (*das Zu-Denkende*). All that Heidegger seeks to accomplish is to open up a sphere, so long closed, for future thought, himself only taking the first preparatory steps. Moreover, this thinking does not and cannot result in a set of sharply defined 'concepts' but only in a simple 'saying' which discloses something of a realm which never finally sheds its mysteriousness.

79. Cf. *Kants These über das Sein*, pp. 32–35.

tion of thinking as representation (*Vorstellen*)—the "oblivion" of Being is at the same time oblivion of the true character of thinking. It follows from this that all "criticisms" of thought (empiricistic or rationalistic, including the Kantian critique of thinking understood as Reason) which have been offered from time to time, have taken a particular form of thinking as embodying the universally valid nature of thought and then proceeded to determine its powers and functions. Heidegger's quest for the truth of Being may be described, therefore, as being also the quest for the true essence of thinking, presupposed in all its historical manifestations but never itself brought to light. It is the most radical "critique" not only of metaphysics but also of the representational thinking that necessarily goes with it and, unlike all previous critiques, it is not destructive but seeks only to uncover the unacknowledged truth or essence of both metaphysics and thought, the source from which both arise and into which they both revert in Heidegger's conception of Identity.[80] The determination of the positive essence of thinking, like that of man (and thinking *is* man in his relationship to Being), must be attempted, according to Heidegger, in terms of the truth of Being, and not the other way round, for, as Heidegger never tires of repeating, the relationship to Being is determined from the side of Being and so must be described in terms of Being itself rather than of man, as metaphysics invariably does.

Thinking in the primary sense is mindfulness, minding or remembrance, the *noein* which, in Parmenides' sentence, belongs together with "Being" in the *to auto*, the Self-same. Thinking as such, as distinguished from the unthinking calculation of science and the "philosophy" about essents, is thinking *of* the Self-same, of Being (where Being is both subject and object), demanded

---

80. Cf. L. Landgrebe, *"Husserl, Heidegger, Sartre"* (*Revue de Metaphysique et de Morale,* No. 4, 1964) where he shows how these three philosophers have contributed, each in his own way, to such a critique and towards the emergence of a new conception of thinking (*pensée méditative,* as Landgrebe calls it) which alone can do justice to the fundamental problems of our epoch.

and brought to pass by Being and in turn a cherishing of it.
Thinking in this primordial sense is cherishing, holding in memory, unceasing and collected abiding, not merely with what is
past but equally with the present and the coming. It is a gathered-
together mindfulness of the has been, the is and the coming in
their unity, the remembrance of Be-ing (*An-wesen,* i.e., Being in
the non-metaphysical sense, not confined to presence), entirely at
the disposal and behest of the *Ereignis* in which it is owned.[81] As
such cherishing and dependence, thinking is man's responsive
relationship to Being, a kind of thanking. It is a thanks-giving for
the gift of our own essence, for the relationship of belongingness
in the truth of Being. Being itself, as itself this relationship,
claims our remembrance and we, as intrinsically belonging in the
Identity, are the mortals that we are in virtue of such remembrance. It is remembrance in and through which what is in itself
thought-worthy, i.e., Being in its truth, is preserved, "trued" and
liberated in its "it gives" and in its coming to us as a gift entrusted to our care. Such cherishing is not something different
from and external to Truth but the latter itself in the way in
which it gives itself to us as what is most worthy and needy of
thought.[82]

Thinking in the above sense is nothing psychological, no "act"
of a supposedly independent agent called man and directed
towards or against some entity standing over against him. With
the emergence of Being (*einai*) as presence (*physis*), itself
needing (*chre*) letting-lie-in-front (*legein, Vorliegen-lassen*) as
well as mindfulness or taking care of (*noein, in-die-Achtneh-
men*), as Parmenides has it, there arises a conception of thinking
which eventually developed into the logical concept of thinking as judgment. The initial coupling together of *noein* (*Vernehmen,* apprehension) and *legein* (stating), however, had as yet

81. Heidegger refers in this context to the myth of Mnemosyne, daughter
of Earth and Heaven, the bride of Zeus and the mother of the nine Muses.
See *Das heisst Denken?,* p. 7 (E.T., p. 11).
82. For this paragraph and the following, see *Was heisst Denken?,*
passim, and the essay with this title in *Vorträge und Aufsätze.*

nothing in it of Reason (*Vernunft*, from *Vernehmen*) and Judgment (*logos*). As yet, thinking is "not a grasping, neither a grabbing at what lies in front, nor an attack on it. What lies in front is not, in *legein* and *noein*, moulded into shape by gripping and handling. Thinking is not (as yet) com-prehending."[83] It is only with the falling out of *legein* and *noein*, originally interwoven and resting on and determined in their unity by the differentiation, the two-foldness (*Zwiefalt*), of Being and beings, from their dependence on Being (as Difference) that they appear later in the form of *ratio*. Thinking is thus transformed into logic; Reason and its concepts (representation) are only *one* mode of thinking, not self-determined but dependent upon the way the Greek *logos* was transformed into *ratio* as European man's specific response to the way the Being of essents disclosed itself to him and claimed him. For such rational, representational thinking, everything turns into an essent, is objectivized and rendered amenable to the taming, subjugating Will of a Subject. Being in its truth eludes its grasp, as also man, world and thing in their essence. It is this inaccessibility of the truth of Being to such thinking that Heidegger strikingly formulates in the statement, "thinking only begins when we have realized that Reason, elevated for centuries into a position of supremacy, is the most pertinacious opponent of thinking."[84] Thinking, as man's relationship to "the region of all regions", must, like all true relationship, maintain and preserve both man and Being in their real nature and it can do so only when it ceases to be representational and conceptual, when it sheds itself of its volitional character and becomes a serene "letting", beyond willing and beyond the will not to will. Thinking in the sense in which alone it is adequate to man's belongingness in the *Ereignis* can only be, as Heidegger says in the Dialogue on Serenity,[85] a kind of waiting (not an awaiting,

83. *Was heisst Denken?*, p. 128 (E.T., p. 211).
84. *Holzwege*, p. 24.
85. Cf. *Gelassenheit*, p. 44 (E.T., p. 68). The term *Gelassenheit* (serenity, calmness, collectedness; transl. by Richardson as 'release') belongs to the vocabulary of German mysticism. Heidegger employs it to indicate man's

which always has an object), a surrender, a tranquil resignation to the Self-same. Such thinking is not a self-assertive act of man but is the expression of his repose in Being; it is not a going beyond or an ascent to something remote from man but is the Instancy (*Inständigkeit,* standing within) in what is nearest, in the nearing region of the *Ereignis* which, as primordial Truth, is nearness (*Nähe*) itself. This thinking does not argue and prove, gives nothing that might be kept as a possession, brings no final conceptual "clarity"; it only points and shows, letting the "region" to which it belongs exhibit itself in all its mystery. And language is not its tool or expression but this thinking itself, its very motion and chant.

IV THE SAVING LEAP

For Heidegger, the Western metaphysical tradition has been a ladder which has enabled him to climb up to the place and moment of its birth and to see this point as pregnant with the entire development which, through its culmination in the scientific and technological mode of thinking dominating the man of today, has assumed a planetary importance, far exceeding the limits of a geographically or historically localized 'culture' or 'civilization'. In this "Europeanization of the earth", Edmund Husserl, the Husserl of the last *Krisis* phase, sees the abiding and universal significance of Western 'philosophy' in its Greek origins, for it is this essentially Greek phenomenon that constitutes the foundation of the rise and development of modern science.[86] Heidegger likewise insists on the basically Greek character of

---

true relation to the Region, a "nay-saying to willing" which is a "higher kind of action that is yet no activity." The corresponding term in *Being and Time* is *Entschlossenheit* (resoluteness). For a summary of the dialogue, *Zur Erörterung der Gelassenheit,* see Richardson (*Heidegger,* pp. 502–510); also Versényi (Heidegger, *Being and Truth,* pp. 142–146) for a brief discussion of both the dialogue and the address entitled *Gelassenheit.*

86. Cf. *Die Krisis der europäischen Wissenschaften,* p. 4 and the whole of Sec. 6. So also, in his own way, does Bertrand Russell. Cf. The "Introduction" to his recent *The Wisdom of the West.*

Western-European philosophy (and there is no other, either Chinese or Indian, as he puts it[87]), which for him is an essentially Western phenomenon, as distinguished from the 'thinking' of the East and from the 'thinking' which has found expression, outside the central 'philosophical' mainstream, within the literary, the religious and the mystical tradition of the West itself. As he remarks,[88] the phrase "Western-European philosophy" is in truth a tautology, because 'philosophy' is in essence Greek; even though it is dominated in its modern form by Christian conceptions, it still remains true that "the West and Europe, and only they, are, in the innermost movement of their history, basically 'philosophical'. This is testified by the rise and dominance of the sciences. Because they originate from the innermost dynamic core of Western-European history, viz. the philosophical, they are in a position today to give its specific contemporary stamp to the history of mankind upon the whole earth." Unlike Husserl, however, Heidegger sees this "complete Europeanization of the earth and of mankind" eating away all substance from things, drying up the very wellsprings of reality.[89] He sees this because, having climbed back to the source from which Western metaphysical thought has sprung up, he not only finds in this source a wellspring hiding in itself much that has remained the Unthought but sustaining foundation of Western philosophy but, taking the step back, leaps from this point into a region which is above the opposition of East and West, beyond the clash of traditions and the conflict of religions. This "region of all regions", suspended in itself, is itself above all regional loyalties and the Babel of conflicting tongues. It is the realm of that universality and simplicity

87 *Was heisst Denken?*, p. 136 (E.T., p. 224).
88. Cf. *Was ist das—die Philosophie?*, p. 13 (E.T., p. 31).
89. Cf. *Unterwegs zur Sprache*, pp. 103 f. As Karlfried Gründer remarks, the problem of the essence, possibility and limitations of science pervades all of Heidegger's writings. Cf. *M. Heideggers Wissenschaftskritik in ihren geschichtlichen Zusammenhängen*, in *Archiv für Philosophie*, 11/3–4, 1962. This article, of which a translation has recently appeared in *Philosophy Today*, is valuable for an understanding of Heidegger's attitude towards science as also for the whole which Hölderlin has played in his thinking.

of primordial truth, the happening of *aletheia*, of overtness, in the belongingness of man and Being in the Self-same, where alone divergent traditions, disfranchised of their exclusive claims and yet without losing their own identity, can meet together as one, as belonging-together in the Self-same. If there is any hope of an ultimate unity of divergent philosophies and religions, it lies not in the throwing of dubious bridges across them, not in questionable syntheses and compromises, but solely, through a going back of each to its own origins, in the leap into this swaying region, vibrant with the possibility of giving voice to its primordial word in a multiplicity of tongues.[90]

This realm is inaccessible to representational thinking; 'philosophy', as conceptual thought, has no entry into this sphere of the *Ereignis*. But neither is it accessible only in the ineffable immediacy of the 'personal' experience of individual men. This realm opens out and reveals itself, Heidegger believes as a thinker, to the unpretentious simplicity and humility of plain 'Thinking', dwelling in the neighbourhood of poetic utterance as a mode of pure saying, itself no more than the spoken echo of the chime of Stillness, to that thinking which is an utterance, revealing and so in a true sense realizing, of man's belongingness, with

90. Cf. the remarks of H-G. Gadamer on the extent to which Western philosophy can be synthesized with Eastern (in "Vorwort" to *Grundriss der allgemeinen Geschichte der Philosophie* by W. Dilthey, Frankfurt, 1949; quoted by Glasenapp in *Das Indienbild deutscher Denker*): *Obwohl die Forschung auf dem Gebiete der Philosophie des Ostens inzwischen weiter gefördert worden ist, glauben wir uns heute eher weiter von ihrem philosophischen Verständnis entfernt: die Schärfung unseres historischen Bewusstseins hat die Übersetzungen oder Übertragungen der Texte . . . von Grund auf problematisch gemacht . . . Von einer aneignung dieser Dinge durch die abendländische Philosophie kann nicht die Rede sein. Nur die negative Einsicht kann als gesichert gelten, dass unsere eigenen, durch die Griechen geprägten Grundbegriffe das Fremde in der Substanz verändern.* To be sure, these remarks are made from a perspective quite different from that of intellectual and cultural "ambassadors", professionally engaged in throwing bridges across. But they deserve more serious attention and a more philosophical response than defenders of the Indian cultural heritage like Helmuth von Glasenapp have been able to offer. Similar doubts were expressed by Professor Heidegger in conversation.

all that is, in the Self-same. The leap out of metaphysical thinking, away from the separateness of man and Being, is not an
abdication of thought, not a leap into the 'mystical', into some
kind of intuitive, unmediated cognitive experience. As a leap of
thought, it is only a transformation of its own nature, such that,
surrendering its conceptuality, its will to grasp, it becomes a
simple co-respondence to the *Ereignis,* content in its function of
letting what is reveal itself, of *letting* Truth shine forth in all its
obscuring-revealing mystery. As a European, Heidegger has only
the ladder of his own central 'philosophical' tradition by which to
climb over to its earliest germination and to take from there the
leap that might, as he hopes,[91] convert "this Land of the Eve-
ning, away beyond Occident and Orient and cutting straight
through the European, into a place from which there may
emanate a new historical destiny (a history governed by the
mutuality of man and Being rather than by the withdrawal of the
latter, as thus far) in the time to come." Perhaps other traditions
have other ladders enabling them to go up to the springboard,
perhaps a ladder is not indispensable.[92] But the leap by which
one can alight on this region, and from there have a complete
view of the birth and development of one's tradition in its entirety, is by itself not enough. The leap is a renunciation of the
might of conceptual, representational thinking—from the point of
view of the latter a renunciation of thought itself—but like all
renunciation, it does not impoverish but gives, bestows upon the

91. *Holzwege,* p. 300. Cf. in this connection Egon Vietta's observations in
his *Die Seinsfrage bei Martin Heidegger* (pp. 93–94): "Indian princes in
particular have ever again sought for a religion which should be equally
valid for all men and above all creeds. The quest of a religion for which all
dogmatic differences become untenable engages every thoughtful East
Asiatic. The East also knows the sage for whom the various religious com-
munities co-exist as of equal value in the eyes of God. But in Oriental
thinking, the sages themselves have not been able to find a way of realizing
in thought this demand. For that reason, we may suggest at least as a
question, whether Heidegger's philosophizing does not offer such a way.
Heidegger's thinking is world-historical, very much as the thinking of Plato
and Kant has determined the course of Western history." See also *Hölderlins
Erde und Himmel* (*Hölderlin-Jahrbuch,* 1958/60, pp. 35–36.)
92. Cf. *Gelassenheit,* p. 51.

thinker "the inexhaustible power of the simple." All that metaphysical thought has sought, in vain, to catch in its conceptual net, the Soul, the World, God (the subject-matter of the three branches of *metaphysica specialis*, Psychology, Cosmology and Theology) comes back in its truth to a thinking that has reverted to its own humble essence. To such renunciation and surrender to the Self-same, Soul, World and God all speak with the true eloquence of simplicity.[93] And the thinker's task, like the poet's, far from being consummated in the transforming leap that enables him to listen to the voice of silence, only *begins* here, for the realm of the *Ereignis* needs, to be truly and effectively the realm of Truth that it is, man's guarding, tending and realizing response. In order that man's collective historical existence should become a true 'dwelling' in this region, it is necessary that he should work unwearyingly, with all self-will transmuted into tranquil resignation (*Gelassenheit*), at building, by means of the inexhaustible wealth of material that language puts at his disposal, a home for humanity on this region.

It is towards such planetary construction (which might be described, in the idiom of contemporary linguistic philosophy, as the construction of a universal, basic language of Truth from which the languages of different philosophical and religious traditions can be derived) that Heidegger seeks to take the first pioneering steps, leaving to the future a task no less vast in its magnitude than it is supreme in its urgency. In this endeavour at planetary thinking, Heidegger realizes, a 'dialogue' with East Asiatic thought is inescapable. Neither side, he believes, is as yet equal to the impending encounter between the ways in which the European and East Asiatic languages speak. And this is no less true about the sphere of a possible dialogue between them for, as he says, "Neither of the two is capable, by itself, to lay open and establish this sphere."[94] The central tradition of Indian thought,

93. *Der Feldweg*, p. 7.
94. *Zur Seinsfrage*, p. 43. Cf. Heidegger's remarks in "From a Dialogue on Language" (*Unterwegs zur Sprache*, pp. 93–94): ". . . Even today the

with its clear vision of the realm of Identity and of the intimacy of man's belongingness in what Heidegger calls the *Ereignis,* has surely a vital contribution to make to this venture at co-operative building.[95] But in an age in which the "Europeanization of the

appropriate word is still to be found. The outlook for the thinking that labours to prove adequate to the essence of language still remains obscure in its full scope. For this reason, I cannot as yet see whether the nature of language as I am attempting to think, *also* suffices to express the nature of east Asiatic language, whether in the end—which would be at the same time the beginning,—it is at all possible to realize in thought an essence of language which might guarantee that European-Western and East Asiatic ways of talking ('saying') can enter into a mutual dialogue in such a manner that a music flowing from a single source can be heard in it." This dialogue between Heidegger and a Japanese scholar brings home the need of extreme caution in every kind of 'comparative' philosophizing and in the employment of Western metaphysical terms to express ideas rooted in another linguistic soil. One consequence of the "all-consuming Europeanization" mentioned above is that even Eastern scholars are tempted to adopt, even outside the scientific sphere, European conceptual thinking as the measure by which to judge, and naturally find deficient, their own non-representational ways of saying, i.e. showing, the truth of things.

In his challenging essay, "Über den paradigmatischen Charakter der griechisschen Kultur" (in *Gegenwart der Griechen im neueren Denken*), Johannes Lohmann takes the extreme position that even among the Indo-European languages, the demythologization of language and the concep-tualization of the verb 'is' has been accomplished only in Greek. He says, "*So kommt nur in Griechenland der Samen, den die indogermanishche Sprache . . . hervorgebracht hat, zum Wachstum, zur Blüte und zur Reife. In Indien geht das e s t i als 'copula' des Satzes . . . praktisch wieder verloren.*" Perhaps a greater familiarity with the Indian thinkers' discovery of *Vak* and their labours to conceptualize the 'is'—with a history covering the period from 500 B.C. to 1600 A.D.—would have enabled Lohmann to see that there is more to Indian thought than a mere elevation of the magic-word *Brahman* to a world-principle. In what specific sense the Greek 'con-cept' is yet unique and in this uniqueness dominates the world today, is an open question which Heidegger has been the first to explore in all its implications. Lohmann's investigations, published in a series of articles in *Lexis* and in his book, *Philosophie und Sprachwissenschaft* (1965), consti-tute a valuable application of Heidegger's insights to linguistic science and a first attempt at analysing how and why different languages speak differently.

95. The task envisaged here is something quite different from "compara-tive philosophy". Suggestions towards an interpretation of early Indian philosophy stimulated by Heidegger's mode of thinking have been made by Leo Gabriel (*Vom Brahma zur Existenz*, 2nd ed., 1956). But as against such attempts, in themselves not without value, what Heidegger speaks about is a "dialogue" between the *languages* of the East and the West, an inquiry into the different ways in which they *speak.*

A good example of the first, comparative type of 'dialogue' is an article by

Earth and of humanity" is no longer a mere threat but has become a harsh reality, when his way of thinking is in most respects
taken up into and dominated by the universal sway of the
metaphysical, the rational, the scientific and the technological,
the thinking Indian faces a challenge to which he was never
exposed before: the compulsion of belonging, irretrievably and
inescapably, to this 'one world' of the *Ge-Stell,* to a world 'one'
only in the desolation of being enveloped within the Nihilistic
metaphysical heritage of the West. The present spiritual situation
and its challenge is utterly new in history because of its universal
and all-enveloping character, because there is neither escaping it
nor a possibility of directly attacking it and because no strategy
of defence can be enduringly effective against it. Its "compulsion" lies in this that there is no other way open, to us in the East,
but to go along with this Europeanization and to go *through* it.
Only through this voyage into the foreign and the strange can we
win back our own self-hood; here as elsewhere, the way to what
is closest to us is the longest way back.[96] This challenge demands a bold, freely undertaken marching out into the alien, the
questionable and the unhomely. And it demands a profounder re-
thinking of our Indian tradition in terms of its own original beginnings, of what was originally 'heard' in it, a more searching
and critical analysis of its historical unfoldment, a clearer vision
of the nature, significance and limitations of metaphysical thinking (i.e., representational, conceptual, logical, scientific thinking
in the Western sense, as also of allied manifestations within our

---

the Japanese philosopher Hajime Tanabe, entitled *Todesdialektik* ('The
Dialectic of Death', in *Martin Heidegger zum siebzigsten Geburtstag,* 1959).
Tanabe approaches Heidegger's philosophy from the point of view of
Mahayana Buddhism, especially Zen, and interprets Heidegger's analysis of
death and his conception of *Ereignis* from this point of view. Heidegger, it
may be added, has deeply influenced contemporary Japanese thinking and
has himself been, ever since the twenties, in intimate contact with Japanese
scholars and, through them, with Buddhist thought.

96. As Heidegger has remarked (*Hölderlins Hymnen,* quoted by Pöggeler, op. cit., p. 226), the appropriation of what is our very own occurs only
as a home-coming, as a return from a journey into the alien and the other;
this is the law of being at home as a making oneself at home. See also the
motto placed at the beginning of this work.

own tradition), a greater sensitiveness to the silent message of language. As a powerful stimulus to such re-thinking—which alone is true appropriating and safe-guarding—of the basic truth of our tradition and as a summons inviting us to participate in the co-operative endeavour of planetary building, Heidegger's thinking, single-minded and yet polyphonic in its beauty, passionate and yet commanding in the sweep of its vision, may not be without some relevance.

As remarked at the very outset, Heidegger's philosophy is not a finished system, lying ready to be submitted to a final critical scrutiny. It is neither a system (being itself an investigation into the implicit basis of all Western philosophical systems) nor something finished and complete. Itself "on the way", it only opens out an unexplored "way" for future thought. Moreover, Heidegger is too close to us in time to afford the distance requisite for an impartial, objective assessment—the contemporary, as Heidegger has himself remarked, is the least understood, being always "untimely".[97] Nevertheless, from the perspective of the exposition of the nature of Being given above, we may address a few questions to Heidegger as a thinker of Being, for whom the "essence" of Time, too, cannot itself be temporal nor eternity a mere word.

It has been suggested here that Heidegger's thinking carries him beyond the limitation of his own tradition into a region of "pure" thinking, the region of Being in *its* truth, unconditioned

97. As will have become evident by now, Heidegger's regular practice, on his 'way' of thought, has been to look back constantly at what he has already thought and interpret it from his present position, while going beyond it all the time. The 'later' Heidegger is thus always, explicitly or implicitly, a commentator and critic of his own former self. Among his explicitly autobiographical statements are the remarks in "Aus einem Gespräch von der Sprache" (in *Unterwegs zur Sprache*), the "Preface" in Richardson's *Heidegger* and remarks in his Address to the Heidelberg Academy of Sciences (in *Jahresheft der Heidelberger Akademie der Wissenschaften*, 1957/58, Heidelberg, 1959; also in Leo Gabriel's *Wege zum Sein* in *Wissenschaft und Weltbild*, vol. 12, 1959). For the controversial problem of the nature and justification of his self-interpretations, see F. W. von Herrmann's *Die Selbstinterpretation Martin Heideggers* (1964).

by the particular tradition *from* which one happens to leap into
it, unconditioned by the particular form of representational thinking—Western "philosophy" or metaphysics—which has historically preceded the leap. In *Gelassenheit,* Heidegger in fact
roundly speaks of two "kinds" of thinking, suggesting that it lies
in the very nature of man's relationship to Being to bifurcate into
these two modes. He says (p. 15), "Thus there are two kinds of
thinking, each of which is in its way legitimate and necessary:
calculative thinking and meditative (recollective) thoughtful-
ness." And yet one does not find in Heidegger an explicit recognition of the possibility that such a universal, historically unconditioned level of thinking, valid for all traditions and yet leaving room for individual variations,—as regards the form assumed
by both the essent-centred as well as the Being-centred thought
—might actually have been realized in some other tradition.
Heidegger admits that thinking in "the manner of conceptual
representation all too easily creeps into every type of human
experience, even where (as in the case of the Japanese) thinking
is in a certain sense non-representational" and that hence "the
metaphysical mode of representation . . . is in some respect inevitable."[98] If this is true of man in general, the origin of such
representational thinking cannot lie in the Western destiny of
Being. May it not be that man *as* man (irrespective of whether
he is Greek, or Chinese, or Indian) has some comprehension of
Being in so far as, as man, he has dealings with essents? May it
not be that, *as* man—Oriental or Occidental—he has the inherent
tendency towards becoming forfeit to the world and, losing himself in it, to interpret Being in terms of the essent; that, always
and everywhere, in becoming forfeit to the world, man relates
himself to the essent, to world and to Being by representing and
conceptualizing it? May this truth not have been realized already
in another tradition?

It may be admitted that the thinking of the *Ereignis,* the reach-

98. *Unterwegs zur Sprache,* p. 116.

ing up to this realm, is mediated in the case of the Western man by the history of his own metaphysical tradition. Does it follow from this that such dwelling in the "Region of all regions" must always be mediated? Does not Heidegger himself admit that it is Being in its truth that is the all empowering, in which all dispensation has its source? And even if it is in some sense necessarily mediated, must its mediation have the unique character of the Western metaphysical destiny? Further, the findings of the analytic of Dasein are presumably not restricted to the *Dasein* of Western man or to a particular epoch in history nor, by the same logic, is what Heidegger later says about the belongingness of man and Being in the Self-same. What Heidegger says about the human state as one of confusion, delusion and error (*Irren, Irre, Irrtum*) in *Vom Wesen der Wahrheit* is not itself a historical manifestation but a characterization of the way history itself (i.e., man's historical existence) always, everywhere *is*. Is it not possible that it is a universal character of thought to lapse into the "metaphysical" and to develop into a tradition of the oblivion of Being as such? Is not the tradition of Indian thought one in which the lapse into representational thinking—of a different complexion than that in the West, to be sure—has already come under the scrutiny of thought, is it not a tradition in which an awareness of the "Difference", of the "Identity" and of the necessity of a "reversal" are present from its earliest beginnings? Perhaps, it is "the Thinker's profound loyalty to his inner limits" of which Heidegger speaks in *Nietzsche* that prevents him from a precipitate and premature answer.

In a letter published immediately after the first world war under the title, *"La Crise de l'esprit,"* Paul Valéry asked, "This Europe, will it become *what it is in reality,* i.e. a little cape of the Asiatic continent? Or will this Europe remain rather *what it seems,* i.e., the priceless part of the whole earth, the pearl of the globe, the brain of a vast body?" Quoting these sentences, Heidegger remarks that perhaps Europe has already become what it is, a mere cape, yet it remains, at the same time, the brain of the entire body of the earth, the brain that carries out our techno-logical-industrial, planetary-interstellar, computations.[99] The contemporary world situation is, in respect of its essential source, through and through European-Western-Greek, and if it is to change, the resources for this must lie, and be sought, in the untapped abundance of this origin, of that great beginning to which there cannot be any mere return but which preserves in itself the saving possibility that may yet in its coming fulfil and heal the present. That is why Heidegger inquires into this 'great beginning', asking whether Europe, this cape and brain, must first become "the land of a sunset", from which the morning of another world history may prepare to dawn. This new dawn, Heidegger admits, cannot remain in its Western isolation but "opens itself to the few other great beginnings which, in what is their very own, belong in the Self-Same of the source of that Infinite Relation which sustains and holds the earth." The *Upan-iṣadic,* mystical tradition of Indian religious and philosophical thought, by going back to its own unspent origins and opening itself out at the same time to the 'unthought' in that other great beginning in the West, can perhaps contribute more substantially towards the preparation of a new dawn than has seemed possible so far.

99. *Hölderlins Erde und Himmel* (*Hölderlin-Jahrbuch,* 1958–60, pp. 35–36.)

Bibliography

I. HEIDEGGER'S WRITINGS

1. "Das Realitäsproblem in der modernen Philosophie." *Philosophisches Jahrbuch der Görres-Gesellschaft*, XXV, 1912.
2. "Neuere Forschungen über Logik." *Literarische Rundschau für das katholische Deutschland*, XXXVIII, 1912.
3. Review of *Kant's Briefe* by F. Ohmann. *Literarische Rundschau für das katholische Deutschland*, XXXIX, 1913.
4. Review of *Zeitlichkeit und Zeitlosigkeit* by N. Bubnoff. *Literarische Rundschau für das katholische Deutschland*, XXXIX, 1913.
5. Review of *Von der Klassifikation psychischer Phänomene* by Franz Brentano. *Literarische Rundschau für das katholische Deutschland*, XL, 1914.
6. Review of *Kant und Aristoteles* by C. Sentroul. *Literarische Rundschau für das katholische Deutschland*, XL, 1914.
7. Review of *Kant-Laienbrevier* by F. Gross. *Literarische Rundschau für das katholische Deutschland*, XL, 1914.
8. *Die Lehre vom Urteil im Psychologismus. Ein kritischpositiver Beitrag zur Logik*. Leipzig, 1914.
9. "Der Zeitbegriff in der Geschichtswissenschaft." *Zeitschrift für Philosophie und philosophische Kritik*, CLXI, 1916. Freiburg Probevorlesung, 1915.
10. *Die Kategorien-und Bedeutungslehre des Duns Scotus*. Tübingen, 1916. Freiburg Habilitationsschrift, 1915.
11. "Abendgang auf der Reichenau." *Das Bodenseebuch*, IV, 1917.
12. "Zur Geschichte des philosophischen Lehrstuhls seit 1866." *Die Philipps-Universitaet zu Marburg 1527–1927*. Marburg, 1927.
13. *Sein und Zeit, Erste Hälfte*. *Jahrbuch für Philosophie und phänomenologische Forschung*, VIII, 1927. Simultaneously published separately; 7th ed., with "Vorbemerkung" and with "Erste Hälfte" left out, Tübingen, Niemeyer, 1953. Variations in reading, as between earlier and later editions, are noted by Macquarrie and Robinson in the English translation. Lecture courses on "Her-

meneutik der Faktizität" date back to 1919/20; lecture course on "Ontologie oder Hermeneutik der Faktizität," 1923; lecture course on Descartes, Marburg, 1923/24; Address on "Die Zeit," 1924 and Address to Marburg theologians, 1924.

14. "Anmerkungen" *zu* Husserl, in part in W. Biemel's "Husserls Encyclopaedia Britannica Artikel und Heideggers Anmerkungen dazu"; complete in *Husserliana Vol. IX*, The Hague, 1962 (pp. 237–301 and 590–600).

15. "Brief" an Husserl, in *Husserliana*, vol. IX, pp. 600f. and Anlagen I & II, pp. 601f.

16. Review of *Philosophie der Symbolischen Formen*, 2 Teil, by Ernst Cassirer. *Deutsche Literaturzeitung für Kritik der Internationalen Wissenschaft*, Neue Folge, V, 1928.

17. "Vorbemerkung des Herausgebers," in "Edmund Husserls Vorlesungen zur Phaenomenologie des inneren Zeitbewusstseins." *Jahrbuch für Philosophie und phänomenologische Forschung*, IX, 1928.

18. *Vom Wesen des Grundes*. Supplementary Volume, *Jahrbuch für Philosophie und phänomenologische Forschung*, 1929. Simultaneously published separately; 3rd ed., with "Vorwort," Frankfurt, 1949.
Conceived, 1928.

19. *Kant und das Problem der Metaphysik*. Bonn, 1929. 2nd ed., with new "Vorwort," Frankfurt, 1951.

20. *Was ist Metaphysik?* Bonn, 1929.
Frieburg Inaugural Lecture, 1929; conceived, 1928. 4th ed., with "Nachwort" and 5th ed., with "Einletung," Frankfurt, 1943 and 1949 respectively.

21. "Die Selbstbehauptung der deutschen Universität," Breslau, 1933. Rectoral speech, Freiburg, 1933.

22. "Hölderlin und das Wesen der Dichtung." *Das innere Reich*, III, Munich, 1936/37. Speech at Rome, 1936.

23. "Wege zur Aussprache." *Allemannenland*. Stuttgart, 1937; also in Schneeberger's *Nachlese zu Heidegger*.

24. "Lettre à M. J. Wahl." *Bulletin de la Société francaise de Philosophie*, XXXVII, 1937; also in *Existence Humaine et Transcendence*. Neuchàtel, 1944.

25. "Prologue." *Qu'est-ce que la metaphysique?*, tr. and ed. Henri Corbin. Gallimard, 1938.

26. "Hölderlins Hymne 'Wie wenn am Feiertage'." Halle, 1941. Speech delivered, 1939.

27. "Platons Lehre von der Wahrheit." *Geistige Überlieferung*, II, 1942; also in *Platons Lehre von der Wahrheit. Mit einem Brief über den 'Humanismus'*." Bern, 1947. Conceived, 1930/31.
28. *Vom Wesen der Wahrheit*. Frankfurt, 1943.
    2nd ed., with enlarged "Schlussanmerkung," 1949.
    Delivered as Address since 1930; lecture course, 1937/38.
29. "Andenken." *Hölderlin Gedenkschrift*, ed. P. Kulckholn. Tübingen, 1943.
30. *Erläuterungen zu Hölderlin*. Frankfurt, 1944, containing "Heimkunft/An die Verwandten" (Address, 1943) and No. 22.
31. "Brief über den 'Humanismus'." *Platons Lehre von der Wahrheit*. Bern, 1947. Published separately as *Über den Humanismus*, Frankfurt, 1949.
32. "Der Zuspruch des Feldweges." *Sonntagsblatt*, 23–10–1949, Hamburg. Also, *Wort und Wahrheit*, V, Wien, 1950. 2nd ed., with the title *Der Feldweg*. Frankfurt, 1956.
33. *Holzwege*. Frankfurt, 1950. Contains:
    "Der Ursprung des Kunstwerkes," dating back to Address delivered during 1935/36; published separately, with "Zusatz" (1956), Stuttgart, 1960; "Die Zeit des Weltbildes," dating back to Address in 1938;
    "Hegels Begriff der Erfahrung," dating back to Seminars and Addresses during 1942/43;
    "Nietzsches Wort 'Gott ist tot'," dating back to Nietzsche lecture courses during 1936–1940 and Address in 1943;
    "Wozu Dichter?" Address, 1946;
    "Der Spruch des Anaximander," part of a treatise written in 1946.
34. *Erläuterungen zu Hölderlins Dichtung*. Frankfurt, 1951. 2nd ed. of No. 30, containing all the four Hölderlin essays mentioned above.
35. "Seinsverlassenheit und Irrnis." *Ernst Barlach*, ed. E. Vietta. Darmstadt, 1951. Included in "Überwindung der Metaphysik" in *Vorträge und Aufsätze*. Written during 1936–46.
36. "Briefe" an Emil Staiger. *Zu einem Vers von Mörike. Trivium*, IX, 1951; also separately, Zürich, Atlantis.
37. "Das Ding." *Jahrbuch der Bayerischen Akademie der Schönen Künste*, I, 1951. With "Nachwort," *Vorträge und Aufsätze*. Address, 1950.
38. "Logos." *Festschrift für Hans Jantzen*. Berlin, 1951. Dates back to lecture course on "Logik," 1944.

THE PHILOSOPHY OF MARTIN HEIDEGGER

39. "Bauen Wohnen Denken," *Mensch und Raum* (Darmstadter Gespräch, II.), Darmstadt, 1952.
Address, 1951.
40. "Was heisst Denken?" *Merkur,* VI, 1952.
41. "Georg Trakl." *Menkur,* VII, 1953; under the title, "Die Sprache im Gedicht" in *Unterwegs zur Sprache.*
42. *Einführung in die Metaphysik.* Tübingen, 1953.
Lecture course, 1935.
43. "Brief" an die Redaktion. *Die Zeit,* XXXIX, 24–9–1953.
44. "Die Frage nach der Technik." *Jahrbuch der Bayerischen Akademie der Schönen Künste,* III, 1954; also in *Die Künste im technischen Zeitalter.* München, 1956. Address, 1953; enlarged form of Address on "Das Gestell" in 1949.
45. "Anmerkungen über die Metaphysik." *Festschrift für Emil Preetorius.* Wiesbaden, 1954. Included in "Überwindung der Metaphysik" in *Vorträge und Aufsätze.* Written during 1936–46.
46. "Wissenschaft und Besinnung." *Börsenblatt für den Deutschen Buchhandel.* Frankfurt, 13–4–1954.
Address, 1953.
47. ". . . dichterisch wohnet der Mensch . . ." *Akzente. Zeitschrift für Dichtung,* I, 1954.
Address, 1951.
48. "Heraklit." *Festschrift der 350. Jahresfeier des Humanistischen Gymnasiums in Konstanz.* Konstanz, 1954. Under the title "Aletheia" in *Vorträge und Aufsätze.* Dates back to lecture course on Heraclitus, 1943.
49. *Vorträge und Aufsätze.* Pfullingen, 1954. Contains:
Nos. 37, 38, 39, 40, 44, 46, 47 and 48; also "Überwindung der Metaphysik" (incorporating Nos. 35 and 45), "Wer ist Nietzsches Zarathustra?" (Address, 1953) and "Moira" (from lecture course on "Was heisst Denken?," 1951–1952).
50. *Aus der Erfahrung des Denkens.* Pfullingen, 1954.
Written, 1947.
51. *Was heisst Denken?* Tübingen, 1954.
Lecture course, 1951–1952.
52. "Über 'Die Linie'," *Festschrift für Ernst Jünger.* Frankfurt, 1955.
Separately, as *Zur Seinsfrage.* Frankfurt, 1956.
53. *Was ist das—die Philosophie?* Pfullingen, 1956.
Address, 1955.
54. "Encuentros con Ortega." *Claviteno, Revista de la Asociacion Internacional de Hispanismo,* Vol. VIII, No. 39, Madrid, 1956.

55. *Der Satz vom Grund.* Pfullingen, 1957. Contains lecture course of 1955/56 and Address, 1956.
56. *Hebel—der Hausfreund.* Pfullingen, 1957.
57. *Identität und Differenz.* Pfullingen, 1957. Contains: "Der Satz der Identität," an Address of 1957 and "Die onto-theologische Verfassung der Metaphysik," the concluding lecture of a Seminar on Hegel's *Wissenschaft der Logik* in 1956/57.
58. "Vom Wesen and Begriff der *physis,*" Aristoteles *Physik* B 1, *Il Pensiero,* III, Milan, 1958. Seminar lectures, 1940.
59. "Grundsätze des Denkens." Jahrbuch für Psychologie und Psychotherapie, VI, 1958.
60. *Unterwegs zur Sprache.* Pfullingen, 1959. Contains: "Die Sprache." Address, 1950; "Die Sprache im Gedicht." No 41 above; "Aus einem Gespräch von der Sprache." Written during 1953/54; "Das Wesen der Sprache." Three Addresses in 1957/58; "Das Wort." Address, 1958; "Der Weg zur Sprache." Address, 1959, published also in *Die Sprache,* Darmstadt, 1959.
61. "Aufzeichnungen aus der Werkstatt." Neue Züricher Zeitung, 26–9–1959.
62. "Antrittsrede." *Jahresheft der Heidelberger Akademie der Wissenschaften,* 1957/58, 1959; also, *Wissenschaft und Weltbild,* XII, Wien, 1959.
63. *Gelassenheit.* Pfullingen, 1959. Contains: "Gelassenheit." Address, 1955 and "Zur Erörterung der Gelassenheit." Aus einem Feldweggespräch über das Denken. Written, 1944/45.
64. "Hegel und die Griechen." *Die Gegenwart der Griechen im neueren Denken.* Tübingen, 1960. Address, 1958.
65. "Hölderlins Erde und Himmel." *Hölderlin-Jahrbuch,* 1958–1960. Tübingen, 1960. Address, 1960.
66. *Nietzsche,* 2 vols. Pfullingen, 1961. Contains:
    A. Lecture course on Nietzsche, consisting of:
    "Der Wille zur Macht als Kunst," 1936/37;
    "Die ewige Wiederkehr des Gleichen," 1937;
    "Der Wille zur Macht als Erkenntnis," 1939;
    "Die ewige Wiederkehr des Gleichen und der Wille zur Macht," 1949;

"Der europäische Nihilismus," 1940;
"Nietzsches Metaphysik," 1940.
  B. Treatises:
"Die seinsgeschichtliche Bestimmung des Nihilismus," 1944/46;
"Die Metaphysik als Geschichte des Seins," 1941;
"Entwürfe zur Geschichte des Seins als Metaphysik," 1941;
"Die Erinnerung in die Metaphysik," 1941.
67. "Sprache und Heimat." *Dauer im Wandel.* Festschrift für Carl J. Burckhardt, München, 1961.
68. *Die Frage nach dem Ding. Zu Kants Lehre von den transzendentalen Grundsätzen.* Tübingen, 1962.
    Lecture course, 1935/36.
69. "Kants These über das Sein." Festschrift für Erik Wolf, *Existenz und Ordnung.* Frankfurt, 1962. Separately, Frankfurt, 1963.
70. "Ansprache zum Heimatabend." *700 Jahre Stadt Messkirch.* Messkirch, 1962.
71. "Aus einer Erörterung der Wahrheitsfrage." *Zehn Jahre Neske Verlag.* Pfullingen, 1962.
    From lecture course, 1937/38.
72. *Die Technik und die Kehre.* Pfullingen, 1962. Contains:
"Das Gestell." Address, 1949, published in enlarged form as No. 44;
"Die Kehre." Address, 1949.
73. "Zeit und Sein." Address, summarized and discussed by H. Rombach and by O. Pugliese, 1962. According to Magda King, delivered in 1961 at the University of Kiel. First published in *L'endurance de la pensée* (Festschrift for Jean Beaufret). Paris, 1968.
74. "Brief" an Richardson, as 'Vorwort' in W. J. Richardson: *Heidegger.* The Hague, 1963.
75. "Aus der letzten Marburger Vorlesung." *Zeit und Geschichte.* Dankesgabe an Rudolph Bultmann. Tübingen, 1964.
    From lecture course in Leibniz, 1928.

II.   ENGLISH TRANSLATIONS

A.   Translations referred to in this book.
An Introduction to Metaphysics (Einführung in die Metaphysik), Ralph Manheim, trans. (New York: Doubleday & Company, 1961).
Being and Time (Sein und Zeit), John Macquarrie and Edward Robinson, trans. (New York: Harper & Row, 1962).

Kant and the Problem of Metaphysics (*Kant und das Problem der Metaphysik*), James S. Churchill, trans. (Bloomington, Ind.: Indiana University Press, 1969).

The Essence of Reason (*Vom Wesen des Grundes*), Terrence Malick, trans. With German text. (Evanston, Ill.: Northwestern University Press, 1969).

Discourse on Thinking (*Gelassenheit*), John M. Anderson and E. Hans Freund, trans. (New York: Harper & Row, 1966).

Hegel's Concept of Experience ("Hegels Begriff der Erfahrung" in *Holzwege*) (New York: Harper & Row, 1970).

Identity and Difference (*Identität und Differenz*), Joan Stambaugh, trans. With German text. (New York: Harper & Row, 1969).

The Question of Being (*Zur Seinfrage*), William Kluback and Jean T. Wilde, trans. With German text. (New Haven, Conn.: College and University Press, n.d.).

What Is Philosophy? (*Was ist das—die Philosophie?*) William Kluback and Jean T. Wilde, trans. With German text. (New Haven, Conn.: College and University Press, n.d.).

What Is a Thing? (*Die Frage nach dem Ding*), W. B. Barton, Jr. and Vera Deutsch, trans. (Chicago: Regnery Gateway ed., 1970).

What Is Called Thinking? (*Was heisst Denken?*) Fred D. Wieck and J. Glenn Gray, trans. (New York: Harper & Row, 1968).

"Remembrance of the Poet" ("Heimkunft/An die Verwandten" and "Hölderlin and the Essence of Poetry" (Hölderlin und das Wesen der Dichtung"), Douglas Scott, trans., In Werner Brock, *Existence and Being*. These are two of the four essays on Hölderlin in *Erläuternungen zu Hölderlin's Dichtung*.

"On the Essence of Truth" (*Vom Wesen der Wahrheit*) and "What is Metaphysics?" (*Was its Metaphysik?*), R. F. C. Hull and Alan Crick, trans. In Werner Brock, *Existence and Being*.

B. The following are some other translations to which no reference is made in the footnotes in this book.

"The Age of the World View" ("Die Zeit des Weltbildes" in *Holzwege*), Marjorie Grene, trans., *Measure*, II (1951), 269–284.

"The Way Back into the Ground of Metaphysics" ("Introduction" to *Was ist Metaphysik?*), Walter Kaufmann, trans., in Walter Kaufmann, *Existentialism* (New York: Meridian, 1957).

"Plato's Doctrine of Truth" (*Platons Lehre von der Wahrheit*), John Barlow, trans.; and "Letter on Humanism" ("*Brief über den 'Humanismus'* "), Edgar Lohner, trans. Both in William Barrett

and Henry D. Aiken, *Philosophy in the Twentieth Century* (New York: Harper Torchbooks, 1971).
"The Origin of the Work of Art" ("Ursprung des Kunstwerkes"), Albert Hofstadter, trans. In Albert Hofstadter and Richard Kuhns, eds., *Philosophies of Art and Beauty* (New York: Random House Modern Library ed., 1964).

III.   SECONDARY LITERATURE CITED

A.   Bibliographies, etc.

Feick, Hildegard. *Index zu 'Sein und Zeit'*. Tübingen, 1961. .
Lübbe, Hermann. *Bibliographie der Heidegger-Literatur 1917–1955*. Meisenheim, 1957.
Schneeberger, Guido. *Ergänzungen zu einer Heidegger-Bibliographie*. Bern, 1960.
Schneeberger, Guido, *Nachlese zu Heidegger*. Bern, 1961.
Martin Heideggers Einfluss auf die Wissenschaften. Bern, 1949.
Anteile. Martin Heidegger zum 60 Geburtstag. Frankfurt, 1950.
Martin Heidegger zum siebzigsten Geburtstag. Pfullingen, 1959.
Richardson, W. J. *Heidegger*. Contains a "Verzeichnis der Vorlesungen und Übungen von Martin Heidegger." This does not, however, include titles of Heidegger's unpublished Lectures and Addresses, for which reference may be made to Otto Pöggeler's *Der Denkweg Martin Heideggers* and Orlando Pugliese's *Vermittlung und Kehre*.

B.   Books and Articles about Heidegger

Allemann, Beda. *Hölderlin und Heidegger*. 2nd ed., Zürich and Freiburg, 1956.
Biemel, Walter. "Heideggers Begriff des Daseins." *Studia Catholica*, XXIV, 1949.
Biemel, Walter. *Le Concept de Monde chez Heidegger*. Louvain, 1950.
Biemel, Walter. "Husserls Encyclopaedia Britannica Artikel und Heideggers Anmerkugen dazu." *Tijdschrift voor Philosophie*, XII, 1950.
Birault, Henri. "Heidegger et la pensée de la finitude." *Revue Internationale de la Philosophie*, No. LII, 1960.
Bretschneider, Willy. *Sein und Wahrheit*. Über die Zusammengehörigkeit von Sein und Wahrheit im Denken Martin Heideggers. Meisenheim, 1965.
Brock, Werner. *Existence and Being*. London, 1949.

Bröcker, Walter. "Heidegger und die Logik." *Philosophische Rundschau*, I, 1953.

Buddeberg, Else. *Denken und Dichten des Seins*. Heidegger/Rilke. Stuttgart, 1956.

Cassirer, Ernst. "Kant und das Problem der Metaphysik." *Kant-Studien*, XXXVI, 1931.

Demske, J. M. *Sein, Mensch und Tod*. Das Todesproblem bei Martin Heidegger. Freiburg/München, 1963.

Demske, J. M. "Heidegger's Quadrate and Revelation of Being." *Philosophy Today*, VIII, 1964.

De Waelhens, A. *La Philosophie de Martin Heidegger*. Louvain, 1942.

De Waelhens, A. & Biemel, W. "Heideggers Schrift 'Vom Wesen der Wahrheit'." *Symposion*, III, 1952.

Fürstenau, P. *Heidegger*. Das Gefüge seines Denkens. Frankfurt, 1958.

Gabriel, Leo. "Wege zum Sein." *Wissenschaft und Weltbild*, XII, 1959.

Gadamer, Hans-Georg. "Zur Einführung." Heidegger: *Der Ursprung des Kunstwerkes*. Stuttgart, 1960.

Gadamer, Hans-Georg. "Martin Heidegger und die Marburger Theologie." *Zeit und Geschichte*. Tübingen, 1964.

Glicksman (Grene), Marjorie. "A Note on the Philosophy of Heidegger." *Journal of Philosophy*, XXXV, 1938.

Grene, Marjorie. *Martin Heidegger*. London, 1957.

Gründer, Karlfried. "M. Heideggers Wissenschaftskritik in ihren geschichtlichen Zusammenhängen." Archiv für Philosophie, XI, 1962.

Hamburg, Carl. "A Cassirer-Heidegger Seminar." *Philosophy and Phenomenological Research*, XXV, 1964.

Henrich, Dieter. "Über die Einheit der Subjectivität." *Philosophische Rundschau*, III, 1955.

Herrmann, F. W. v. *Die Selbstinterpretation Martin Heideggers*. Meisenheim, 1964.

Hünerfeld, Paul. *In Sachen Heidegger*. München, 1961.

Jonas, Hans. "Heidegger and Theology." *Review of Metaphysics*, XVIII, 1964.

Kanthack, K. *Das Denken Martin Heideggers*. Berlin, 1959.

King, Magda. *Heidegger's Philosophy*. A guide to his basic thought. New York, 1964.

Krüger, Gerhard. "M. Heidegger und der Humanismus." *Studia Philosophica*, IX, 1949; also, *Theologische Rundschau*, XVIII, 1950.

Landgrebe, Ludwig. "Husserl, Heidegger, Sartre." *Revue de Metaphysique et de Morale*, No. 4, 1964.

Langan, T. *The Meaning of Heidegger*. A Critical Study of an Existentialist Phenomenology. London, 1959.

Leidecker, Kurt F. (trans.) *Essays in Metaphysics: Identity and Difference.* New York, 1960.

Levy, H. "Heidegger's Kant-Interpretation." *Logos,* XXI, 1932.

Liebrucks, Bruno. "Idee und ontologische Differenz." *Kant-Studien,* XLVIII, 1956/57.

Lipps, Hans. "Pragmatismus und Existentialismus." *Die Wirklichkeit des Menschen.* Frankfurt, 1954.

Löwith, Karl. *Heidegger—Denker in dürftiger Zeit.* Frankfurt, 1953.

Macquarrie, John. *An Existentialist Theology.* London, 1955.

Marx, Werner. "Heidegger's New Conception of Philosophy." *Social Research,* XXII, 1955.

Marx, Werner. *Heidegger und die Tradition.* Stuttgart, 1961.

Meulen, J. van der. *Heidegger und Hegel.* Meisenheim, 1954.

Müller-Lauter, W. *Möglichkeit und Wirklichkeit bei Martin Heidegger.* Berlin, 1960.

Noack, Hermann. "Gespräch mit Martin Heidegger." *Anstösse,* I, 1954.

Ortega y Gasset, J. "Heidegger und die Sprache der Philosophie." *Universitas,* VII, 1952.

Ott, Heinrich. *Denkin und Sein.* Der Weg Martin Heideggers und der Weg der Theologie. Zürich, 1959.

Pflaumer, R. "Sein und Mensch im Denken Martin Heideggers." *Philosophische Rundschau,* XIII, 1966.

Pöggeler, Otto. "Jean Wahls Heidegger-Deutung." *Zeitschrift für philosophische Forschung,* XII, 1958.

Pöggeler, Otto. "Sein als Ereignis." *Zeitschrift für philosophische Forschung,* XIII, 1959.

Pöggeler, Otto. "Metaphysik und Seinstopik bei Heidegger." *Philosophisches Jahrbuch,* LXX, 1962.

Pöggeler, Otto. Review of *Index zu 'Sein und Zeit'. Philosophischer Literaturanzeiger,* XV, 1962.

Pöggeler, Otto. *Der Denkweg Martin Heideggers.* Pfullingen, 1963.

Pugliese, Orlando. *Vermittlung und Kehre.* Grundzüge des Geschichtsdenkens bei Martin Heidegger. München, 1965.

Richardson, W. J. *Heidegger.* Through Phenomenology to Thought. The Hague, 1963.

Ryle, Gilbert. Critical Notice of *Sein und Zeit. Mind,* XXXVIII, 1929.

Schöfer, Erasmus. *Die Sprache Heideggers.* Pfullingen, 1962.

Schrey, H-H. "Die Bedeutung der Philosophie Martin Heideggers für die Theologie." *Martin Heideggers Einfluss auf die Wissenschaften.* Bern, 1949.

Schultz, Walter. "Über den philosophiegeschichtlichen Ort Martin Heideggers." *Philosophische Rundschau*, I, 1953/54.

Seidel, G. J. *Martin Heidegger and the Pre-Socratics*. Lincoln, 1964.

Szilasi, Wilhelm. "Interpretation und Geschichte der Philosophie." *Martin Heideggers Einfluss auf die Wissenschaften*. Bern, 1949.

Versényi, Laszlo. *Heidegger, Being, and Truth*. New Haven, 1965.

Vietta, Egon. *Die Seinsfrage bei Martin Heidegger*. Stuttgart, 1950.

Vycinas, Vincent. *Earth and Gods*. An Introduction to the Philosophy of Martin Heidegger. The Hague, 1961.

Wild, John. "An English Version of Martin Heidegger's 'Being and Time'." *Review of Metaphysics*, XVI, 1962.

Wiplinger, Fridolin. *Wahrheit und Geschichtlichkeit*. Eine Untersuchung über die Frage nach dem Wesen der Wahrheit im Denken Martin Heideggers. Freiburg/München, 1961.

C. OTHER WORKS

Biemel, Walter. *Die Bedeutung von Kants Begründung der Aesthetik für die Philosophie der Kunst*. *Kantstudien-Ergänzungsheft* LXXVII, Köln, 1960.

Bollnow, O. F. *Dilthey*. Stuttgart, 1955.

Brentano, Franz. *Von der mannigfachen Bedeutung des Seienden nach Aristoteles*. Hildesheim, 1960.

Brock, Werner. *Introduction to Contemporary German Philosophy*. Cambridge, 1935.

Bröcker, Walter. *Aristoteles*. 2nd ed., Frankfurt, 1957.

Bultmann, Rudolph. *Zeit und Geschichte*. Dankesgabe an Rudolph Bultmann. Tübingen, 1964.

De Waelhens, A. "Die phänomenologische Idee der Intentionalität." *Husserl und das Denken der Neuzeit*. The Hague, 1959.

Dilthey, Wilhelm. *Gesammelte Schriften*, V, VII & VIII. Stuttgart, 1957–60.

Dilthey, Wilhelm & Yorck, Paul. *Briefwechsel zwischen Wilhelm Dilthey und dem Grafen Paul Yorck v. Wartenburg 1877–1897*. Halle, 1923.

Fink, Eugen. *Zur ontologischen Frühgeschichte vom Raum-Zeit-Bewegung*. The Hague, 1957.

Fink, Eugen. *Sein, Wahrheit, Welt*. The Hague, 1958.

Fink, Eugen. *Alles und Nichts*. The Hague, 1959.

Fink, Eugen. *Spiel als Weltsymbol*. Stuttgart, 1960.

Friedländer, Paul. *Platon I*. 2nd ed., Berlin, 1954.

Gabriel, Leo. *Vom Brahma zur Existenz*. 2nd ed., München, 1956.

Gadamer, Hans-Georg. *Wahrheit und Methode*. Tübingen, 1960.

266 THE PHILOSOPHY OF MARTIN HEIDEGGER

Gadamer, Hans-Georg. "Die phänomenologische Bewegung." *Philosophische Rundschau*, XI, 1963.
Gadamer, Hans-Georg. "Enleitung." R. G. Collingwood: *Denken. Eine Autobiographie*. Stuttgart, 1957.
Gadamer, Hans-Georg. "Hermeneutik und Historismus." *Philosophische Rundschau*, IX, 1961.
Gadamer, Hans-Georg. *Die Gegenwart der Griechen im neueren Denken*. Festschrift für Hans-Georg Gadamer. Tübingen, 1960.
Gadamer. Hans-Georg. "Die Universalität des hermeneutischen Problems." *Philosophisches Jahrbuch*, LXXIII, 1966.
Gadamer, Hans-Georg. "Vorwort". W. Dilthy: *Grundriss der allgemeinen Geschichte der Philosophie*. Frankfurt, 1949.
Heller, Erich. *The Disinherited Mind*. New York, 1959.
Hodges, H. A. *The Philosophy of Wilhelm Dilthey*. 1952.
Husserl, Edmund. *Ideen*, 3 vols. The Hague, 1950–1952.
Husserl, Edmund. *Logische Untersuchungen*. 3rd ed., Halle, 1922.
Husserl, Edmund. *Die Krisis der europäischen Wissenschaften*. The Hague, 1954.
Kanthack, K. *Nicolai Hartmann und das Ende der Ontologie*. Berlin, 1962.
Kaufmann, Walter. *Nietzsche*. New York, 1959.
Landgrebe, Ludwig. *Philosophie der Gegenwart*. Bonn, 1952.
Landgrebe, Ludwig. *Phänomenologie und Metaphysik*. Hamburg, 1949.
Landgrebe, Ludwig. *Der Weg in die Phänomenologie*. Gütersloh, 1963. Contains selected essays from the preceding; also article mentioned next.
Landgrebe, Ludwig. "Husserls Abschied vom Cartesianismus." *Philosophische Rundschau*, IX, 1961.
Löwith, Karl. *Nietzsches Philosophie der ewigen Wiederkehr des Gleichen*. Stuttgart, 1958.
Lohmann, Johannes. "Über den paradigmatischen Charakter der griechischen Kultur." *Die Gegenwart der Griechen im neueren Denken*. Tübingen, 1960.
Lohmann, Johannes. *Philosophie und Sprachwissenschaft*. Berlin, 1965.
Manasse, E. M. "Bücher über Platon I." *Philosophische Rundschau*, V, Beiheft I, 1957.
Misch, G. *Lebensphilosophie und Phänomenologie*. Leipzig, 1931.
Misch, G. "Einleitung." W. Dilthey: *Gesammelte Schriften*, V.
Möller, Joseph. *Existenzial Philosophie und katholische Philosophie*. Baden-Baden, 1952.

Müller, Max. *Existenzphilosophie im geistigen Leben der Gegenwart.* 2nd ed., Heidelberg, 1958.

Oltmanns, K. *Meister Eckhart.* 2nd ed., Frankfurt, 1958.

Paton, H. J. *Kant's Metaphysic of Experience,* 2 vols. London, 1936.

Plessner, Helmuth. "Offene Problemgeschichte." *Nicolai Hartmann— Der Denker und sein Werk.* Berlin, 1952.

Pöggeler, Otto. "Das Wesen der Stimmungen." *Zeitschrift für philosophische Forschung,* XIV, 1960.

Pöggeler, Otto. "Zur Deutung der Phänomenologie des Geistes." *Hegel-Studien,* I, 1961.

Pöggeler, Otto. "Hermeneutische und mantische Phänomenologie." *Philosophische Rundschau,* XIII, 1965.

Pöggeler, Otto. Review of books by Viehweg and Hennis. *Philosophischer Literaturanzeiger,* XVIII, 1965.

Pos, H. J. "Recollections of Ernst Cassirer." *The Philosophy of Ernst Cassirer.* Evanston, 1949.

Rombach, Heinrich. *Die Gegenwart der Philosophie.* München, 1962.

Sartre, J-P. *Being and Nothingness.* London, 1956.

Schleiermacher, F. *Hermeneutik.* Ed. H. Kimmerle. Heidelberg, 1959.

Schulz, Walter. *Die Vollendung des deutschen Idealismus in der Spätphilosophie Schellings.* Stuttgart, 1955.

Schulz, Walter. *Der Gott der neuzeitlichen Metaphysik.* Pfullingen, 1957.

Siewerth, G. *Das Schicksal der Metaphysik von Thomas zu Heidegger.* Einsiedeln, 1959.

Spiegelberg, Herbert. *The Phenomenological Movement,* 2 vols. The Hague, 1960.

Tanabe, Hajime. "Todesdialektik." *Martin Heidegger zum siebzigsten Geburtstag.* Pfullingen, 1959.

Volkmann-Schluck, K-H. *Plotin als Interpret der Ontologie Platos.* 2nd ed., Frankfurt, 1957.

Volkmann-Schluck, K-H. "Zur Gottesfrage bei Nietzsche." *Anteile. Martin Heidegger zum 60. Geburtstag.* Frankfurt, 1950.

Wild, John. "Man and His Life-World." *For Roman Ingarden.* The Hague, 1959.

Wittgenstein, Ludwig. *Notebooks 1914–1916.* Oxford, 1961.

Index

Absolute, the, 167, 171–173, 201
actualitas, 152, 167, 194, 196
actus purus, 197
adequatio intellectus et rei, 98
aei on, 35, 151
agathon (*idea tou agathou*), 28, 95, 151, 151n, 159, 176n, 199
aion, 93n
aition, 93n, 197
aletheia, 15n, 45, 46n, 100, 143, 148–9, 169, 185, 199, 211, 219n, 230–232, 246
    see also truth
aliquid, 193n
Allemann, Beda, 41n, 74
analogia entis, 155
Anaximander, 42, 45, 48, 108, 134, 139, 140
Andenken, see remembrance
animal rationale, 210
Anwesen (*-heit*), *see* presence
anxiety, 83
arche, 89, 93, 194, 197
Aristotle, 13, 14, 28, 29n, 30, 36, 42, 45, 45n, 60, 67, 71, 71n, 89, 91, 104, 114, 138n, 147, 150, 152, 152n, 155, 156, 174n, 176, 190, 193, 195f, 198, 201, 203n, 225
ars inveniendi, 120n
art, 41n
Augustine, St., 13, 14, 29n, 205n
Austrag, see issue

Beaufret, J., 76, 117
Being
    and becoming, 142
    and beings, *see* Ontological Difference

Being (*continued*)
    and language, *see* language and Being
    and man, 116–119, 117n, 118, 118n, 208–211, 215f, 217
        see also Ereignis
    and the Ought, 151
    and seeming, 142f
    and thought, 60n, 143–152, 233f, 240–244
    and time, 153, 171, 233
    as *a priori*, 198f
    as condition of possibility (*agathon*), 151, 158f, 199f
    as crossed out, 216
    as essence (*idea*, with 'what'), 195f
    as existence (*energeia*, actuality), 196f
    as *Ereignis*, 201, 213, 213n, 239
    as the Fourfold, 217–223
    as Ground, 159, 200f, 203
    as *physis, see physis*
    as presence (constancy of), 14, 35–36, 139, 142, 142n, 151, 190, 233
        see also presence and *ousia*
    as objectivity (representedness), 164f
    as substance, 194n
    as transcendence, 197f
    as a universal, 197f, 198n
    as value, *see* value
    as Will, 234f, 235n
    Aristotle's view of, 152, 153n, 193f, 195f
    destiny (dispensation), of, 59, 68, 130f, 141, 159n
    eschatology of, 236–7